Counter-Enlightenmer

The Enlightenment is a key organising concept in philosophy, social theory and the history of ideas and its legacy is still being actively debated today. *Counter-Enlightenments* is the first general, book-length study of the history and development of Enlightenment criticism from its inception in the eighteenth century through to the present. It examines the various ways in which the Enlightenment has been both constructed and attacked by its enemies on the left, the right and in the centre.

Engaging in a critical dialogue with Isaiah Berlin's seminal work on this subject, this book analyses the concept of Counter-Enlightenment and some of the most important conceptual issues and problems that it raises. Graeme Garrard explores the diverse forms of Counter-Enlightenment thought with a wide-ranging review of the Enlightenment's principal opponents of the past two hundred and fifty years, and concludes with an assessment of the persuasiveness of some of the most common and important criticisms of it.

Graeme Garrard teaches political theory and European thought at Cardiff University, UK.

Routledge studies in social and political thought

Counter-Enlightenments

From the eighteenth century to the present

Graeme Garrard

Routledge
Taylor & Francis Group

LONDON AND NEW YORK

First published 2006
by Routledge
2 Park Square, Milton Park, Abingdon, Oxon, OX14 4RN (UK)

Simultaneously published in the USA and Canada by Routledge
711 Third Avenue, New York, NY 10017 (US)

First issued in paperback 2013

Routledge is an imprint of the Taylor & Francis Group, an informa business

© 2006 Graeme Garrard

Typeset in Garamond by Wearset Ltd, Boldon, Tyne and Wear

British Library Cataloguing in Publication Data
A catalogue record for this book is available from the British Library

Library of Congress Cataloging in Publication Data
A catalog record for this book has been requested

ISBN 0–415–18725–7
ISBN 978-0-415-85296-8 (Paperback)

To the Memory
of
Frank Ernest Garrard

Contents

Preface

My interest in Counter-Enlightenment thought was first sparked when I read Isaiah Berlin's essay on 'Joseph de Maistre and the Origins of Fascism' in the *New York Review of Books* in the autumn of 1990.[1] It was not long before I was reading his essay on 'The Counter-Enlightenment' (1973) which, by situating Maistre within a much broader context of ideas, opened a door through which I gingerly stepped into a strange, fascinating, eclectic, sometimes morbid, frequently exaggerated but not *wholly* misguided intellectual world in which I have been immersed (although I hope not lost) ever since. I then greedily devoured all of what Berlin had published on the Enlightenment and its enemies in preparation for my first direct encounter with him during my first term at Oxford, the first of many we had over the next five years. This volume grows directly out of that experience with Berlin and his work on the Enlightenment and its enemies. It is, in part, a critical dialogue with him on the subject, one that attempts to build and, I would like to think, improve upon his pioneering work in this area, rather than simply to bury his work and him with it, or to leave it untouched as the 'definitive' map of Counter-Enlightenment thought.[2]

The other significant influence on my outlook has been James Schmidt. His approach to the Enlightenment and its enemies could hardly be more different from Berlin's, although I do not think that they are entirely incompatible. Berlin's approach to intellectual history has an impressive range, boldness and sweep that I find irresistibly attractive and stimulating. But scholarship on the Enlightenment has undergone a revolution in the past thirty years, and scholarly standards and methods in the historical study of ideas have changed dramatically since Berlin retired as Chichele Professor of Social and Political Thought at Oxford in the 1960s. So the time is now right to revisit his work on Counter-Enlightenment thought in light of these changes, and James Schmidt has helped me to appreciate the need for this.

This book attempts to strike a balance between these two approaches, combining some of the expansiveness and range of Berlin's work with a good measure of the scholarly rigour and precision of Schmidt's. It is bound to be both less colourful than Berlin's and less rigorous than Schmidt's as a consequence. But I believe that it is possible to have enough of what is valuable from each to satisfy most of my readers, and I hope that I have found that *juste milieu* here, a good part of the time at least.

This study makes no pretence to being exhaustive. Even if it were possible for a single volume to encompass *all* of the Enlightenment's enemies over the past two centuries, it would likely end up being too superficial to be of much value. By restricting the range of material covered by focusing on a limited number of examples, I have tried to avoid this hazard and to strike a balance between breadth and depth. The result, while necessarily selective, is not wholly arbitrary, for I have followed two rules of inclusion.

First, as a work of intellectual history, this study concentrates on what may be called 'high Counter-Enlightenment', which is not to deny either the existence or the importance of a 'low Counter-Enlightenment'. A *complete* picture of Counter-Enlightenment thought (if such were possible) would have to span not only its entire temporal, geographical and ideological range, but its full cultural and social breadth as well. Such a work would necessarily be a massive history of several movements, high and low, far and wide, covering over two centuries across a broad range of national contexts and ideological perspectives, probably running to several volumes. By strolling along the summits of 'high Counter-Enlightenment', to adapt a metaphor of Friedrich Meinecke's, this study offers at most some insight into one stratum of Counter-Enlightenment thought (even at this level it is necessarily selective and incomplete), although it tries to do so as widely as possible. I aim simply to show that there are more summits than Berlin imagined without denying that there is much of interest in the valleys below, as historian Darrin McMahon has recently shown.[3]

Second, I have included only those thinkers who offered *some* conception of what we now call 'the Enlightenment'. This is partly to limit the scope of my study to manageable proportions, and partly because I am interested not only in the ways in which the Enlightenment has been *attacked*, but also the ways it has been *depicted* by its enemies, which is no less interesting and important. To make something an object of criticism requires that one first have a particular conception of that object. A history of the Enlightenment's opponents must therefore be a history of their *constructions* of 'the Enlightenment' as well as their *destructions* of it. Thus I have paid considerable attention here not only to the many different criticisms of the Enlightenment over the past 250 years, but also to the different ways it has been portrayed to suit the particular beliefs, prejudices, agendas and interests of its enemies. There are many thinkers who have attacked specific tenets of Enlightenment thought and have exerted great influence on its critics without actually offering a clear conception of it as a historical movement. One such is Martin Heidegger (1889–1976), who plays almost no part in the story I tell. For Heidegger, the roots of the crisis that afflicts Western modernity are to be found well before the Enlightenment; Descartes plays a much more central part in his attack on modernity than do his eighteenth-century successors. In fact, Heidegger's work says virtually nothing about the latter.[4] This explains the absence from my text of some writers who might otherwise have been included among the enemies of the Enlightenment.

This study lies somewhere between a textbook and a narrowly specialised monograph, although it is rather closer to the latter than to the former. It is broad and synthetic rather than narrow and analytical, aiming, like John Burrow's exemplary *The Crisis of Reason* (2000), to provide a context for more specialised studies without being a substitute for them.[5] It is also thematic; it does not try to provide a comprehensive account of the ideas of each of the thinkers with which it deals. Rather, it focuses on one particular theme (the Enlightenment and its alleged shortcomings) across a broad range of writers and how each of them dealt with it. Like most books in intellectual history, it does not fit neatly within the boundaries of conventional academic disciplines, and I have not adhered strictly to any particular methodological orthodoxy.

Acknowledgements

Part of this book was written in the congenial surroundings of Boston University, where I spent a term as a Visiting Scholar in the University Professors Program. I then crossed the Charles River to spend a stimulating and enjoyable term as a Visiting Fellow at the Minda de Gunzburg Center for European Studies at Harvard University. I owe much to friends and colleagues at both institutions, and I am glad to have this opportunity publicly to thank them for welcoming me into their ranks for a time.

From Cambridge I took my manuscript with me to rural New England, where I spent a delightful year teaching at Dartmouth College in New Hampshire, followed by a happy and productive year at Williams College in western Massachusetts. I had the greatest pleasure teaching Mark Yohalem and Steve Menashi at Dartmouth, and thank them for reminding me of just how rewarding teaching can be. The friendship and intellectual companionship of James Murphy made my New England sojourn truly memorable and enjoyable. The same must be said of my Williams friend and colleague Sung-Ho Kim – citizen, scholar, 'man of vocation', gastronomer.

I am grateful to Gunnar Beck for reading and commenting upon earlier drafts of some of the chapters that follow, correcting my German, and for his advice and intellectual companionship over many years. I have benefited a great deal from the work of Darrin McMahon, and from our occasional exchanges on the subject of Counter-Enlightenment. I am indebted to Richard Lebrun for reading and commenting on Chapter 3.

The friendship of my colleagues Chris Ealham, David Hanley and Sean Loughlin has made my time at Cardiff University as stimulating and pleasant as it could be.

The final stage of the manuscript was completed while I was on sabbatical leave in Paris during 2003 and 2004. I am very grateful to the UK Arts and Humanities Research Board for providing me with funding that made it possible for me to give my undivided attention to this work for an extended period. Without such support it is certain that this book's completion would have been much delayed.

Paris, summer 2004

1   Introduction

Like it or not, the West today (and not only the West) is a legacy of what has come to be known in English as 'the Enlightenment'. Many of the values, practices and institutions of our present civilisation are rooted in the eighteenth century, which helped to liberate a vast human potential that determined much of the shape and direction of the world we now inhabit. Michel Foucault's claim that the Enlightenment 'has determined, at least in part, what we are, what we think, and what we do today' is beyond serious dispute.[1]

Assessing this legacy is much more difficult than merely acknowledging its scale and significance. On the one hand, the Enlightenment was a 'great leap forward' in many ways, leading to an unprecedented expansion of scientific discovery and application, political reform, social liberation and individual empowerment. Its legacy of religious toleration has been a precious gift for reasons made obvious by the long history of religious persecutions and crusades in the pre-Enlightenment West and the fundamentalist excesses so common in our time. Its faith in the potential of modern science to enhance human knowledge – and thereby power – has been vindicated to a degree far exceeding the wildest dreams of the most optimistic *philosophes*. On the other hand, the experience of the twentieth century has revealed the dark side of knowledge to a degree that may have startled many of the Enlightenment's eighteenth-century proponents. With increased freedom and mobility, the spread of literacy, the decline in infant mortality, the prolongation of human life and the alleviation of physical suffering through modern medicine have come a potentially catastrophic degradation of the natural environment, the depletion of vital and irreplaceable natural resources, the advent of nuclear, chemical and biological weapons, and the dystopic possibilities of genetic engineering. The destructive potential at the disposal of the human appetite for power, cruelty, stupidity and hatred is now enormous and growing. In addition, the increase in individual freedom of conscience, religious expression, mobility and self-determination that the Enlightenment helped to facilitate has undermined many traditional sources of conflict while fostering others. For many today, the balance between the costs and the benefits of living in an enlightened civilisation – if we really can call ours such – cannot sustain the buoyant optimism usually associated with the Enlightenment. For increasing numbers of others, the balance clearly favours a deeply pessimistic – even apocalyptic – reading of the trajectory of human history since the eighteenth century. Either way, few now retain the relatively simple faith in science, progress, reason and the natural goodness of human beings commonly associated with the age we now call the Enlightenment. Given this scepticism, it is hardly surprising that the re-emergence of 'enlightenment' as a key organising concept in philosophy, social and critical theory, and the history of ideas since the Second World War has been shadowed by a proliferation of new forms of Counter-Enlightenment thought, resulting in yet another round in the continuing war between the Enlightenment and its enemies.

Although criticism of the Enlightenment has been a central theme in twentieth-century thought – particularly in intellectual movements such as critical theory, hermeneutics, pragmatism, feminism, post-modernism and communitarianism – and the *term* 'Counter-Enlightenment' is now quite well established and widely used,[2] the *concept* of Counter-Enlightenment is underdeveloped, lagging at least a generation behind the scholarly literature on the Enlightenment, the sophistication of which has increased dramatically in the past quarter of a century. Indeed, the only significant scholarly study devoted exclusively to this subject in general is Isaiah Berlin's 1973 essay 'The Counter-Enlightenment', which is the necessary starting point of any discussion on the concept in English.[3]

As far as I have been able to discover, the term 'the Counter-Enlightenment' made its first appearance in English in William Barrett's 1949 *Partisan Review* essay on 'Art, Aristocracy and Reason', where it is mentioned only in passing.[4] He also employs it as follows in his popular 1958 book on existentialism, where he writes: 'Existentialism is the counter-Enlightenment come at last to philosophic expression; and it demonstrates beyond anything else that the ideology of the Enlightenment is thin, abstract, and therefore dangerous.'[5] Barratt says little about Enlightenment criticism beyond this. The German expression '*Gegen-Aufklärung*' is older, probably coined by Nietzsche at the end of the nineteenth century, although he only uses it in passing.[6]

The first significant use of the term in English occurs in a chapter on 'The Counter-Enlightenment' in Lewis White Beck's study of *Early German Philosophy* (1969), which is about Counter-Enlightenment in Germany, since it focuses exclusively on J. G. Hamann, J. G. Herder and F. H. Jacobi.[7] He argues that, at the height of the *Aufklärung*, 'there was a reaction which I shall call the "Counter-Enlightenment"'.[8] After decades of enlightened despotism under Frederick II (1712–1786), Beck claims, a counter-movement arose in Germany attacking what it saw as Frederick's soulless, secular authoritarian state. This enlightened conception of the state reflected the mechanical Newtonian view of disenchanted nature that dominated Enlightenment thought in the eighteenth century. In opposition to this, the 'faith and feeling' philosophers of the Counter-Enlightenment, epitomised by Hamann, favoured a more organic conception of social and political life, a more vitalistic view of nature, and an appreciation for beauty and the spiritual life of man that, they thought, had been neglected in the eighteenth century.

It has only been since the republication in 1981 of Berlin's essay 'The Counter-Enlightenment' in a popular collection of essays that the term has been widely used.[9] Like Beck, Berlin claims that the Germans 'rebelled against the dead hand of France in the realms of culture, art and philosophy, and avenged themselves by launching the great counter-attack against the Enlightenment'.[10] Both believe that it was in late-eighteenth century Germany that Counter-Enlightenment thought really took off, starting with the Königsberg philosopher Hamann, 'the most passionate, consistent, extreme and implacable enemy of the Enlightenment'.[11] This German reaction to the imperialistic universalism of the French Enlightenment and Revolution, which had been forced on them first by the Francophile Frederick II, then by the armies of Revolutionary France, and finally by Napoleon, was crucial to the epochal shift of consciousness that occurred in Europe at the time, leading eventually to Romanticism. According to Berlin, the surprising and unintended consequence of this revolt against the Enlightenment has been pluralism, which owes more to the Enlightenment's enemies than it does to its proponents, most of whom were monists whose political, intellectual and ideological offspring have often been terror and totalitarianism.[12]

In *Liberalism and the Origins of European Social Theory* (1983), Steven Seidman distinguishes between three distinct strands of Counter-Enlightenment thought, only one of which is primarily German: Conservatives (e.g. Joseph de Maistre, Louis de Bonald, Edmund Burke, the Historical School of Jurisprudence); German Romantics (e.g. Friedrich Schiller, Friedrich von Schelling, Auguste Wilhelm and Friedrich von Schlegel, Friedrich von Hardenberg ['Novalis'], Johann Gottlieb Fichte, Friedrich Schleiermacher); and French Revolutionaries (e.g. François Noël Babeuf and Louis-Auguste Blanqui).[13] Rejecting the stark dualism of Enlightenment versus Counter-Enlightenment, Seidman recasts the latter as a transitional phase between a traditional social order that was in retreat in the eighteenth century and an emergent new form of industrial civilisation that typified the nineteenth century. The Counter-Enlightenment was a 'transmitter' of innovations in social theory originally made by the Enlightenment, refining and adapting them in the process. For example, Seidman argues that the Enlightenment rejected the methodological individualism and atomistic assumptions of classical social contract theory in favour of a belief in 'the interpenetration of the individual and society'.[14] Rather than rejecting these views, the Enlightenment's enemies adopted them and 'insinuated them into the centre of the intellectual milieu of the nineteenth century. In short, the counter-Enlightenment formed a bridge between the eighteenth and nineteenth centuries which was of immense significance.'[15] For Seidman, Enlightenment and Counter-Enlightenment are forms of communitarianism, united in their basic belief in social holism, but divided in their particular views on culture and politics. The real difference between the Enlightenment and its enemies is that the latter replaced the pluralistic ideal of the Enlightenment with 'the ideal of a uniform and common culture which integrates and harmonizes the interests of the individual and the community'.[16]

Like Seidman, John Gray has also emphasised the continuity between the Enlightenment and Counter-Enlightenment, which he regards as currents of thought 'watered by the same stream of humanism, which flowed into and strengthened one another'.[17] For example, a belief in a universal human narrative is common to both the Enlightenment and its reactionary opponents such as Joseph de Maistre. According to Gray, both belong to a single tradition of Western thought and culture that he traces back to antiquity. The differences that separate them exist within a broad consensus about the narrative structure of history, the unity of truth and the objectivity and compatibility of values that was not seriously challenged until late modernity, above all by Nietzsche.

Darrin McMahon, taking his cue from historian Robert Darnton, has recently examined the early enemies of the Enlightenment in France from below, documenting the existence of a long-forgotten 'Grub Street' literature in the late eighteenth and early nineteenth centuries aimed at the *philosophes*.[18] In *Enemies of the Enlightenment* (2001) he delves into the obscure and at times unseemly world of the 'low Counter-Enlightenment' that attacked the *encyclopédistes* and fought an often dirty battle to prevent the dissemination of Enlightenment ideas in the second half of the eighteenth century.[19] By extending it both back to pre-Revolutionary France and down to the level of 'Grub Street', this approach marks a major advance in scholarship on Counter-Enlightenment thought.

All of these authors end their accounts fairly abruptly in the early nineteenth century, thereby reinforcing the idea that 'the Counter-Enlightenment' is a period term like 'the Enlightenment', which it is not. Although the trend of recent scholarship has been to broaden the geographical, intellectual and social range of Counter-Enlightenment thought beyond Germany, its temporal scope remains narrowly circumscribed. No balanced account of this subject can ignore the fact that criticism of the Enlightenment has returned in the twentieth century with a vengeance. One of the principal objectives of the present study is to challenge the idea of *the* Counter-Enlightenment as a single historical movement, more or less restricted to the late eighteenth and early nineteenth centuries. I do so primarily by focusing as much on the Enlightenment's twentieth-century critics as on its earlier opponents. Each of the Enlightenment's enemies depicted it as they saw it or wanted others to see it, resulting in a vast range of portraits, many of which are not only different but incompatible. *The* Counter-Enlightenment, understood as a single movement, is a fiction, and not a particularly useful one at that. There were – and are – *many* Counter-Enlightenments.[20] This is most apparent when seen from a perspective that encompasses the full breadth of Enlightenment criticism in Germany and beyond, and from the mid-eighteenth century to the present.

Cleaning the stables

A major obstacle impeding intelligent discussion of this subject is the confusing and inconsistent use of terms, a problem that not only divides writers from each other but often divides them against themselves. Above all, the interchangeable use of 'enlightenment', 'Enlightenment', 'the enlightenment' and 'the Enlightenment' utterly confounds sensible discussion of this subject. Examples abound. In a single passage in his study of *Nietzsche and the Political*, for example, Daniel Conway refers to the 'dialectic of enlightenment', 'dialectic of Enlightenment', 'historical enlightenment', the 'dream of the Enlightenment' and the 'image of Enlightenment'.[21] In an otherwise admirable translation of Hegel's *Phenomenology of Spirit*, A. V. Miller renders 'die Aufklärung' as 'Enlightenment', 'the Enlightenment' and 'the enlightenment', all on a single page, thereby imposing distinctions on Hegel that are not at all apparent in his German text.[22] Charles Frankel's *The Faith of Reason* contains the following sentence: 'It was in France that enlightenment had its most lively career, and it was from France, which was the social centre of the Enlightenment, that such tenets of enlightenment as the belief in progress were most widely disseminated. The Enlightenment was a movement that transcended national boundaries; it fostered and was in turn sustained by a European culture.'[23] George Friedman gives us the following usages, all in one paragraph: 'The crises of Enlightenment . . . the purpose of Enlightenment . . . the crisis of the Enlightenment . . . the crisis of Enlightenment.'[24] One might go on indefinitely.

It is not at all clear to what the terms 'Enlightenment' and 'the enlightenment' refer. They add nothing but confusion to the debate and are therefore best avoided. I shall restrict myself to 'enlightenment' (no definite article, small 'e') as a generic concept referring to both the general goal and the process of replacing darkness with light, taken metaphorically to refer to wisdom or insight (however defined) replacing ignorance or a lack of understanding, and 'the Enlightenment' (definite article, capital 'E') to designate one historically specific conception of this process, usually associated with Europe and America after (roughly) 1750, with many national variations (e.g. the French Enlightenment, the Scottish Enlightenment, the German Enlightenment). A *concept* offers only a vague and general account of something, whereas a *conception* is a specific interpretation of it.[25] While there is one generic *concept* of enlightenment, there are many particular *conceptions* of it. For example, we may speak, as the philosopher and classical scholar Hans-Georg Gadamer does, of 'the enlightenment of the classical world' ('Die antike Aufklärung'[26]) when, as he puts it, 'the view of life enshrined in the epics and myths of Homer and Hesiod was dissolved by the new passion for discovery', epitomised by the allegory of the cave in book seven of

Plato's *Republic*.[27] Another conception of enlightenment may be found in Buddhism, where it refers to the 'experience in which one is said to "see" things as they really are, rather than as they appear to be. To have gained enlightenment is to have seen through the misleading textures of illusion and ignorance, through the dark veils of habitual comprehension, to the light and clarity of truth itself.'[28] The necessary path to enlightenment thus understood is through spiritual self-transcendence, something completely missing from the conception that emerged in Europe and America in the eighteenth century, epitomised by, although by no means confined to, the Paris-based *philosophes* such as Diderot, d'Alembert, Voltaire and Condorcet. This *conception* emphasised the centrality of reason and sensory experience as sources of knowledge, looked to modern science as the principal vehicle of human progress, and championed religious toleration. Each of these particular conceptions (ancient Greek, Buddhist, eighteenth-century European – to name just a few) exhibit distinctive, even incompatible, features, yet all are instances of the general *concept* of enlightenment, since all involve replacing ignorance or darkness with knowledge or insight of *some* kind. My concern in this study is confined to the opponents of that particular conception of enlightenment now known in English as 'the Enlightenment' of the eighteenth century.

So what was *the* Enlightenment? This question raises its own semantic problems. No such term was used by the *philosophes* in eighteenth-century France. While they did use the general *concept* of enlightenment (*éclaircissement*) and sometimes referred to themselves as 'les hommes d'éclaircissement' (men of enlightenment), they never used it to refer to a particular historical period, let alone a movement. However, the French expression 'le siècle des Lumières' (the century of lights) was used from the late eighteenth century, while 'Lumières' on its own has been popular in French only since the 1950s to refer to what is known in English as the Enlightenment.[29] But there is no 'l'Eclaircissement' in French (definite article, capital 'E') even now. The term 'the Enlightenment' came into use in English only long after the eighteenth century, and it was not until after the Second World War that it usurped the expression 'the Age of Reason' in common parlance, as in Isaiah Berlin's *The Age of Enlightenment* (1956), Jack Lively's *The Enlightenment* (1966), and in particular Peter Gay's influential two-volume study *The Enlightenment: An Interpretation* (1966–1969).[30] Philosopher John Grier Hibben appears to have been the first to use the term in the title of a book in English, *The Philosophy of the Enlightenment* (1910), and historian Alfred Cobban used it throughout his study of *Edmund Burke and the Revolt Against the Eighteenth Century* (1929).[31] The 1932 publication of Carl Becker's Storrs lectures at Yale, which uses 'the Enlightenment', and the 1951 translation of Ernst Cassirer's widely read *Die Philosophie der Aufklärung* (1932) into English as *The Philosophy of the Enlightenment*, appear to have been important milestones in this shift towards the use of 'the Enlightenment' as a period concept in English.[32] In German, 'die Aufklärung' has been used from the late eighteenth century to refer to the particular historical movement we know in English as 'the Enlightenment', as distinct from 'Aufklärung', which is the same as the English word 'enlightenment'. Thus Kant's famous essay 'Was ist Aufklärung?' (1784) is properly rendered in English as 'What is enlightenment?' rather than 'What is *the* Enlightenment?' ('Was ist *die* Aufklärung?').

It is now much harder to answer the question 'What is *the* Enlightenment?' than it was a generation ago. The term has been extended both horizontally, to encompass a much wider geographical range than France, and vertically, to include a broader spectrum of social groups than just the Paris-based *encyclopédistes*. It is now widely acknowledged that the influence of the Enlightenment was felt, and adapted in significantly different ways, throughout the old and new worlds. Recent scholarship on the Enlightenment in Scotland, Germany, Switzerland, the Netherlands, Sweden, Russia, Italy, Austria, Latin America, Bohemia, Japan and the USA has revealed the extent of the variations among these diverse contexts and their effects on the reception and development of Enlightenment ideas.[33] The work of social and cultural historians such as Robert Darnton, Margaret Jacob and Roger Chartier has further complicated, and enriched, our picture of 'the' Enlightenment by examining its more practical and concrete aspects, such as the publishing history of the *Encyclopédie*, the reading habits of the public, and the development of social movements in the eighteenth century.[34]

In the face of this mounting complexity, some have advocated abandoning the term 'the Enlightenment' altogether, on the grounds that it is an essentialising concept that homogenises many disparate movements and obscures important distinctions. Historian J. G. A. Pocock has taken this path, opting for 'enlightenments' over 'the Enlightenment'.[35] On this view, there is insufficient unity beneath the particular national contexts of eighteenth-century 'enlightenments' to justify a single encompassing expression like 'the Enlightenment'. Sankar Muthu heartily endorses Pocock's conclusion: 'It is indeed high time that we pluralise our understanding of "the Enlightenment" both for reasons of historical accuracy and because, in doing so, otherwise hidden or understudied moments of Enlightenment-era thinking will, as it were, come to light.'[36]

This is an over-reaction to the unavoidable vagueness of language and creates many problems of its own. The fact that a word is vague does not mean that it is entirely useless. The boundaries of 'Asia' are uncertain and there are many different meanings of the word 'Asian', but it is still a useful, if imperfect, word. As H. L. A. Hart argues in *The Concept of Law* (1961), when it is not clear whether a general term (such as 'vehicle') applies in a borderline case (for example, to a rollerskate), there are unlikely to be any clear conventions or consensus to which appeal can be made to resolve the matter once and for all. In such circumstances, one can only ask whether the borderline case resembles plain cases sufficiently and in relevant respects to count as an instance of the same, even though what counts as 'sufficient' or 'relevant' – let alone 'plain' – will itself never be beyond dispute. In the end, 'because we are men, not gods', as Hart put it, a choice is necessarily thrust upon us when trying to resolve such issues, and the choice will always be open to reasonable disagreement.[37] Setting a higher standard than this will only guarantee the irrelevance of most of our general concepts and lead us into a kind of conceptual and linguistic anarchy. This applies to historical categories such as 'the Enlightenment' and 'the Renaissance', terms that are now too well entrenched in both popular and scholarly usage to be abandoned any time soon, notwithstanding the preferences of some *dix-huitièmistes*.[38]

The present study is 'hermeneutical', a work of (mostly) uncritical intellectual history rather than philosophy, dealing principally with the meaning rather than the truth of propositions. As such, it does not directly address the question of the fairness of these depictions and criticisms of what we now call 'the Enlightenment' until the concluding chapter, and then only to a limited degree. Even if 'the Enlightenment' did not really exist as a single movement, it *did* exist in the minds of many writers. So I shall not attempt to answer the question 'What is the Enlightenment?' here. Rather, I shall concentrate on how those who opposed the Enlightenment answered this question, and the diversity of their criticisms of it, rather than on the accuracy or fairness of their answers. The latter is the subject of a different book, although I do assess some of the most common and important criticisms of the Enlightenment in the final chapter.

The distinction between 'enlightenment' and 'the Enlightenment' forces on us another distinction, between 'counter-enlightenment' and 'Counter-Enlightenment', the former being opposition to the concept of enlightenment in general, while the latter (with a capital 'E') is opposition to the Enlightenment of the eighteenth century. Counter-Enlightenment is based on a rejection of only one particular conception of enlightenment, whereas counter-enlightenment is a much more radical view, rejecting the concept of enlightenment per se, in *all* of its diverse forms. Two points need to be stressed here. First, Counter-Enlightenment is a form of enlightenment because *any* attempt to explain the ways in which the Enlightenment was wrong, harmful, dangerous or deluded is itself an attempt to enlighten. As some of the Enlightenment's detractors have rightly insisted, enlightenment is not the exclusive property of *the* Enlightenment. Indeed, the proponents of the Enlightenment were frequently denounced as 'sophisters of darkness' and 'slaves of prejudice'[39] who led people away from *true* enlightenment into 'illusion, error and darkness',[40] as the counter-Revolutionary Augustin Barruel put it. This only *appears* contradictory or paradoxical in the absence of the important distinction I have been insisting on between enlightenment and the Enlightenment. Counter-Enlightenment is that particular form of enlightenment which opposes the Enlightenment and seeks to enlighten us about its errors and dangers.

Second, counter-enlightenment (small 'e') is also a form of enlightenment. Whereas Counter-Enlightenment opposes itself to only one particular conception of enlightenment (namely 'the Enlightenment'), and is therefore consistent with some other conceptions and, of course, with the general concept of enlightenment, counter-enlightenment is an example of what Jürgen Habermas (1929–) calls a 'totalising critique', an attempt to 'leap out of the dialectic of enlightenment' entirely.[41] Such critics inevitably get caught in the 'performative contradiction', as Habermas calls it, of making claims and arguments the particular *content* of which is inconsistent with the *act* of making them because the act itself presupposes the very distinctions between truth and falsehood, knowledge and ignorance, accurate and inaccurate that are being explicitly denied. In this case, the *act* of countering enlightenment *in general* implicitly presupposes *some* conception of enlightenment, *some* critical perspective from which it is being judged. So there is simply no way to jump out of the dialectic of enlightenment, any more than it is possible to deny truth itself, assuming one values logical consistency. That is why enlightenment is as necessary to the Enlightenment's enemies as it is to the Enlightenment itself. To the extent that we are beings who reason and debate, we are proponents of enlightenment in *some* form, whether we reason and debate for *the* Enlightenment or against it. For this reason, I have banished 'counter-enlightenment' from my text along with 'the enlightenment' and 'Enlightenment'. My sole concern is with opposition to *the* Enlightenment.

Not all of the Enlightenment's critics wished to undermine it, let alone destroy it. Criticism of something is not necessarily the same thing as outright rejection of it. Some of the Enlightenment's critics have been sympathetic to its basic values and goals while rejecting some of its assumptions and prescriptions. Such criticisms are ultimately intended to strengthen rather than to undermine the Enlightenment. Just as some twentieth-century Marxists have revised some of Marx's original claims in order to strengthen the *general* theory in light of our knowledge and experience of the world since the nineteenth century, many have sought to revise the original assumptions and arguments of the eighteenth-century *philosophes* and *Aufklärer* in favour of a 'self-enlightened Enlightenment', or what the Germans call 'ein aufklärung über die Aufklärung'. Isaiah Berlin thought that the German philosopher J. G. Herder (1744–1803) was an early example of this, describing him as 'not an enemy but a critic of the French Enlightenment'.[42] The leading contemporary proponent of this position is Jürgen Habermas, a neo-Kantian sympathetic to, but critical of, the Enlightenment of the eighteenth century. Many other writers who do not fit neatly into one camp or the other might also best be seen as 'friendly critics' rather than outright enemies of the Enlightenment.[43] Those who were critical of *some* aspects of the Enlightenment should not, for that reason alone, be lumped in with the likes of Hamann and Maistre. This study is concerned only with those who sought to *undermine* the Enlightenment – its *enemies* – and therefore has relatively little to say about 'friendly critics' like Herder and Habermas.

Unfortunately, it is impossible to specify precisely in the abstract where the line should be drawn between enemies of the Enlightenment and friendly critics. It is a matter of the degree of opposition to the Enlightenment, even though any answer to the obvious question 'To what degree?' is always bound to be provisional and reasonably contestable, for reasons already discussed above. Any such demarcations will necessarily be debatable because of the unavoidably open texture of language, as a consequence of which many general concepts can rarely be reduced to a single agreed meaning with clear boundaries.

The term '*the* Counter-Enlightenment'? faces the same sorts of problems that confront us with 'the Enlightenment', only much more so. One of the principal claims of this study is that it makes little sense to refer to '*the* Counter-Enlightenment' as though it is a single movement, which it most definitely is not. Although a good case can be made for viewing the Enlightenment as a movement, the same is not true of 'the' Counter-Enlightenment. The range of Counter-Enlightenment thought extends far and wide, much further and wider than the Enlightenment itself, from the mid-eighteenth century to the present; it appears in a variety of national contexts, and comes from all points of the ideological compass, from conservative Catholics and German Romantics to liberals, neo-Marxists, feminists, environmentalists and postmodernists. Each opponent of the Enlightenment has their own particular conception of what it was, and their own specific reasons for opposing it, although there is much overlap and many strange bedfellows among them. That is why it is best to follow Arthur Lovejoy, who favoured 'Romanticisms' over 'Romanticism'.[44] I will therefore use only 'Counter-Enlightenment' and 'Counter-Enlightenments', rather than '*the* Counter-Enlightenment', a term that, in the interests of conceptual clarity and historical accuracy, I propose we retire along with 'the enlightenment', 'Enlightenment' and 'counter-enlightenment'.[45] It is therefore necessary to deconstruct 'the Counter-Enlightenment' into many different Counter-Enlightenments. That, essentially, is the project of this book.

The Enlightenment perversion of reason

Is there anything that the diverse enemies of the Enlightenment, encompassing diametrically opposed positions and spanning two and a half centuries, have in common? The answer is yes, although much less than might be assumed, and certainly far less than would justify using the term *the* Counter-Enlightenment as though it were a single movement. But all forms share at least three basic characteristics, which constitute the common core of Counter-Enlightenment thought: (1) all offer some conception of what we now call 'the Enlightenment', typically involving a cast of 'usual suspects' that almost always includes Voltaire, Rousseau, Helvétius and Condorcet (particularly the first two, who had been 'Panthéonised' together during the

Revolution), and an assortment of more peripheral characters, such as Diderot, Kant, Hume, d'Alembert, Bentham and the Baron d'Holbach, with some prominent seventeenth-century thinkers such as Locke, Hobbes, Bacon, Newton and Descartes occasionally thrown in as well; (2) all attack the Enlightenment as deluded and dangerous in some fundamental ways (hence *Counter*-Enlightenment); and (3) all contest what I shall call 'the Enlightenment perversion of reason': distorted conceptions of reason of the kind each associates with the Enlightenment in favour of a more restricted view of the nature, scope, and limits of human rationality. The third *New International Webster's Dictionary* definition of enlightenment as including a belief in the 'untrammelled but frequently uncritical use of reason' (p. 754) reflects the extent to which this view has taken root. It plays an important (in most cases central) part in *every* depiction of the Enlightenment by its enemies, from the mid-eighteenth century to the present, and from the far left to the far right. Yet none of the enemies of the Enlightenment has been prepared to abandon reason *entirely*. The battle has been over the scope, meaning and application of reason, not over whether it is good or bad, desirable or undesirable, essential or inessential per se. It is important not to misrepresent this conflict as one between friends and enemies of reason, any more than it is between friends and enemies of enlightenment. Although objections have consistently been raised against what has been taken as the 'typical' Enlightenment view of reason by its opponents, this has almost never been generalised to reason as such by Counter-Enlightenment thinkers.

Overview of the book

The organisation of what follows is chronological (more or less). The first half focuses on the Enlightenment's early opponents in the second half of the eighteenth and early nineteenth centuries; the second deals with its twentieth-century enemies. I have grouped thinkers together by generation, which is meant to be indicative without being either airtight or exhaustive. Each chapter focuses on a small number of representative figures who lived and wrote contemporaneously and opposed what we now call 'the Enlightenment'. This is *not* to imply that thinkers with different and often conflicting views were really ideological or intellectual kindred spirits because they shared a common enemy. A common opposition to Hitler did not make Churchill and Stalin allies in all respects. Even though the Enlightenment has been attacked from many different – even incompatible – directions, its enemies do not necessarily have anything else in common, let alone constitute a single movement. That is why I have abandoned the term *'the* Counter-Enlightenment'.

My story begins in the mid-eighteenth century, just as the Enlightenment in France was becoming conscious of itself as a movement seeking to eradicate superstition, clerical oppression and religious intolerance. I argue in Chapter 2 that the first major shot fired in the war between the Enlightenment and its enemies came from the pen of Jean-Jacques Rousseau (1712–1778), contrary to Berlin's claim that he was, at most, only an occasional critic who shared much more with the *philosophes* than he rejected. Rousseau's famous 'illumination' on the road to Vincennes in 1749 resulted in his *Discourse on the Sciences and the Arts* (1750), which prompted the *philosophe* Jean d'Alembert (1717–1783), co-editor of the *Encyclopédie*, to reply in his *Preliminary Discourse to the Encyclopédie* (1751). Although this early skirmish was a relatively polite affair compared to the vicious battles that later raged between Rousseau and the *philosophes* (particularly Voltaire), it was the first of its kind and marks the opening of what would become a 250-year war over the Enlightenment and its legacy. Not long afterwards, Johann Georg Hamann (1730–1788) had his own 'illumination' while visiting London, which gave birth to the *Aufklärung*'s first serious opponent in Germany. Together, Rousseau and Hamann launched a two-front war against the Enlightenment in France and in Germany, and set the tone for much of the subsequent debate between the Enlightenment and its enemies.

The first major assault on the Enlightenment came during the French Revolution, which is the subject of Chapter 3. In the minds of many at the time – and many since – the Enlightenment was inextricably connected to the Revolution. This presumed link gave rise to an explosion of Counter-Revolutionary hostility to the Enlightenment, beginning with Edmund Burke's (1729–1797) popular and enormously influential *Reflections on the Revolution in France* (1790). In it and the works that followed he raged against the *philosophes* for corroding the delicate fabric of *ancien régime* France with their radical ideas, and blamed a cadré of zealous revolutionaries for violently imposing wild theories inspired by the *philosophes* on an innocent and unsuspecting public. In the French-speaking world, the former Jesuit and *émigré* writer Augustin Barruel (1741–1820) took this argument even further in his best-selling *Mémoires pour servir à l'histoire du jacobinisme* (1798), which makes the case that the Revolution was the result of a deliberate conspiracy hatched by a coalition of *philosophes*, freemasons and the Order of the Illuminati to overthrow throne, altar and society in Europe. Burke read Barruel's book and was much impressed. The Savoyard Catholic Joseph de Maistre (1753–1821) read it and was not. He saw the hand of God rather than that of humans in the terrible events of the 1790s and depicted the Revolution as divine punishment for the sins of the *philosophes*. He left virtually no space for human agency in his account of the French Revolution, unlike Burke and Barruel, who seemed to regard the upheavels of the age as proof that humans had too much freedom to act.

Chapter 4 looks at the views of three Romantic writers on the Enlightenment. All were major figures in early Romanticism and all attacked the *philosophes* for being the architects of a world empty of beauty, imagination and spirit. They were also at the intellectual fore of the religious revival that swept Europe in the late eighteenth and early nineteenth centuries in reaction to decades of anti-clericalism and religious scepticism. The Romantic writers of this period emphasised spirituality, inwardness and the centrality of emotion in our mental life, all of which they believed had been systematically deprecated during the eighteenth century. The German poet and philosopher Friedrich von Hardenberg (1772–1801) regarded his as an age of transition from the beauty and faith of the Middle Ages, which was gone forever, to a new age of spirituality that he was convinced would soon dawn. Between these two periods lay the eighteenth century, epitomised by the soulless 'factory state' of Frederick II's enlightened Prussia. Another poet and philosopher, Samuel Taylor Coleridge (1772–1834), spent a crucial year of his life in Germany in his twenties when the Romantic Movement was just beginning to flower there. It marked an important step in his turn against the 'demagogues of this "enlightened age"' who, he believed, had undermined faith and helped to spawn the French Revolution.[46] After a period of youthful radicalism, the increasingly conservative Coleridge grew more and more hostile to the beliefs and values of the *philosophes*, particularly Voltaire. The French Romantic novelist and statesman François-René, vicomte de Chateaubriand (1768–1848), returned from exile in England very early in the nineteenth century and finished *Le Génie du Christianisme* (*The Genius of Christianity*, 1802), his best-selling defence of Christianity which gives the beauty and mystery of faith a centrality absent during an age when natural religion was in the ascendant and atheism was gaining ground.

Although criticism of the Enlightenment did not disappear entirely in the middle decades of the nineteenth century, it did go into remission. Despite occasional voices raised against the Enlightenment (by Thomas Carlyle, for example), it was not until the years immediately following the Second World War that it re-emerged as a key organising concept in social and political thought, this time in the context of debates about twentieth-century totalitarianism. An important exception to this is Friedrich Nietzsche (1844–1900). The Enlightenment never had the centrality for him that it would come to have for many of his twentieth-century epigones. In fact, as we shall see in Chapter 5, he enthusiastically supported it during his 'middle period' and he never lost his admiration for Voltaire – the single most vilified figure among the Enlightenment's enemies. Even so, the radical assaults on reason, truth, progress and morality in his later works mark a major turn against Enlightenment beliefs and values. In the decade prior to his complete mental breakdown in 1889, Nietzsche reversed his opinion of the Enlightenment and issued a call-to-arms against the entire eighteenth century, which his many admirers and followers in the second half of the twentieth century have taken up with zeal.

The Enlightenment acquired a central role in the story of twentieth-century totalitarianism for a generation of intellectuals born in *fin-de-siècle* Europe, when Nietzsche's work was beginning to win widespread recognition. Although these writers came from all points of the ideological compass, all were deeply affected by the experience of totalitarianism, which they associated with the Enlightenment in various ways, as I show in Chapter 6. Max Horkheimer (1895–1973) and Theodor Adorno (1903–1969) led the attack from the left with *Dialectic of Enlightenment* (1947), which loosely outlines the various ways in which the particular Western conception of enlightenment from antiquity to the present (including the Enlightenment of the eighteenth century) has had totalitarian tendencies that have come to fruition in the twentieth century, when it 'radiates disaster triumphant'. Cold War liberals such as Jacob Talmon (1916–1980) and Isaiah Berlin (1909–1997) traced the origins of twentieth-century totalitarianism back to beliefs about nature and truth shared by the *philosophes*, who sought to 'unbend the crooked timber of humanity' to make it conform to their intolerant beliefs. From the right the German *émigré* Eric Voegelin (1901–1985) and the English philosopher Michael Oakeshott (1901–1990) assaulted the rationalism of the *philosophes* for its disastrous effects on the social and political order of the West. One of the characteristics shared by most of these thinkers is the idea that the Enlightenment produced an unintended result in the twentieth century that was diametrically opposed to the intentions of the eighteenth-century *philosophes*, what I shall call 'the inversion thesis of the Enlightenment' – the unforeseen reversal that occurs when human actions unexpectedly produce the very opposite of their author's intentions, with tragic consequences, as in ancient Greek drama (known as a 'peripeteia'). This idea, for which George Crowder coined the term 'the inversion thesis' to describe a crucial aspect of Isaiah Berlin's thought, recurs in many different forms among the Enlightenment's opponents, particularly in the twentieth century.[47]

In their deconstruction of common Western assumptions about truth, reason and nature, many postmodern writers have, not surprisingly, turned their sceptical attention to the Enlightenment, which has come to epitomise those features of modernity that many of them find most pernicious and destructive. In Chapter 7 I show how Michel Foucault's (1926–1984) account of the emergence of a 'disciplinary society' ('*la société disciplinaire*') during what he called 'the classical age' (*l'âge classique*) in eighteenth-century Europe echoes Horkheimer and Adorno who, he admitted, 'had tried, earlier than I, to say things I had also been trying to say for years'.[48] In books like *Madness and Civilization* (1961), *The Birth of the Clinic* (1963) and *Discipline and Punish* (1975), Foucault describes the advent in the late seventeenth and eighteenth centuries of a deeply sinister and highly effective new form of social control that developed in conjunction with a rhetoric which was, on the surface, deceptively liberal and humane. Among the harshest critics of the Enlightenment in the twentieth century are postmodern feminists, many of whom write under Foucault's intoxicating influence. Jane Flax, for example, repeats many of Foucault's criticisms of the supposed 'purity' of Enlightenment reason, which she claims is really a form of androcentrism that suppresses vital gender differences and serves male interests. Like Nietzsche, the 'postmodern bourgeois liberal' Richard Rorty (1931–) is wholly dismissive of what he calls the 'philosophical' Enlightenment's strong assumptions about truth, reason and nature. Yet, unlike Nietzsche, he also declares himself to be unflinchingly loyal to the 'political' Enlightenment, whose 'liberal' values of toleration, moderation and humaneness he shares with the *philosophes*, albeit for 'ethnocentric' reasons utterly at odds with their universalism.

It was Nietzsche more than anyone else who put the concept of nihilism at the centre of the debate about the decline of European civilisation in the twentieth century. Several writers in the postwar West have applied his influential account of nihilism to the purported failure of the 'Enlightenment project' to construct a universal morality, the subject I explore in Chapter 8. For Lester Crocker (1912–2003), the destructive side of this project – directed primarily at Christianity – was an unqualified success, but the *philosophes* proved utterly incapable of constructing anything positive to replace what they had so effectively torn down. The best expression of the nihilistic impasse that ensued from this failure may be found in the writings of the Marquis de Sade, according to Crocker. Alasdair MacIntyre (1929–) agrees that the moral project of the Enlightenment has been an abject failure. He argues that this failure has left the West with just two options – to continue going beyond the Enlightenment deeper into Nietzschean nihilism or to go back before the Enlightenment to the ethical naturalism of Aristotle. (He opts for Aristotle.) John Gray's (1948–) strong antipathy to the Enlightenment owes much to Nietzsche, whose influence he readily acknowledges. For Gray, like Horkheimer and Adorno, the Enlightenment is the last and most destructive phase in a long Promenthean drive to master the world that began in Western antiquity. Although the Enlightenment project has failed, Gray believes that it still has the power to devastate vulnerable natural and human environments outside of the West, having gutted those within it.

I conclude in Chapter 9 with a brief assessment of some of the most common criticisms that the Enlightenment's enemies have made of it since the eighteenth century. This is the only critical chapter in the book, although it by no means constitutes a final, overall assessment of the Enlightenment and its opponents, or a complete list of criticisms. However, it is sufficient to establish that, while many palpable hits have been made against the Enlightenment, many of the shots fired at it have fallen very wide of the mark.

2 First shots

The enlightenment of our century (*Die Aufklärung unsers Jahrhunderts*) is therefore a mere northern light, from which can be prophesied no cosmopolitical chiliasm except in a nightcap & by the stove. All prattle and reasoning of the emancipated ones ... all this is a cold, unfruitful moonlight without enlightenment for the lazy understanding (*ohne Aufklärung für den faulen Verstand*) and without warmth for the cowardly will – and the entire response to the question which has been posed is blind illumination (*eine blinde Illumination*) for every immature one who walks at noon.[1]

(J. G. Hamann)

Introduction

The Enlightenment's first two truly serious, formidable opponents were among its first defectors: Jean-Jacques Rousseau (1712–1778) and Johann Georg Hamann (1730–1788). Like many of the Enlightenment's early critics, both had once been sympathetic to it. After his arrival in Paris in 1743, Rousseau became an *homme de salon*, friend of the *philosophes* and regular contributor to the *Encyclopédie*. As a student in Prussia, Hamann had been 'a typical young German of the *Aufklärung*' and a 'disciple of the French *lumières*'.[2] However, the trajectory of their views changed dramatically following transformative personal experiences each had which ultimately led them to turn against the French and German Enlightenments respectively. According to his *Confessions*, this experience occurred for Rousseau in 1749 while he was on his way to see his imprisoned friend Diderot, editor of the *Encyclopédie*. It was then that he had his famous 'illumination' on the road to Vincennes while reading about an essay contest sponsored by the Academy of Dijon. 'From the moment I read these words,' he later recorded, 'I saw another universe and I became another man.'[3] The intellectual product of this epiphany was Rousseau's *Discourse on the Sciences and the Arts* (1750), the principal contention of which is that 'our souls have been corrupted in proportion to the advancement of our Sciences and Arts to perfection'.[4] He continued to denounce the 'fatal enlightenment of Civil man' (*des lumières funestes de l'homme civil*) for the rest of his life, and fought a long and increasingly bitter war with the leading *philosophes*.[5]

Just under a decade later Hamann had a similar life-altering experience of a more directly religious kind while living in London in 1758.[6] Isolated and deeply depressed in a foreign country, his mission on behalf of his friend and employer a failure, he immersed himself in the Bible. As he read he was 'seized with the awareness that he was not simply reading the history of Israel, but the record of his own life'.[7] He emerged from this experience transformed, to the great chagrin and bewilderment of his enlightened friends back home. From this point Hamann took up arms against the *Aufklärung*, just as Rousseau had done against the *philosophes* almost a decade earlier.[8] Between them, they set the terms within which the great clash between the Enlightenment and its enemies took place for generations to come.

Isaiah Berlin has written that Hamann was both 'the first out-and-out opponent of the French Enlightenment of his time' and its 'most passionate, consistent, extreme and implacable enemy',[9] whereas Jean-Jacques Rousseau was only an occasional critic of 'this or that error or crime of the new culture' of the Enlightenment, who 'shares more presuppositions with the Encyclopaedists than he denies'.[10] It is possible that Hamann was a more passionate and consistent enemy of the Enlightenment than was Rousseau (I do not intend to argue the point either way), but the latter's *Discourse on the Sciences and the Arts* was the first major shot fired in the war between the Enlightenment and its enemies. Hamann did not turn decisively against the Enlightenment until after the spiritual crisis he experienced in England in 1758, whereas Rousseau's earlier discourse (1750) directly challenged many of the basic assumptions and objectives of the Enlightenment. In addition, Rousseau was far more than an occasional critic of the Enlightenment, as the *philosophes* knew only too well. He was a pivotal figure in the emergence of the movement that gradually developed against the Enlightenment in the second half of the eighteenth century, eventually giving rise to a rejection of its central ideas and assumptions by many writers in the early nineteenth century, particularly, although by no means exclusively, those associated with Romanticism.[11] Rousseau's writings represent the first serious intellectual challenge to the Enlightenment in France, and Hamann's work occupies a comparable position in the context of the German Enlightenment, where they gave 'a mighty stimulus to the currents of irrationalism that were present in the *Sturm und Drang* and Romanticism'.[12]

The Counter-Enlightenment republic of virtue

Throughout much of the 1740s Rousseau was a close friend and supporter of the leading *philosophes* of the day. The editor of the *Encyclopédie*, who was one of his closest friends at the time, assisted him in publishing his first *Discourse*; he owed the circulation of many of his works in France to

Malesherbes, the Director of Publications, who was sympathetic to the *philosophes* and their ideas; he corresponded with Voltaire, he contributed to the *Encyclopédie*, and he was a *habitué* of the salons of Paris. Charles Palissot's popular satirical comedy of the period, *Les Philosophes* (1760), parodied Rousseau along with other leading *lumières* without distinguishing between them.

However, Rousseau's upbringing in the Calvinist city-state of Geneva prevented his complete absorption into the sophisticated culture of eighteenth-century Paris. He continued to think of himself as a 'citoyen de Genève' for most of his life. His eventual alienation from the world of enlightened Paris was partly rooted in the simple provincial values which he carried with him when he left Geneva as a young man. Rousseau retained an image of his native city as the ideal community, a small, virtuous, self-contained fraternity of independent people of simple faith and strong morals, which he contrasted favourably with the fragmentation and immorality of modern, sophisticated urban civilisation, epitomised by Paris, the 'capital city' of the Enlightenment, where 'the whole order of natural sentiments is reversed'.[13] He rallied to the defence of his beloved homeland when he thought that it was threatened by the insidious spread of Parisian values through the modern theatre that Voltaire had recently introduced. Rousseau's idealised Geneva was as much a small, cohesive city-state of robust, 'masculine' virtue as Paris was a sprawling 'abyss' full of decadent, 'scheming, idle people without religion or principle'.[14] To his mind, these two cities symbolised the best and the worst of collective life under modern conditions, one a monument to sophistication and enlightenment, the other a model of simplicity and virtue.

In reaction to the sophisticated milieu of enlightened Paris from which he grew progressively alienated, Rousseau eventually undertook an 'intellectual and moral reformation', forsaking the lifestyle and values with which he had associated since his arrival in Paris a decade earlier, having then been '[s]educed for a long time by the prejudices of my century'.[15] He eventually abandoned Paris and fell out with those *philosophes* with whom he was still on speaking terms.

That serious trouble lay ahead was already apparent in Rousseau's *Discourse on the Sciences and the Arts*, which praises ignorance and argues that the strength and purity of morals are inversely related to the presence of the universal arts and sciences. Many *philosophes*, such as Voltaire, were amazed and repelled by this argument, and in his *Preliminary Discourse to the Encyclopédie* (1751), d'Alembert treated it as a kind of 'Preliminary Discourse to an anti-*Encyclopédie*'. This became the first significant skirmish in what would eventually develop into a full-scale war between Rousseau and the *philosophes*.

However, open warfare did not come until Rousseau's *Letter to d'Alembert* (1758), which attacked the performance of modern theatre on Genevese territory when Voltaire was staging plays at his estate near Geneva and persuading its citizens to take part in them. Rousseau blamed 'that buffoon'

Voltaire for ruining his homeland by corrupting its morals. In response, Voltaire denounced Rousseau as an 'arch-fool'[16] and the 'Judas of his *confrères*'.[17] He wrote to a friend asking: 'What about Jean-Jacques's book against the theatre? Has he become a priest of the church?'[18] The fact that the orthodox Jesuit priest Guillaume-François Berthier (1704–1784) admired Rousseau's letter was simply grist for Voltaire's mill. Many of Rousseau's associates among the *philosophes* were further amazed and infuriated by what they took to be the apostasy of his subsequent writings as well, seeing in them further evidence that, as Voltaire wrote to Mme d'Epinay, 'Jean-Jacques has gone off his head'.[19] Even d'Alembert, who often tried to temper Voltaire's attacks on 'that lunatic Jean-Jacques',[20] was led to conclude that 'Jean-Jacques was mad'.[21] After Rousseau's *débâcle* with the good-natured David Hume in 1766, the latter denounced him as 'absolutely lunatic'.[22] Eventually, as Peter Gay notes, Rousseau 'was treated as a madman by other philosophes long before his clinical symptoms became obtrusive',[23] no doubt due to his seemingly inexplicable 'betrayal' of the Enlightenment.

The core of the critique of the Enlightenment developed by Rousseau lies in his decisive modification of its rejection of social contract theory. Their many differences notwithstanding, virtually all of the *philosophes* criticised social contract theory, affirming instead their belief in both the indispensability of society to the formation of a fully human identity, and the existence of natural human sociability, understood as the innate disposition of human beings towards society. While Rousseau agreed with the former, he rejected the latter. Unlike the *philosophes*, he argues in his *Discourse on Inequality* (1755) that man in the state of nature is an isolated creature whose exclusive, instinctual concern is with its own physical preservation and well-being, remarking on 'the little care taken by Nature to bring Men together through mutual needs and to facilitate their use of speech, one at least sees how little it prepared their Sociability, and how little it contributed to everything men have done to establish Social bonds'.[24]

Rousseau not only claimed that humans are naturally asocial. In his *Discourse on Inequality* he argues that the otherwise benign natural self-regard of human beings in the state of nature (*amour de soi*) is transformed into a powerful and aggressive form of selfishness in society (*amour-propre*), which eventually leads to a state of social warfare. When natural accidents such as floods and earthquakes forced human beings into collective action in the state of nature, their closer proximity increased their awareness of each other. Eventually, individuals began to compare themselves, as a result of which the natural differences between them became increasingly apparent. This eventually developed into an obsessive and ceaseless comparison with others, leading to divisive social competition and even warfare while increasing our dependence on others as we compete for their esteem and recognition.

Like Hobbes, therefore, Rousseau denied that the providentially directed harmony in nature applies to society, as the *philosophes* assumed, and dismissed what he saw as the unfounded optimism lying behind the new morality of commercial society, according to which an 'invisible hand' turns 'private vice' into 'public virtue'. This discontinuity between natural order and social disorder is conveyed very clearly in Rousseau's *Emile* (1762):

> But when next I seek to know my individual place in my species, and I consider its various ranks and the men who fill them, what happens to men? What a spectacle! Where is the order [of nature] I had observed? The picture of nature had presented me with only harmony and proportion; that of mankind presents me with only confusion and disorder! Concert reigns among the elements, and men are in chaos! The animals are happy; their king alone is miserable![25]

By retaining an important aspect of the Hobbesian view, albeit in a modified form, Rousseau insinuated a discordant note of social pessimism into the Enlightenment critique of contractualism, and thereby played an important role in placing the problem of order at the centre of social theory. He reintroduced the radical pessimism of Hobbes and, more importantly, linked it to the principle of enlightenment by claiming that the latter exacerbates this social war of all against all. Rousseau argued that the naivety and simplicity of the *philosophes* blinded them to the deep tensions and complexities of collective life and the powerful disintegrative forces that pose a constant threat to social order. He maintained that, by disseminating philosophy, science and letters, attacking the common moral life, practices and 'good opinion' of society and subjecting religion and religious institutions to systematic criticism and doubt, the French Englightenment has undermined the very conditions of peaceful social life itself, inflaming *amour-propre*, releasing the powerful self-will of the individual and thereby plunging society into a Hobbesian state of war.

While the *philosophes* took human sociability for granted, Rousseau was primarily concerned to explore ways of manufacturing social cohesion and counteracting the powerful atomising force of *amour-propre*. Negatively, this required preventing, or at least minimising, the development and popularisation of philosophy, science and letters, and devaluing reason and the intellect in favour of direct, non-rational sources of moral perception such as conscience and instinct. For Rousseau, ignorance (of the 'right' kind) was not only a desirable condition for most people, but was actually necessary for the preservation of moral, political and social order, all of which rest on foundations that are not primarily rational. Indeed, he believed that the pursuit and acquisition of knowledge and the cultivation of reason only exacerbate the socially disintegrative power of *amour-propre*. Rousseau therefore set himself foursquare against the French Enlightenment project of disseminating and popularising knowledge, particularly of the arts and sciences.

Positively, Rousseau turned to religion and patriotism as the best means of artificially promoting the sociability naturally lacking in human beings. Contrary to virtually all the *philosophes*, he did not believe that human nature and reason are sufficient to sustain the precarious bonds of society in the face of the powerful disintegrative forces constantly pulling against them. Instead, he claimed that particular religious and political institutions and beliefs are needed to promote the strengthening of 'sentiments of sociability', in the absence of which society will become a Hobbesian battleground. With the assumption of natural human sociability, the *philosophes* could confidently rely on the self-regulating powers of civil society to maintain social order (more or less). Given his rejection of this crucial Enlightenment assumption, Rousseau was forced to rely on religion and the state to manufacture sociability. The disorder that he identifies with society can only be controlled by means of the artificial promotion of social order through institutions and habits that reshape the identity and beliefs of individuals, causing them to identify with the common interests of all rather than their own narrowly defined, particular interests, thereby transforming the war of all against all in the spirit of community. Principal among these, Rousseau argues, are a strong and exclusive sense of national identity, the intervention of a quasi-divine legislator, and the integration of religion, society, morality and the state, in emulation of the city-states of antiquity. All play an indispensable part in the process of artificially adapting individuals to society and together constitute his republican Counter-Enlightenment answer to the enlightened 'republic of letters' of the *philosophes*.

For the *philosophes*, the acquisition and dissemination of 'all useful knowledge of Benefit to Mankind in General' was at the core of their goal of dispelling ignorance and spreading enlightenment. This was thought particularly true of scientific knowledge, the application of which held the greatest promise of promoting human well-being by extending man's control over the natural world. Such popularisation of knowledge, according to Condorcet, is what distinguishes the eighteenth century from earlier centuries. 'Up to this stage,' he wrote in 1794, 'the sciences have been the birthright of very few; they were now becoming common property and the time was at hand when their elements, their principles, and their simpler methods would become truly popular.'[26] This Enlightenment mission of disseminating useful knowledge is epitomised by the *Encyclopédie*, to which virtually every *philosophe* contributed and all supported, to a greater or lesser extent. This ambitious project represents the Enlightenment 'body and soul'.[27] It sought to provide a comprehensive compendium of modern learning in the natural and human sciences in a collection of articles written by virtually all the leading *philosophes* of the day in France, including d'Alembert, Diderot, Duclos, Naigeon, Grimm, Jaucourt, Raynal, Turgot, Holbach, Saint-Lambert, Marmontel, Morellet and Voltaire.[28] The Attorney-General of France acknowledged the importance of the *Encyclopédie* as a *machine de guerre* of the Enlightenment, the weapon of 'a society organised to propagate materialism, to destroy Religion, to inspire a spirit of independence, and to nourish the corruption of morals',[29] when he attacked it before the Parlement of Paris in January 1759, just before it was banned.

Despite contributing to the *Encyclopédie* himself (almost exclusively articles on music), Rousseau held that popularising philosophy and practical science is both a cause and an effect of the corruption of civilised societies. Their popularity is symptomatic of moral debasement, since 'the Sciences and Arts owe their birth to our vices'.[30] At the same time, their popularisation is destructive of whatever residues of morality and religion still remain in such decadent contexts. The taste for philosophy, letters and science so characteristic of 'enlightened societies' only inflames *amour-propre*, further 'loosen[ing] in us all the bonds of esteem and benevolence that attach men to society'.[31] That is why Rousseau openly rejected the fundamental goal of the Enlightenment in France as a recipe for certain disaster and called for ignorance and simplicity where the *philosophes* called for knowledge and sophistication. His preference was for the 'happy ignorance' of Sparta over Athens, that 'fatherland of the Sciences and Arts' so much admired by the *philosophes*.[32]

Rousseau linked philosophy to *amour-propre* in his first major political essay. 'Philosophy,' he wrote pessimistically in *The Discourse on the Sciences and the Arts*, 'will always defy reason, truth, and even time, because it has its source in human pride, stronger than all those things'.[33] He repeated this connection again towards the end of his life, when he wrote in his 'Dialogues' (written between 1772 and 1776) that '[t]he proud despotism of modern philosophy has carried the egoism of amour-propre to its furthest extent'.[34] Given that Rousseau associated 'proud philosophy' with *amour-propre* and blamed the latter for giving rise to a Hobbesian state of war in society, philosophy is, by implication, fundamentally socially destructive. Hence his description in *Emile* of the enervating effects of 'the reasoning and philosophic spirit' on society, which causes 'attachment to life, makes souls effeminate and degraded, concentrates all the passions in the baseness of private interest, in the abjectness of the human *I*, and thus quietly saps the true foundations of every society'.[35] For Rousseau, ignorance 'never did any harm . . . error alone is fatal'.[36] In his reply to the King of Poland's criticisms of the first *Discourse*, Rousseau offered an unapologetic defence of such 'happy ignorance':

> There is another, reasonable kind of ignorance, which consists in confining one's curiosity to the extent of the faculties which one has received; a modest ignorance, which is born from a lively love of virtue and inspires only indifference towards all things that are not worthy of filling a man's heart and do not contribute to his betterment; a sweet and precious ignorance, the treasure of a soul that is pure and content with itself, that finds all its felicity in retreating into itself, in confirming itself in its innocence, which places all its happiness in

turning inward, bearing witness to its innocence, and has no need to seek a false and vain happiness in the opinion others may have of its enlightenment.[37]

It follows that the happiest societies are those that are the most ignorant of the arts and sciences. '[T]he beautiful time, the time of virtue for each People was that of its ignorance', Rousseau wrote, summarising the principal thesis of his essay to a critic. 'And to the extent to which it has become learned, Artistic, and Philosophical, it has lost its morals and its probity.'[38] The opposite of this golden age is Rousseau's own society, peopled by 'happy slaves' who are entirely oblivious to the fact that 'the Sciences, Letters, and Arts ... spread garlands of flowers over the iron chains with which men are burdened'.[39] The effect of the popular dissemination of the arts and sciences in virtuous societies is to undermine the 'good opinion' of ordinary citizens. Enlightenment, understood as the popularisation of knowledge, is therefore antithetical to virtue and social harmony.

> But when peoples began to be enlightened and to believe themselves to be philosophers also, they imperceptibly accustomed themselves to the most peculiar propositions, and there was no paradox so monstrous that the desire to distinguish oneself did not cause to be maintained. Even virtue and divinity were put into question, and since one must always think differently from the people, philosophers were not needed to cast ridicule on the things they venerated.[40]

That is why philosophers are, for Rousseau, 'the enemies of public opinion' who go everywhere 'armed with their deadly paradoxes, undermining the foundations of faith, and annihilating virtue. They smile disdainfully at the old-fashioned words of Fatherland and Religion, and devote their talents and Philosophy to destroying and debasing all that is sacred among men.'[41]

Although Rousseau's estimate of the cognitive capacities of ordinary men and women was not high, it mattered little to him, since he did not value this capacity very highly anyway. For Rousseau, a strong moral sense is much more important than knowledge or cognitive ability. It is the strength and purity of virtue, a good heart rather than the possession of knowledge, that is decisive. The innate faculty of conscience, which naturally inclines us towards the good, is of infinitely greater value than the faculty of reason, which usually leads most people astray. Often, knowledge obscures our intuitive disposition towards the good, and the intellect more often than not diverts us from our immediate impulse to do what is right. Philosophers, relying on reason rather than the 'inner light' of conscience, have allowed their empiricism to wipe away the greatest human faculty. Throughout his works Rousseau repeatedly stresses the importance and power of intuitive feeling and sentiment over reason, which he regards as too weak and unreliable to act as a basis for morality or politics, unlike the infallible 'voix intérieur' of conscience, which is the individual's pre-cognitive link with the divine. Rousseau thought of reason as a very weak and unreliable human faculty anyway, more often than not eclipsed by more powerful passions. In a political fragment, he explicitly stated that '[t]he mistake of most moralists has always been to consider man as an essentially reasonable being. Man is a sensitive being, who consults solely his passions in order to act, for whom reason serves only to palliate the follies his passions lead him to commit.'[42] In a letter to Jacob Vernes in 1758 Rousseau announced that 'I have abandoned reason and consulted nature, that is, the inner feeling which directs my belief independently of reason'.[43] In other words, Rousseau took a decisive step, both for himself and for the history of thought generally, away from the Enlightenment's reliance on reason towards a stress on the inner life and feelings of the individual, which he linked directly to the inner world of the spirit, something he thought the *philosophes* denigrated or totally disregarded.

Rousseau also implicates reason in the destructive strengthening of *amour-propre*. In his *Discourse on Inequality*, for example, he writes that reason 'engenders amour-propre and reflection fortifies it; reason turns man back upon himself, it separates him from all that bothers and afflicts him. Philosophy isolates him; because of it he says in secret, at the sight of a suffering man: perish if you will, I am safe.'[44] For Rousseau, the more men reason, the more wicked they become, because of the links between reason and *amour-propre*. Given his hostility to popular enlightenment, it is hardly surprising that Rousseau expressed such a strong preference for Sparta, which 'chased the Arts and Artists, the Sciences and Scientists away from [its] walls',[45] over Athens, 'the abode of civility and good taste, the country of Orators and Philosophers' which is 'the pure source from which we received the Enlightenment of which our century boasts'.[46]

Although Rousseau believed that *amour-propre* is as inescapable as society itself, he thought that, under very rare circumstances, it may be used to strengthen social bonds. He was deeply pessimistic about the likelihood that such circumstances would emerge even under the best of conditions, and he considered the civilisation of modern Europe to be the *least* favourable to their promotion. However, he did see *some* faint hope for preserving a semblance of Sparta in those obscure corners of modern Europe that the *philosophes* regarded as among the most backwards: Poland, Geneva and Corsica.[47] By the end of his life, he appears to have abandoned even this faint hope in favour of individual salvation by isolating himself completely from the corrupting influences of his age and retreating from the human to the natural world.

Given his overwhelmingly pessimistic social assumptions, Rousseau argues that sentiments must be fostered artificially by means of institutions and beliefs that systematically reshape the individual's antisocial passions in a way that promotes the formation and strengthening of social bonds. There is a vital connection, in other words, between sociability and the institutions and ethos of society. Since social sentiments are not naturally found in human beings they must be instilled and maintained from outside. 'Good institutions,' Rousseau writes in *Emile*, 'are those that best know how to denature man, to take his absolute existence from him in order to give him a relative one and transport the *I* into the common unity, with the result that each individual believes himself no longer one but part of the unity and no longer feels except within the whole.'[48] By denying that society is naturally self-sustaining, in other words, Rousseau introduced a link between sociability and politics, one function of which became to manufacture sentiments of sociability where none naturally exist. This provided a basis for the state's involvement in social life.

Rousseau insisted that any solution (or partial solution) to the social predicament must be based on an acceptance of the fact that individuals in society are necessarily dominated by *amour-propre*, the aggressive social form of *amour de soi*. However, he believed that it is possible to mitigate the social divisiveness of *amour-propre* by refocusing it, away from individuals and towards national communities. The 'well-ordered society' is one that maintains institutions, practices and beliefs that 'lead us out of ourselves', diffusing our individual selfishness throughout society and minimising the distance between our particular interests and the common interests of all. By uniting individual wills and interests with the social will and the common interest in this way, *amour-propre* becomes an extended form of social, rather than individual, selfishness. Love of *one*self thus becomes love of *our*selves. 'Let us extend *amour-propre* to other beings', Rousseau writes in *Emile*. 'We shall transform it into a virtue.'[49]

However, Rousseau warned that a global diffusion of *amour-propre* would be unable to generate a sufficiently strong bond of attachment between individuals to preserve social unity. '[T]he feeling of humanity evaporates and weakens as it is extended over the whole world', he writes in his *Encyclopédie* article 'Economie Politique' (1755). 'Interest and commiseration must in some way be confined and compressed to be activated.'[50] According to this essay, the optimal extension of *amour-propre*, one that mitigates the powerful effects of individual selfishness without completely dissipating it through over-extension, focuses on national communities. The republican Rousseau maintained that a strong sense of national identity is crucial to counteract the strength of particular wills by redirecting them, rather than actually repressing them, towards a common end. '[T]he greatest miracles of virtue have been produced by love of fatherland', Rousseau wrote. 'By combining the force of amour-propre with all the beauty of virtue, this sweet and ardent sentiment gains an energy which, without disfiguring it, makes it the most heroic of all the passions. It produced the many immortal actions whose splendour dazzles our weak eyes.'[51]

Since individuals do not naturally identify themselves with particular communities, Rousseau argues that something external to the individual self is necessary to engineer this extension of *amour-propre*. The figure of the legislator, who occupies a central position in both *The Social Contract* (1762) and *The Government of Poland* (written between 1771 and 1772; published 1782) is introduced by Rousseau to overcome this problem. Citing the examples of Mohammed, Lycurgus, Moses, Numa and Calvin, he contends that such semi-divine individuals are vital to the establishment of a well-ordered society. In the *Government of Poland* he writes admiringly of Lycurgus, Numa and Moses in particular for creating 'ties that would bind citizens to the fatherland and to one another. ... All three found what they were looking for in distinctive usages, in religious ceremonies that invariably were in essence exclusive and national.'[52] The 'genius' of these ancient lawgivers lay in their ability to engineer *moeurs*, customary habits and foundational laws and beliefs that shaped lasting communities of public-spirited citizens from a fractious body of essentially self-regarding individuals. Their task, in other words, is that of 'changing human nature' so that *amour-propre* is focused on the national community rather than on the individual.

The manufacture of sociability is central to Rousseau's essay on *The Government of Poland*. The key to the political health of Poland, he argued, is the existence of a powerful sense of national solidarity. One of the principal duties of the state, as we have seen, is the artificial cultivation of 'sentiments of sociability' which, in the case of Poland, is best achieved through the promotion of 'that patriotic fervour which raises men – as nothing else can raise them – above themselves'.[53] 'Sublime' Sparta is the model to which Rousseau urged Poles to turn for inspiration. He rejected the view put forth by the *philosophes* that the universal arts and sciences are an adequate basis for political community, advising the Poles strictly to curtail their development, the debilitating effects of which would be fatal to their vigorous *moeurs* and exclusive national spirit. '[I]t is education,' he writes in *The Government of Poland*, 'that you must count on to shape the souls of the citizens in a national pattern and so to direct their opinions, their likes, and dislikes that they shall be patriotic by inclination, passionately, of necessity. The newly-born infant, upon first opening his eyes, must gaze upon the fatherland, and until his dying day should behold nothing else.'[54]

Rousseau contrasted what he took to be the social fragmentation and moral depredation of the 'enlightened' cosmopolitan civilisation of eighteenth-century Europe (epitomised by Paris) with an idealised image of the cohesive, homogeneous communities of past ages when virtue reigned supreme and all aspects of life were tightly integrated. This may be seen in the admiration he often expressed for pre-modern societies and non-Western (i.e. non-Enlightenment) cultures, such as Sparta, Persia, Scythia, Germany and republican Rome, and in his praise for the great legislators of antiquity, who embody the union of religion, politics and morality he proposed. Most *philosophes* also thought in terms of a contrast between modern European civilisation and the cultures of other times and places. However, the latter were typically described in terms such as 'barbaric' and 'primitive' when compared to the modern (European) age. This contrast was central to the philosophical history of the French Enlightenment, according to which mankind has gradually (in some cases *very* gradually indeed) ascended from a state of ignorance and barbarism to a condition of enlightened civilisation, the apogee of which was eighteenth-century Europe. This progression was interpreted as a development from national and subnational particularism and narrowness to universalism and openness. Rousseau inverted this Enlightenment account in his first major political work, the *Discourse on the Sciences and Arts*, and it remained a central theme of his writings thereafter. He openly and repeatedly attacked eighteenth-century civilisation for its artificiality, immorality, inauthenticity and absence of a strong binding sense of patriotic community, and he poured scorn on its sustaining myths.

Religion, like patriotism, was for Rousseau an indispensable ingredient of social and political life because of its power to shape men's souls so that *amour-propre* is extended beyond the individual. Most of the *philosophes* were prepared to grant that religion is necessary to the maintenance of morality, at least among the unenlightened masses. Even the militantly anti-clerical Voltaire conceded that, 'if God did not exist, it would be necessary to invent him'.[55] This, in fact, was the moderate position of the French Enlightenment, as found, for example, in the *Encyclopédie* article 'Société'. In *The Spirit of the Laws* the moderate *philosophe* Montesquieu notes that 'religion, even a false one, is the best warrant men can have of the integrity of men'.[56] For such *philosophes*, a benign – if remote – God is a necessary condition for moral order, a view that aligned them with the critics of the radical Enlightenment, and distinguished them from the minority of atheists such as Diderot, La Mettrie, Baron d'Holbach, Helvétius and Naigeon.

What so offended the *philosophes*, and alienated Rousseau from atheists and deists alike, was his rejection of the Enlightenment idea of a secular, rational state. Rousseau wished to tear down the wall between church and state that the *philosophes* had sought to erect, defending a civil religion and arguing against religious diversity modelled on ancient Sparta and Calvinist Geneva. Hence his praise for Hobbes, who called for the union of the 'two heads of the eagle': religion and the state. This is one of the principal reasons for Rousseau's deep admiration of the civic cults of antiquity, in which religion and politics were united. The 'religion of the citizen,' as he called it, 'combines the divine cult and love of the laws, and by making the fatherland the object of the Citizens' adoration, it teaches them that to serve the State is to serve its tutelary God. It is a kind of Theocracy.'[57]

Rousseau's own version of this 'catechism of the citizen' in *The Social Contract* elicited a predictably hostile response from most of the *philosophes*, precisely because of its call for the union of religion and politics. Voltaire wrote in the margin of his copy that '[a]ll dogma is ridiculous, deadly. All coercion on dogma is abominable. To compel belief is absurd. Confine yourself to compelling good living.'[58] Shortly after *Emile* had been officially condemned in France, Diderot wrote to his mistress that Rousseau 'has the devout party on his side. He owes their interest in him to the bad things he says about the *philosophes*. . . . They keep hoping that he will be converted;

they're sure that a deserter from our camp must sooner or later pass over into theirs.'[59] The same thought occurred to Voltaire, who asked: 'Has he [Rousseau] become a priest of the church?'[60]

Rousseau's eagerness to eradicate the wall that the *philosophes* were anxious to build between church and state can be better understood when it is borne in mind that he was a proud citizen of Geneva, which had no tradition of such a separation. For the general will to be generated and then to be sovereign, it is necessary that the structure of society be so closely unified that there is no room left for any kind of independent association within the body politic which might constitute a rival will with an interest of its own. Such dissensus is fatal to political unity and inimical to the formation and sovereignty of the general will. Rousseau therefore strongly disapproved of religious nonconformity, which creates conflict rather than unity. It was in deference to this principle that he justified his return to Protestantism during his visit to Geneva in 1754.

> Far from shaking my faith, frequentation of the Encyclopedists had strengthened it as a result of my natural aversion for disputations and for factions ... I also judged that everything that is form and discipline in each country fell within the competence of the laws. From this principle – which is so sensible, so social, so pacific, and which has drawn such cruel persecutions on me – it followed that, wanting to be a Citizen, I ought to be a Protestant and return into the worship established in my country.[61]

Given the divisive presence of *amour-propre* and the absence of natural social bonds, Rousseau believes that social and political life would be impossible without a civil religion, one practical function of which is to stimulate artificially the individual's identification with his national community and its laws and institutions. This identification will diminish the strength of his particular will, which is inversely related to the strength of the general will. Thus, in the first version of *The Social Contract*, Rousseau begins the chapter on civil religion with the statement that, '[a]s soon as men live in society, they must have a Religion that keeps them there. A people has never subsisted nor ever will subsist without Religion, and if it were not given one, it would make one itself or would soon be destroyed.'[62] In fact, Rousseau had said as much himself five years earlier in his *Discourse on Inequality*, in which he linked religion with the weakness of reason.

> [T]he frightful dissensions, the infinite disorders that this dangerous power would necessarily entail demonstrate more than anything else how much *human Governments needed a basis more solid than reason alone*, and how necessary it was for public repose that divine will intervened to give Sovereign authority a sacred and inviolable character which took from the subjects the fatal Right of disposing of it.[63]

Prophet of the secret heart

As a young man, Johann Georg Hamann struggled to reconcile the Enlightenment ideas whose influence he felt while growing up in Königsberg under Frederick II (1712–1786) and as a university student in the early 1750s with the values and beliefs of his Pietist upbringing, just as the Genevan Protestant Rousseau tweaked the conscience of Rousseau the Paris *salonnière*.

The *Aufklärung* was institutionalised in eighteenth-century Prussia to a greater degree than the Enlightenment was in pre-Revolutionary France. Whereas most *philosophes* stood outside and opposed to the church and state establishment in France, in eighteenth-century Prussia the *Aufklärer* were closely allied to both, largely because of the Francophile Frederick II, ally of the *philosophes* and practitioner *par excellence* of 'enlightened despotism'. By the second half of the eighteenth century most educated Prussians like Hamann had been moulded by the enlightened policies of Frederick to some degree.[64] But eighteenth-century Germany was also the centre of the Pietist reform movement within the Lutheran Church led by Count Nikolaus von Zinzendorf (1700–1760), which set itself firmly against the rational theology propounded by *Aufklärer* like Christian Wolff (1679–1754). It preached a life of simple piety modelled on the early church, the inner experience of faith, the sovereignty of individual conscience, and the centrality of feeling and intuition over reason. In this it followed the anti-rationalism of Martin Luther (1483–1546) himself, for whom reason was a 'whore' not to be trusted. It is not hard to see why Isaiah Berlin regarded Pietism as 'the root of romanticism' in Germany, given its enormous influence on the generations of eighteenth-century German writers who would eventually rebel against the *Aufklärung*.[65]

The contest for supremacy within Hamann came to a head in the spiritual crisis he experienced in London in 1758, when pietism won a final victory over the *Aufklärung* in the struggle between his heart and his head. Writing later about this pivotal moment in *Gedanken über meinen Lebenslauf (Thoughts on the Course of My Life*, 1759), he recounted that 'The Spirit of God continued to reveal to me more and more the mystery of divine love and the blessing of faith in our gracious and only Saviour in spite of my great weakness, in spite of the long resistance which I had until then offered to his testimony and his compassion . . . I feel now, thank God, my heart calmer than ever before in my life.'[66] As a consequence of this experience, Jesus became the 'one single truth' to which Hamann henceforth devoted his intellectual life. According to Frederick Beiser, this was decisive not only for Hamann personally, but for German thought in general, since it marked 'one of the starting points of the *Sturm und Drang* and the reaction against the Enlightenment' in Germany.[67]

The cold, heartless centre of everything that Hamann had come to oppose in the German-speaking world of his time after his London experience was Berlin, to which he professed a deep, personal antipathy. It was the Prussian

counterpart to Rousseau's Paris, the capital city of the French Enlighten-
ment that Rousseau abominated. Hamann even identified his hatred for
Babel – his preferred name for Berlin – as 'the true key to my writings'.[68]
The Berliners, he told his friend and ally against the *Aufklärung* Friedrich
Heinrich Jacobi (1743–1819), are 'my adversaries and philistines, on whom
I avenge myself'.[69] The evil brain of Frederick's 'enlightened' Prussian State
was the Berlin Academy, or the 'Academy of Satan', as Hamann dubbed it in
characteristically religious terms,[70] which Frederick had revived and which
became an important source of policies and ideas.

If Berlin was the capital city of 'the enemy' for Hamann, their leader was
'le philosophe de Sans Soucy', Frederick II himself, supported by his 'grand
vizier' Voltaire and a court that included some of the leading French
philosophes, such as the atheist Julien Offray de la Mettrie (1709–1751) and
Maupertuis (1698–1759), President of the Berlin Academy. Hamann called
the period in which he lived the 'age of Voltaire'[71] and regarded Frederick's
enlightened, paternalistic court as an alien presence in his native land, arro-
gantly imposing foreign ideas and institutions on its supposedly 'immature'
people. '[T]rue enlightenment' (*daß wahe Aufklärung*), he asserted, 'consists
in a departure of the immature man out of a *supremely self-incurred* guardian-
ship' of the kind epitomised by the Frederician state and rationalised by
Aufklärer like Kant.[72] Writing about Frederick's court in *Aesthetica in Nuce*
(1762), Hamann remarked that 'The prince of this aeon makes favourites of
the greatest villains against themselves; his court-jesters are the worst
enemies of beautiful nature'.[73] Frederick's Francophile court was composed
of mere 'hunting dogs and laps dogs, whippets and bear-biters' who arro-
gantly seemed to expect gratitude from the ordinary Prussian people for its
despotism.[74] Hamann's 1772 essay *Au Salomon de Prusse* (*To the Solomon of
Prussia*) took its ironic title from Voltaire's ode to the young Frederick upon
ascending the throne – 'Solomon of the North brings light'. In it, he appeals
to the king to rid his realm of the French *philosophes* who dominated the
Berlin Academy and the court, and to recognise and promote the talents of
his own subjects instead. He accuses Frederick and his philosophical followers of completely ignoring the spiritual dimension of life and he traces the
king's apparent tolerance back to his materialism and even his homosexual-
ity. The fact that Hamann was often subject to demanding and sometimes
oppressive French and French-speaking officials in his work as a tax collector
may have prejudiced him even more against this Gallican influence on his
homeland.

Hamann referred to the *philosophes* and *Aufklärer* of his time as 'modern
Athenians', which he intended as an insult, since he regarded ancient Athens
as a decadent culture fatally infected with abstract philosophy and dead to
matters of the heart and spirit. He complained that these latter-day Athenians value the 'code of bon sens' while ignoring 'la politique du St.
Evangile'.[75] Like so many of the religious enemies of the Enlightenment,
Hamann repeatedly depicted these 'children of unbelief'[76] as dogmatists of a

new secular religion, whose 'bible', the *Encyclopédie*, is a barren substitute for the Holy Bible, the 'Encyclopaedia of the Genius-Creator', to whose fundamental truths they were deaf.[77] They are mere 'dogma makers' whom Hamann condemned as 'the biggest stainers of the wonderful works of God'.[78] He complained bitterly about the 'pharisaical sanctimoniousness' of the pedantic 'lettered men of our enlightened century' (*unfers erleuchteten Jahrhunderts*)[79] – a 'tragi-comic century'[80] – and declared that his sole purpose was to turn his readers away from the worship of the 'idol in the temple of learning, which bears beneath its image the inscription "The History of Philosophy"', and towards God.[81] To Hamann, the *philosophes* and *Aufklärer* were anti-Christian zealots against God. This is his version of what I shall call the 'iron law of religiosity' advanced by many of the Enlightenment's religious opponents, who hold that the zealous affirmation of religious disbelief among the *philosophes* was itself a form of religious zealotry. In short, there is no escape from religion, since to deny it is to affirm it in another form. Therefore atheism is impossible.

According to Hamann, the *Aufklärer's* intellectualism and taste for otherworldly abstractions led them away from the real roots of existence in the material world of nature and history. 'The truth must be dug out of the earth,' he instructed Jacobi, 'and not drawn from the air, from artificial words, but must be brought to light from earthly and subterranean objects by means of metaphors and parables, which cannot be direct but only reflected rays.'[82] In an obvious allusion to the story of Adam and Eve, he asked Jacobi in 1784: '[O]ught not the tree of life to be a little more dear to us than the tree of knowledge?'[83] For Hamann, we are sensuous beings with 'fleshly intellect'[84] whose reason is materially grounded in 'flesh and blood'.[85] Since rationality flows from materiality, one must always keep one's feet firmly planted in the ground in order to stay close to the truth. This explains why Hamann described himself as an opponent of Kantian 'Platonism', and placed himself in the 'common sense' empirical tradition of Locke and Hume. He accused modern philosophers like Kant of carving up the natural unity of things to fit their procrustean theories, and he denounced philosophical analysis as a violent dissection of nature and 'a hindrance to truth'.[86] Hamann wanted to 'lower' the species, bringing us back down to the roots of existence and the sources of meaning in things that are common and familiar rather than airy and remote.

Hamann distinguished modern philosophy, which he dismissed as 'mere bombast'[87] belonging to 'the high tastes of this enlightened century [*das erleuchteten Jahrhunderts*], where the denial of the Christian name is a condition without which one ought to dare to lay claim to be a philosopher',[88] from genuine philosophy, which is not hostile to faith. In his highly influential *Sokratische Denkwürdigkeiten* (*Socratic Memorabilia*, 1759), he depicts Socrates as an example of the latter, a forerunner of Jesus who was 'before faith' rather than against it. Socrates' significance for Hamann lay less in the philosophical views attributed to him than in the fact that he had 'lured his

fellow citizens out of the labyrinths of their learned Sophists to a truth in
the inward being, to a wisdom in the secret heart'.[89] Like Rousseau's
Socrates, his genius lay in his inner *daimon* and attentiveness to 'the voice in
his heart', which set him apart from lesser thinkers.[90] Hamann also shared
Rousseau's admiration for Socrates' humble profession of ignorance, which
he interpreted as evidence of a fundamentally Christian sensibility. '[T]he
last fruit of worldly wisdom,' he wrote to his friend Johann Lindner, 'is the
recognition of human ignorance and human weakness.'[91] Ignorance and
genius, not abstract philosophy and reason, were the keys to Socratic greatness as Hamann understood it.[92]

Central to Hamann's critique of the *Aufklärung* is his objection to its conception of reason. He had this in mind when he wrote in exasperation to his
friend J. G. Herder that '[a]ll chatter about reason is pure wind'.[93] Yet this
outburst is misleading when taken in isolation; he was actually ambivalent
about reason in general. 'Are not reason and freedom the noble gifts to
mankind and both at the same time the sources of all moral evil?', he
asked.[94] He wrote to Jacobi that reason is 'the source of all truth and of all
errors. It is the tree of knowledge of good and evil. Therefore, both parties
are right and wrong which deify it and which vilify it. Faith, likewise, is the
source of unbelief and of superstition. "Out of the same mouth proceed
blessing and cursing." '[95] For Hamann, reason has its place within its proper,
limited sphere, but the *Aufklärer* grossly exaggerated and thereby distorted
its power and importance to the exclusion of other sources of insight. For
them it had become a new religion, 'Holy Reason', which 'orders us to genu-
flect in worship before "rational consciousness" '.[96] Hamann scoffed that '[a]ll
the propositions of your so-called universal, sound and scientific reason are
lies'[97] and answered his own question 'what is this highly praised reason
with its universality, infallibility, boundlessness, certainty, and evidence?'
with the claim that it is 'an idol, to which a shrieking superstition of unreason ascribes divine attributes'.[98] He was much impressed by David Hume's
(1711–1776) deflation of the pretensions of reason in his *Treatise of Human
Nature* (1739–1740). Hamann enthusiastically agreed with Hume that
reason is 'the slave of the passions',[99] arguing that there is more feeling than
reason in what we think and do and that this is nothing to lament. 'The
heart beats before the *head* thinks – a good *will* is of more use than an ever so
pure reason.'[100]

Hamann's most systematic treatment of reason appears in his posthumously published 'Metacritique of the Purism of Reason' (written in 1784),
a review of Kant's *Critique of Pure Reason* (1781). In it he attacks Kant's
belief in the autonomy, universality and above all the purity of reason.
Anticipating Nietzsche, he claimed that reason is not a disinterested faculty
of cognition but an instrument of the will with an essentially material, psychological foundation, necessarily embedded in language and experience and
shaped by culture, nature and history. This is an aspect of Hamann's deep
aversion to the obsession with purity which was, he believed, one of the

defining characteristics of his age. The Enlightenment distate for messy, concrete reality was most apparent in Kant's neat dualisms of pure and impure, thought and experience, noumena and phenomena. Such crisp dichotomies were essential for Kant because he wished to separate reason completely from its connection to nature, experience, tradition, language, sensuality and other sources of heteronomy. Hamann argued that this 'purification' of reason unfolded in three stages. First, empiricism sought to free reason from its dependence on external influences such as custom and tradition in order to ensure its autonomy.[101] Kant then went beyond empiricism by divorcing reason, which he situated in the elevated noumenal realm, from experience, which he consigned to the sphere of mere phenomena. According to Hamann, the final stage of this 'purification' set itself the impossible task of purging reason of its dependence on language itself.

Hamann's opposition to this inflation and purification of reason is also apparent in his assaults on rational theology of the kind that was dominant in enlightened circles in both Germany and France in the eighteenth century. The basis of religion, he thought, lies 'outside the sphere of our cognitive powers'.[102] Hamann appears to have had no qualms about enlisting the sceptical Hume in support of his own fideistic belief that '[f]aith is not the work of reason, and therefore cannot succumb to its attack; for faith happens for reasons just as little as tasting and sensing do'.[103] He translated Hume's anti-deistic *Dialogues Concerning Natural Religion* (1779) into German and wrote to Herder that their author 'is always my man, because he has at least ennobled the principle of faith and included it in his system'.[104] In *Golgatha und Scheblimini!* (1784), Hamann attacked the *Aufklärer* Moses Mendelssohn's essay on *Jerusalem, or Religious Power and Judaism* (*Jerusalem, oder über religiose Macht und Judentum*, 1783) for its deistic version of Judaism, which he believed was a fundamental betrayal of its author's own ancient religious heritage. He describes Mendelssohn's rationalistic and anaemic Judaism as empty, artificial and devoid of passion; his faith is simply an 'empty puppet-play', the 'vain, botched work of human artifice'.[105] Hamann also disputed the deist's distinction between the natural and the supernatural; the central lesson of Christianity, he thought, is that heaven and earth are not completely separate because God expresses himself through the material world. He ended up accusing Mendelssohn of atheism, a charge he later regretted when the Jewish *Auklärer* died in unfortunate circumstances.[106]

Hamann's hostility to the eighteenth-century purification of reason is also evident in his attacks on language reform of the kind promoted by the Old Testament scholar Johann David Michaelis (1717–1791), whom Hamann took to task in *Aesthetica in Nuce* (1762) for criticising the language of the Bible for being too figurative, sensual and concrete, and Christian Tobias Damm (1699–1778), an *Aufklärer* and disciple of Christian Wolff. In his *Reflections on Religion* (1773), Damm inveighed against the silent 'h' in

German as a useless anachronism that should be purged from the language. Hamann fought back in his *Neue Apologie Buchstaben h* (*New Apology for the Letter h*, 1773), valiantly defending the beleaguered letter for speaking 'with a human voice'.[107] He points out that pronunciation is not the sole guide to spelling because language addresses itself to the whole person, to feeling as well as to reason.[108] Purging it of such allegedly useless 'irrationalities' is an assault on the colour, beauty, texture, character, virility, history, and even spirituality of language. 'The purity of a language diminishes its riches; a too strict correctness diminishes its strength and manhood.'[109]

According to Hamann, a universal, rational language of the kind he believed the *Aufklärung* favoured would be a 'baking-oven of ice'.[110] In addition, given Hamann's belief in the essential divinity of language, Damm's reforms are nothing less than blasphemous, a 'stiff-necked stupidity in the guise of philosophy and a wrenching brutality in sheep's clothing against the one true God and the image of His invisible being in human nature!'[111] That is why it is mere hubris on the part of humans to tamper with language: God is an author whose 'writings' in the form of language and nature should be studied and revered rather than judged, corrected and purified.

Like Rousseau, Hamann believed that poetry preceded prose among the forms of human expression.[112] Poetry is 'the mother-tongue of the human race' and the principal means by which God communicates with man.[113] Because 'God is a poet, not a geometer',[114] the language of nature is poetical rather than mathematical. God expresses himself 'through nature and the Scriptures, through creatures and seers, through poets and prophets'.[115] According to Hamann, at the opposite extreme from poetry is French, the preferred language of Frederick and the *Aufklärer*, which is why Hamann composed those of his essays which focus on Frederick and his philosophical supporters in that language rather than in his native German. Like Rousseau, he disapproved of French for being a cold, rigid, abstract, rationalistic language. Hamann shared Rousseau's admiration for the rich languages of earlier, more 'primitive' peoples, who enjoyed an immediate relationship to nature, which brought them closer to God. He seemed to believe that, through a Rousseau-like return to the kind of natural language that characterised the poetic tongues of primitive peoples, a partial return to this original state of linguistic innocence and enchantment might be possible.

Although Hamann's own 'tumultuous, obscure and perverse' style of writing appears to have possessed a certain magic which even Goethe confessed to find bewitching, it was completely devoid of primitive simplicity and directness.[116] His style stands as a major obstacle to understanding his meaning, which was his intention. He did not *want* to be easily understood, and successfully employed an array of techniques to ensure this. He often wrote in deliberately compressed, paratactic sentences, composed of aphorisms and epigrams intended to squeeze 'the most thoughts in the fewest words'.[117] His writings are also densely saturated with classical and biblical references and allusions, many of which are thickly layered with meanings. In addition to the liberal use of paradox, irony, imagery and analogy, Hamann relied heavily on literary devices such as autonomasia, periphrasis and what he called 'metaschematism' that would enable him to communicate his insights obliquely.[118] 'Truths, principles, systems I am not up to,' he confided to Johann Lindner. 'Rather scraps, fragments, crotchets, thoughts.'[119] Even Hegel, with his own well-deserved reputation for opacity, criticised Hamann's work for its 'unintelligibility', describing it as 'an enigma, indeed an exhausting one'.[120] If 'it so happens that I cease to be clear to myself as soon as I have cooled off.' Hamann wrote to Jacobi, 'how little should I be surprised that I am not sufficiently clear to others?'[121] Small wonder that, looking back on his own work, he admitted that 'in some cases I can no longer understand it myself'.[122]

One reason Hamann chose to write in this fashion was to affirm stylistically his opposition to the superficial clarity of contemporary philosophical writing. He thought that his dense and epigrammatic style corresponded better to the inherent mystery and complexity of things than did the superficially polished and elegant style prevalent in his day. Witty and sophisticated 'beaux esprits' such as the *philosophes* and their German admirers may have mastered the art of the clever *bon mot*, but they were oblivious to the deeper mysteries and wonder of language and its divine author. Hamann's essays are a deliberate challenge to 'the despotism of Apollo' – the God of the philosophers – which 'fetters truth and freedom in demonstrative proofs, principles and conclusions'.[123] He compared his own method of composition to that of Heraclitus, whose sentences often *seem* unconnected, but are actually joined beneath the surface 'like a group of small islands for whose community the bridges and ferries of system were lacking'. Hamann does not make his thought-connections explicit because he expected his readers to be able to 'swim'.[124]

3   Counter-Enlightenment and Counter-Revolution

> Enlighten nations; that is to say, efface from the minds of the people what we call religious and political prejudices; make yourself master of the public opinion; and this empire once established, all the constitutions which govern the world will disappear.[1]
>
> (Augustin Barruel)

Introduction

When the leaders of the French Revolution canonised Voltaire and Rousseau (by putting them in the Panthéon in Paris, in 1791 and 1794 respectively), counted the Marquis de Condorcet (1743–1794) among their enthusiastic supporters (at least until they sentenced him to be guillotined), and made basic Enlightenment themes such as reason, progress, anti-clericalism and emancipation central to their own revolutionary vocabulary, it was inevitable that a backlash against the Revolution would fuel opposition to the Enlightenment as well.[2] By the mid-1790s in Germany the term 'Jacobiner' was practically synonymous with 'Aufklärer'.[3] In France, the idea that the Revolution was 'la faute à Rousseau, la faute à Voltaire' had become deeply entrenched and widespread among both its advocates and its opponents by the early 1790s, despite the fact that Rousseau admitted to having 'the greatest aversion to revolutions' and Voltaire preferred government for the people rather than by the people.[4] With the establishment of this link in the minds of so many, the violent excesses of the Revolution tainted the Enlightenment and spawned a new generation of enemies. The advent of what I shall call the 'continuity thesis' between the Enlightenment and the Revolution – the belief that they were connected in some intrinsic way, as cause and effect, for example, or crime and punishment – proved seriously damaging to the former as the latter became increasingly steeped in blood.

Edmund Burke (1729–1797) was among the first of the Revolution's enemies to blame the ideas propounded by the *philosophes* for the disastrous collapse of political authority and social order in France in the 1790s. His enormously influential *Reflections on the Revolution in France* (1790) – the first sustained counter-revolutionary text of its kind in Europe – did much to popularise the idea of the Enlightenment as a principal cause of the Revolution.[5] His hostility to the Enlightenment came as a surprise to many of Burke's contemporaries, since he was a Whig politician who had hitherto fitted quite comfortably within the Enlightenment of moderate *philosophes* such as Montesquieu, a 'genius' whom he admired even after 1789.[6] As Conor Cruise O'Brien notes in his study of Burke, he was, like Rousseau, 'a child of the early Enlightenment, that of Locke and Montesquieu'.[7] Like so many of his generation (and social position), the Revolution had a huge impact on Burke's attitude to what preceded it. He raged not only against the Revolutionaries, but also against the *philosophes* for providing the leaders of the Revolution with the theories on which they based their disastrous political schemes. He regarded the revolutionaries as nothing more than politicised *philosophes* whose self-appointed mission was to unbend the naturally 'crooked timber of humanity' (to borrow Kant's phrase) to conform to an abstract ideal, an undertaking that had had fatal consequences in France and that Burke feared might spread to England.

Abbé Augustin Barruel (1741–1820) was a conservative writer and former Jesuit who fled from revolutionary France to England in 1792, not returning until Napoleon made his peace with the Church a decade later. Unlike Burke, his hostility to the *philosophes* was well known and well developed long before 1789. In the decades before the Revolution he had been on the editorial staff of the popular anti-*philosophe* literary journal *Année littéraire*, founded in 1754 by Elie-Catherine Fréron. The author of many books, including the satirical *Les Helviennes, ou lettres provinciales philosophiques* (1781–1788), an anti-*philosophe* novel in five volumes, Barruel is best known for his enormously successful *Memoirs Illustrating the History of Jacobinism* (*Mémoires pour servir à l'histoire du jacobinisme*, 1798), which became one of the most widely read books of its day.[8] In it he blames the French Revolution on a conspiracy of *philosophes*, Freemasons and the secret Order of the Illuminati who together plotted the overthrow of throne and altar in Europe.

Joseph de Maistre (1753–1821) fled into exile from his native Savoy before the advancing armies of revolutionary France in the same year as Barruel (1792). However, unlike the abbé, he saw the Revolution as God's violent answer to the Enlightenment, more a work of divine retribution for the sins of the *philosophes* than of misguided men trying to implement the ideals of the Enlightenment, or the consequence of a vast conspiracy. Maistre depicted the revolutionary storm as an overwhelming force of nature unleashed on Europe by God that mocked human pretentions. For Burke and Barruel, by contrast, the destruction wrought by the revolutionaries was largely wilful, perpetrated by men who knew only too well what they were doing, even if they were largely blind to the unintended effects of their actions. There is almost no space for such human agency in Maistre's providential view of these events.

A philosophic revolution

Burke's immediate reaction to the French Revolution was ambivalent. In his earliest known comment on it, in a letter to Lord Charlemont dated 9 August 1789, he professed his astonishment at 'the wonderful Spectacle' of the French 'struggle for Liberty', the spirit of which he found 'impossible not to admire'. Yet he also sensed something 'paradoxical and Mysterious' about it and warned that they would need a 'Strong hand like that of their former masters to coerce them'.[9] Burke's attitude to the Revolution quickly soured. By 17 September he admitted to his friend William Windham that he had 'great doubts whether any form of Government which they [the French] can establish will procure obedience'.[10] When news reached him on 10 October that a mob had forced its way into the Royal Palace at Versailles to escort the king and his family to the Tuiléries Palace in the centre of Paris, he wrote ominously to his son about 'the portentous State of France – where the Elements which compose Human Society seem all to be dissolved, and a world of Monsters to be produced in the place of it'.[11] By the end of the year, Burke had basically made up his mind about the essentially negative character of the Revolution and, towards the end of January 1790, he decided to sound the alarm against it in order to save England from a similar fate.[12] He feared that the great and delicate fabric of English social and political life that had been carefully spun over centuries would be completely torn apart by domestic Jacobins inspired by the example of their French brethren. In the process these 'illuminators of the world'[13] would, he predicted, dispel the 'sober shade of the old obscurity'[14] with their garish light, bringing ruin in their wake.

Although Burke generally favoured reform over revolution, he did concede that recourse to the latter is sometimes justified under extraordinary circumstances. Hence his sympathy for both the 'Glorious' Revolution of 1688 to 1690 and the American Revolution that began in 1776. However, he distinguished very clearly between these limited, pragmatic revolutions, as he saw them, and those based on grand philosophical or metaphysical principles, which are always undesirable and invariably do more harm than good. The quintessential 'philosophic revolution',[15] he believed, was the French Revolution.

For Burke, it was the role of philosophy in the French Revolution that was its most distinctive and destructive feature. France after 1789 had become a 'Republic of Philosophy'[16] governed by 'philosophic lords',[17] 'political Men of Letters'[18] and 'politicians of metaphysics'[19] who had had 'their minds seasoned with theories',[20] 'dangerous and delusive first principles',[21] 'metaphysic propositions'[22] and 'rash speculation'.[23] The French Revolution was fundamentally unlike the Revolution of 1688 to 1690 and the American Revolution, which were essentially defensive and moderate, undertaken to preserve a traditional balance of settled customs, time-honoured rights and well-established institutions that had passed the test of time, rather than to implement new modes and practices derived from first principles.

> The present Revolution in France seems to me to be quite of another character and description [than the 'Glorious' Revolution], and to bear little resemblance or analogy to any of those which have been brought about in Europe, upon principles merely political. *It is a Revolution of doctrine and theoretic dogma.* It has a much greater resemblance to those changes which have been made upon religious grounds, in which a spirit of proselytism makes an essential part. The last revolution of doctrine and theory which has happened in Europe is the Reformation.[24]

The French Revolution was not only fundamentally 'philosophic' in its nature, according to Burke, but had been *caused* by the spread of philosophical speculation and abstract theoretical reflection in France in the second half of the eighteenth century. As a result, he argued, a 'false philosophy passed from academies into courts; and the great themselves were infected with the theories which conduced to their ruin'.[25] As the abstract theories of the *philosophes* gradually seeped into the minds of those who held – or would hold – actual political power in France, 'literary men [were] converted into a gang of robbers and assassins; never before did a den of bravoes and banditti assume the garb and tone of an academy of philosophers' as during the French Revolution.[26]

By 'philosophy', Burke has in mind the ideas of 'grave, demure, insidious, spring-nailed, velvet-pawed, green-eyed philosophers'[27] such as Condorcet, Rousseau, Voltaire, d'Alembert, Diderot and Helvétius (all named) that he held most culpable for bringing about the Revolution. Of these, Burke singled out Rousseau and Condorcet in particular, since the former was both an *encyclopédiste* and 'the insane Socrates of the National Assembly' of Revolutionary France,[28] and the latter was simultaneously the 'last of the *philosophes*' and 'the most furious of the heads of the Jacobin Club'.[29] Burke refers to the revolutionary leaders as Rousseau's 'scholars'[30] whose 'blood they transfuse into their minds and into their manners' and who looked upon his writings as 'holy writ'.[31] This is spelled out most fully in his *Letter to a Member of the National Assembly* (1791), which contains a diatribe against the pernicious influence of this 'great professor and founder of *the philosophy of vanity*'.[32] Ironically, Burke's view of Rousseau was essentially Voltairean, even though he detested Voltaire and regarded these two mortal enemies as kindred spirits. Like the *philosophes* he despised, Burke focused more on Rousseau's character and alleged influence than on his theories per se. In the circumstances, what the *philosophes* actually wrote was less important to Burke than the uses that had been made of them by the revolutionaries in France and the ideas that had been attributed to them.

> [T]hey [the Revolutionary leaders] erect statues to a wild, ferocious, low-minded, hard-hearted father, of fine general feelings, – a lover of his kind, but a hater of his kindred ... Through Rousseau, your masters are resolved to destroy these aristocratic prejudices ... they infuse into their youth an unfashioned, indelicate, sour, gloomy, ferocious medley of pedantry and lewdness, – of metaphysical speculations blended with the coarsest sensuality ... the writings of Rousseau lead directly to this kind of shameful evil.[33]

Burke also singled out 'the impious sophistry of Condorcet'[34] as an example of the link between the Enlightenment and Revolution in France. As with Rousseau, Burke's hostility towards Condorcet and the 'geometric spirit' he embodied focuses predominantly on his role in, and influence upon, the Revolution, rather than on his theories per se, even though it would be difficult to imagine anything more alien to Burke's outlook than the 'social mathematics' of Condorcet. 'That wretched man,' he complained of him to a French correspondent in 1791, 'stands as a great example, to shew that when the heart is vitiated nothing can be sound ... the Condorcets and the whole of that sect of Philosophic Robbers and Assassins ... delight in the destruction of mankind.'[35]

Burke's main objection to this 'philosophic' form of revolution is that it is based on a fundamental misunderstanding of the essential nature of social and political life and is therefore destined to end in practical disaster. The most durable and humane political systems, he thought, are basically pragmatic, emerging 'naturally' by trial and error over a very long period of time and adapting prudentially to particular circumstances as required. In this process of gradual evolution, habits and prejudices emerge that regulate the system's operation, maintaining its equilibrium and balancing its intricately interconnected parts. According to Burke, the paradigmatic example of such a system – as perfectly balanced and finely tuned as any human regime could be – is to be found in England. Such a system can only be the product of time, common sense and patient, piecemeal development, and it was Burke's self-appointed mission to protect it from the dangers posed by the virulent spread of France's 'philosophic' brand of revolution.

The antithesis of the slow, 'natural', evolutionary English approach to politics, Burke argues, is Jacobinism, which seeks to apply 'wild, visionary theories'[36] that are devoid of a sense of history and completely ignore local circumstances and practicalities. Its practitioners imagine themselves as political architects, erecting elaborate systems based only on '[p]ure metaphysical abstraction',[37] in the process 'destroying all docility in the minds'[38] of both leaders and led, inevitably culminating in '[m]assacre, torture, hanging'.[39] Words such as design, speculation, theory, system, metaphysics, philosophy and abstraction recur throughout Burke's post-revolutionary writings as terms of opprobrium used to describe the Jacobin approach to politics, just as prudence, prescription, habit, prejudice, custom and convenience are used approvingly in his account of its antithesis: the English political system.

> What is Jacobinism? It is an attempt (hitherto but too successful) to eradicate prejudice out of the minds of men, for the purpose of putting all power and authority into the hands of the persons capable of occasionally enlightening the minds of the people. For this purpose the Jacobins have resolved to destroy the whole frame and fabrick of the old Societies of the world, and to regenerate them after their fashion. . . . This I take to be a fair description of the principles and leading maxims of the enlightened of our day, who are commonly called Jacobins.[40]

According to Burke, the test of a political system should be broadly utilitarian, not theoretical. The question that should be asked is not whether a political system conforms to some abstract ideals, but whether it 'works' pragmatically, by which he meant whether it fosters peace, order and good government over the long term, given the particular context in which it is situated. The only reliable test for this is the test of time, which alone can establish the viability and durability of a political system. For Burke, political problems should be approached in terms of their likelihood of promoting good or evil, and not their conformity to truth or falsehood, which is a ruinously inappropriate standard in practical human affairs. Unfortunately for France, the Jacobins, in failing to realise this, built their politics 'not on convenience, but on truth'.[41] They are just politicised *philosophes*, 'political Men of Letters' seeking a wholesale reordering of political life to make it conform to a standard of abstract truth and universal justice.

> Men of Letters, fond of distinguishing themselves, are rarely averse to innovation. Since the decline of the life and greatness of Lewis the XIVth, they were not so much cultivated either by him, or by the regent, or the successors to the crown; nor were they engaged to the court by favours and emoluments so systematically as during the splendid period of that ostentatious and not impolitic reign. What they lost in the old court protection, they endeavoured to make up by joining in a sort of incorporation of their own; to which the two academies of France, and afterwards the vast undertaking of the Encyclopaedia, carried on by a society of these gentlemen, did not a little contribute. . . . They were possessed with a spirit of prosyletism in the most fanatical degree; and from thence, by an easy progress, with the spirit of persecution according to their means. . . . These Atheistical fathers have a bigotry of their own . . . this system of literary monopoly. . . . A spirit of cabal, intrigue, and proselytism, pervaded their thoughts, words, and actions. . . . Writers . . . have great influence on the publick mind.[42]

The French revolutionaries also shared with the *philosophes* a profound contempt for religion in general, according to Burke. He regarded both as either atheists in fact or in effect, the difference between the two being practically irrelevant. 'The philosophers,' he claimed, 'had one predominant object, which they pursued with a fanatical fury – that is, the utter extirpation of religion'[43] which the French revolutionaries put into practice. Hence the 'great Object of the Jacobins,' Burke wrote, 'is the seduction of that part of mankind from the principles of religion, morality, subordination, and social order.'[44]

While Burke thought of the principled 'atheism' of the *philosophes* as a sacrilege against the 'city of God', disastrous to the souls of men and women in the life to come, he saw the practical 'atheism by establishment' of the revolutionaries in his day as socially and politically disastrous to the 'city of Man', since religion is what 'held the materials of the fabric' of society together.[45] Although a true-believing Christian, like many *philosophes* Burke also believed in the utility of religion as an indispensable foundation of political legitimacy and form of social cement, in the absence of which he thought that institutions would crumble and society atomise. His depiction of the *philosophes* as atheists who fatally weakened the moral and social order of Europe is a major theme of much early Counter-Enlightenment writing, as we have already seen in the case of both Rousseau and Hamann, and is strongly echoed by Barruel and Maistre as well.

The triple conspiracy against throne, altar and society

Burke admired Augustin Barruel's *Mémoires* and told him so. 'I cannot easily express to you how much I am instructed and delighted by the first volume of your History of Jacobinism', he wrote to the delighted abbé in May 1797, just over two months before Burke's death. 'The whole of the wonderful Narrative is supported by documents and Proofs with the most juridical regularity and exactness. Your Reflexions and reasonings are interspersed with infinite Judgement and in their most proper places, for leading the sentiments of the Reader and preventing the force of plausible objections.' Burke even personally corroborated Barruel's conspiracy thesis by revealing to him that 'I have known myself, personally, five of your principal Conspirators; and I can undertake to say from my own certain knowledge, that so far back as the year 1773 they were busy in the Plot you have so well described and in the manner and on the Principle you have so truly presented. To this I can speak as a Witness.'[46] Barruel was deeply flattered by these words from 'the immortal Burke', whom he appears to have held in the highest esteem.

Burke was a late-comer to the theory of a *philosophe* conspiracy to overthrow throne and altar, compared to Barruel, who wrote for the popular conservative journal *Année littéraire* where the theory was first formulated in the mid-1770s.[47] This was after Barruel had returned from his first exile, following the expulsion of the Jesuits from France in the 1760s. For years after his return he warned his compatriots that the *philosophes* were conspiring to topple the traditional institutions of France, and must be stopped. In addition to his anti-*philosophe* novel *Les Helviennes*, he wrote several books attacking the Revolution, including *Le Patriote véridique, ou Discours sur les vraies causes de la Révolution actuelle* (1789) and *Questions nationales sur l'autorité et sur les droits du peuple et du gouvernement* (1791). Barruel then went into exile a second time, in 1792, living in London where he devoured Burke's *Reflections* and penned a *Histoire du clergé pendant la Révolution française* (1793), as well as his *chef d'oeuvre* on the Revolution – the best-selling *Mémoires*.

At the same time, John Robison, Professor of Natural Philosophy at the University of Edinburgh, was writing his *Proofs of a Conspiracy Against All the Religions and Governments of Europe, carried on in the secret meetings of Free Masons, Illuminati and Reading Societies*, which was published in London in 1798 and quickly translated into French and German. Barruel wrote in the Preface to the third volume of his *Mémoires* that Robison's *Proofs* had been published just as his own third volume was going to press. 'Its author had not then met with my two first volumes', he notes, with a faint hint of disappointment. '[B]ut in a second edition he is pleased to mention them in his appendix. Without knowing it, we have fought for the same cause, with the same arms and pursued the same course.'[48] Despite the many similarities in their arguments and conclusions, Barruel was quite critical of Robison for his sloppiness, correctly pointing out that his own book devoted much more attention to detail and to the key philosophical texts than the good professor's had done.[49]

The four thick volumes of Barruel's *Mémoires* present a mass of evidence (what was to *his* eyes evidence) in support of his central charge that the French Revolution was the consequence of a 'triple conspiracy' of *philosophes*, Freemasons and the Order of the Illuminati who together formed 'one continuous chain of cunning, art and seduction'[50] intended to bring about 'the overthrow of the altar, the ruin of the throne, and the dissolution of all civil society' throughout Europe.[51] The first volume focuses on the anti-Christian conspiracy launched in 1728 by Voltaire when he 'consecrated his life to the annihilation of Christianity' upon his return to France from England.[52] This conspiracy took Voltaire's famous war-cry against Christianity – *écrasez l'infame!* – as its slogan. Barruel's second volume concentrates on the anti-monarchical conspiracy, whose leading intellectual lights were Rousseau and Montesquieu, who campaigned under the watchwords 'Independence and Liberty' to destroy all governments.[53] The anti-Christian principles of the first conspiracy were grounded in the passions (above all a passionate, blind hatred of Christianity), whereas reason was the basis for the principles of the second.[54] Barruel's third and fourth volumes address the antisocial conspiracy that was the objective of the Freemasons and the Order of the Illuminati inaugurated and led by the Bavarian radical Adam Weishaupt (1748–1811). Together, these three groups constituted a single 'sect' numbering 300,000 'adepts', supported by two million sympathisers in France alone, 'all zealous for the Revolution, and all ready to rise at the first signal and to impart the shock to all other classes of the people'.[55]

Although the *philosophes* styled theirs the 'century of philosophy par excellence', as d'Alembert famously put it in his *Eléments de philosophie* (1759), it was really an 'age of pretended Philosophy',[56] or 'philosophism', according to Barruel. Philosophism is a term of abuse that would be used by Joseph de Maistre, William Wordsworth and Michael Oakeshott as well, to refer to the outlook of the *philosophes*, which all were at pains to distinguish from *true* philosophy as they understood it. Barruel defines 'philosophism' as 'the error of every man who, judging of all things by the standard of his own reason, rejects in religious matters every authority that is not derived from the light of nature. It is the error of every man who denies the possibility of any mystery beyond the limits of reason, of everyone who, discarding revelation in defence of the pretended rights of reason, Equality and Liberty, seeks to subvert the whole fabric of the Christian religion.'[57] Their differences notwithstanding, the *philosophes*, the Freemasons and the Illuminati were united in their zealous commitment to liberty and equality, 'these principles of pride and revolt' at the heart of philosophism.[58]

Among the leaders of the anti-Christian conspiracy who fought to destroy the Church in France were Voltaire, its 'chief', d'Alembert, its 'most subtle agent', Frederick II, their 'protector and adviser', and Diderot, its 'forlorn hope'.[59] While Voltaire directed his attention and efforts to the highest strata of European society – its kings, emperors, princes and ministers – his more wily lieutenant d'Alembert deftly worked on the secondary 'adepts' of the conspiracy, on whom he employed his natural cunning and skill for intrigue in the *cafés* of Paris no less than in its learned academies, which he successfully infiltrated. Barruel makes much of the private correspondence between Voltaire and d'Alembert – these two great 'sophisters of impiety' – which (he claims) reveals the extent of the 'subterranean warfare of illusion, error and darkness waged by the Sect' to destroy Christianity.[60]

The close association between Frederick II, Voltaire and d'Alembert also underscored for Barruel the degree to which the Prussian leader collaborated in this anti-Christian crusade.[61] He points out that these leaders of the plot even employed secret names for each other in their private correspondence – Voltaire was 'Raton', d'Alembert 'Protagoras', Frederick 'Luc' and Diderot 'Plato'. Collectively they were known as the 'Cacouac' and the phrase 'the vine of Truth is well cultivated' was code for the fact that the *philosophes* were making steady progress in their plans to ruin Christianity.

In league with these four 'chiefs' of the conspiracy, Barruel reveals, was a phalanx of fanatical 'adepts', the most important of whom was 'the monster Condorcet'.[62] He was not only 'the most resolute atheist' who acted in close concert with Voltaire and d'Alembert,[63] but he was also a Freemason who had been elected to the Legislative Assembly, and was a leading member of the Society of 1789, thereby embodying the links between the various elements of the conspiracy that Barruel claims to expose in his *Mémoires*. He also lists the Baron d'Holbach, Buffon, La Mettrie, Raynal, Abbé Yvon, Abbé de Prades, Abbé Morrelet, La Harpe, Marmontel, Bergier and Duclos among the devout members of the 'synagogue of impiety'.[64] Barruel appears to have read the work of many of these *philosophes*, and had a very good knowledge of the writings of Voltaire, Rousseau, d'Alembert and Diderot in particular. Unlike Burke, he quotes them directly and extensively, and frequently cites their private correspondence to support his contentions. This is unusual among the enemies of the Enlightenment, who rarely distracted themselves by actually reading the works of the *philosophes* and *Aufklärer* they were attacking, although this is not surprising in a former editor of the leading literary journal of the period in France.

According to Barruel, the conspiracy extended far beyond this society of men of letters; Joseph II of Austria and Catherine II of Russia were also adepts of Voltaire, and the court of Louis XV was a veritable 'Voltairean ministry'[65] of powerful men such as the Marquis d'Argenson, who 'formed the plan for the destruction of all religious orders in France',[66] the Duc de Choiseul, 'the most impious and most despotic of ministers',[67] Archbishop Briennes, 'friend and confidant of d'Alembert',[68] and Malesherbes, 'protector of the conspiracy' and surreptitious ally of the *philosophes*.[69] Even the king's mistress, Mme de Pompadour, was a confidante and supporter of Voltaire.

Although the conspirators focused most of their attention on the highest orders of society, a strategy that proved enormously successful (in Barruel's eyes), they also tried to disseminate their radical ideas more broadly in order to 'imbue the minds of the people with the spirit of insurrection and revolt'.[70] That is the main reason behind the *Encyclopédie*, 'a vast emporium of all the sophisms, errors, or calumnies which had ever been invented against religion'.[71] According to Barruel, the *philosophes* even shamelessly went from house to house asking for subscriptions for the reprinting of 'the most profligate and impious productions of Voltaire, Diderot, Boulanger, La Mettrie, and of other Deists or Atheists of the age, and this under the specious pretence of enlightening ignorance'.[72] Some of them, such as the wealthy Baron d'Holbach, disseminated their 'poisons' in books and pamphlets printed and distributed at their own expense, scheming and conspiring tirelessly and effectively to advance their revolutionary cause.

But this popular strategy for 'philosophising mankind'[73] proved much less successful than the conspirators had hoped, because the bulk of the nation remained stubbornly attached to its faith throughout the eighteenth century. For Barruel, the Revolution was not a spontaneous popular uprising expressing a long-suppressed general will but the consequence of a 'united faction against the majority of the nation' who used force, subterfuge and terror to impose their will on an innocent and unsuspecting population.[74] He claims that a rising generation of 'literary sophisters' such as Voltaire, Rousseau and d'Alembert not only supplied most of the *philosophes* and scientists who led the conspiracy against Christianity, but it was from this class 'that the revolutionary ministers Necker and Turgot started up; from this class arose those grand revolutionary agents, the Mirabeaux, Sieyès, Laclos, Condorcets; these revolutionary trumps, the Brissots, Champforts [*sic*], Garats, Cheniers; those revolutionary butchers, the Carras, Frerons, Marats'.[75] Lawyers, clerks and other members of the bourgeois professions, epitomised by Robespierre, were 'universally carried away by the torrent of the French Revolution' after studying the writings of the *philosophes*.[76]

The second major target of the conspirators was the monarchy, according to Barruel. In the second volume of his *Mémoires*, devoted to the 'anti-monarchical' conspiracy, he starts out by analysing and criticising Montesquieu's *The Spirit of the Laws* (1748) and Rousseau's *Social Contract* (1762), since the application of their ideas had 'given birth to that disquieted spirit which fought to investigate the rights of sovereignty, the extent of their authority, the pretended rights of the free man, and without which every subject is branded for a slave—and every king a despot'.[77] Barruel was well aware of the mutual antipathy between Voltaire and Rousseau, something that Burke chose to overlook, but regarded it as secondary to their common project to destroy Christianity and the monarchy in France. In this he agreed with the revolutionaries, who had had the remains of Voltaire and Rousseau transferred to the Pantheon as joint 'fathers' of the French Revolution. Like Burke and Maistre, this act of homage did not escape Barruel's notice. All three agreed that it revealed a fundamental truth about the nature of the relationship between the *philosophes* and the Revolution in particular, and between philosophy and politics in general, and all commented on it:

> Follow the Jacobin to the Pantheon; see to whom he has decreed honours, to whom he does homage; ask him how Voltaire and Jean-Jacques can have deserved such tribute, such honours. He will tell you that those men are no more, but that their spirit has survived them in their writings, and more powerfully combat for the cause of Jacobinism than all their armed legions. Here they prepared the minds and hearts of the people for our principles; there they win over the public opinion to our course.[78]

Although Rousseau did eventually secede from the ranks of the *philosophes*, he did not secede from their ideals, which he continued to promote in his own, idiosyncratic way, according to Barruel. Rousseau still subscribed to the values of liberty and equality that were shared by all of the conspirators, and so continued to carry on their war separately.[79]

Like many conservatives at the time, Barruel equated rejection of monarchy with rejection of government in general, just as many orthodox Christians equated attacks on their faith with attacks on religion in general. The principles of liberty and equality underlying the eighteenth-century attacks on monarchy, he believed, apply 'not only against kings, but against every government, against all civil society'.[80] The stark choice that Barruel presents to his readers is between monarchy and the 'reign of anarchy and absolute independence'.[81] According to this syllogism, Rousseau and Montesquieu were anarchists because they were anti-monarchists. This is somewhat surprising, given that Burke, whom Barruel so much admired, thought very highly of Montesquieu.

According to Barruel's thesis, the eighteenth-century philosophers who had conspired against Christianity and the monarchy paved the way for the 'antisocial' conspiracy that was led by the Freemasons and the Illuminati. Since the Freemasons were 'the children of the *Encyclopédie*'[82] and 'all the French philosophists became Masons',[83] they worked together in perfect concert as part of a single conspiracy that sought 'the total dissolution of all society'.[84] The French Revolution was the deliberate consequence of the tripartite coalition of 'the sophisticated writers of Holbach's Club, the sophisters of the Masonic and the Illuminsed Lodges'.[85]

The Order of the Illuminati was founded in 1776 by the Freemason Adam Weishaupt, Professor of Canon Law at Ingolstadt University in Bavaria. He was a Catholic who had been educated by the Jesuits, as Maistre, Barruel and Voltaire had been. However, he was closer to the latter than to the former in his heterodox religious beliefs, and was eventually forced to abandon his academic post and flee from Bavaria after a series of laws were passed in the 1780s proscribing the secretive order that he had founded. Weishaupt had originally tried to take control of the Freemasons from within. When this strategy failed, he created his own secret society modelled partly on the Jesuits, whom he admired for their secrecy, self-discipline and organisational efficiency. Wrapped in a 'mantle of darkness', the secretive Weishaupt and his shadowy band of conspirators then 'coalesced with the Encylopedists and Masons' to overthrow the established political, religious and social order of Europe through violent revolution.

In these obscure and sinister machinations Weishaupt was supported intellectually by Immanuel Kant (1724–1804). Despite the calm surface of his dense scholarly writing, Barruel alleges that the actual doctrines propounded and defended by the Königsberg philosopher had a revolutionary effect on his audiences:

> [They] thirst after that great day when the children of Equality and Liberty are to reign. His colleagues in the universities do not teach his principles with his coolness; the disciples become violent; the Jacobins smile; and as the system spreads, the offspring of both these teachers unite and form alliances in their tenebrous abodes. Under pretence of this perpetual peace that is to be enjoyed by future generations, they have begun by declaring a war of cannibals against the whole universe; nor is there to be found scarcely one of their offspring that is not ready to betray his country, his laws, and his fellow citizens, to erect that Cosmopolitan Empire announced by the Professor Kant, or to enthrone the Man-King of the modern Spartacus.[86]

From the ideas of Weishaupt and Kant there emerged a 'new species of Jacobin' that made 'amazing progress' in Germany.[87]

For Barruel, the 'grand object' of the coalition of the *philosophes*, the Freemasons and the Illuminati was 'consummated by the proscriptions and horrid massacres of the Jacobins'.[88] Indeed, the Jacobin Clubs were actually formed by the 'adepts of impiety', the 'adepts of rebellion' and the 'adepts of anarchy' acting in concert to implement their radical agenda. Not only were these groups united in their basic beliefs and goals, but they agreed on the means that should be employed to advance them, foremost among which were 'violent and sanguinary edicts, decrees of deportation and of death'.[89] The only difference between the Jacobins and their precursors is that the latter *wanted* to do these things, whereas the former actually *did* them in their violent struggle to establish the 'reign of reason and the empire of Philosophy'.[90]

Crime and punishment

Joseph de Maistre shared none of Burke's high regard for Barruel's conspiracy theory of the Revolution, which he dismissed as 'foolish'.[91] He made several pages of notes on the *Mémoires* and found much fault with it, particularly in its account of Freemasonry. This is hardly surprising given that Maistre was a Freemason himself.[92] Indeed, he was an active and senior Freemason for nearly twenty years (1773 to 1792), and retained his interest in the order even after he was no longer involved with it directly.[93] His 'Mémoire sur la Franc-Maçonnerie' and 'Mémoire au Duc de Brunswick' (written in 1782) defend Freemasonry against the charge that it was politically subversive and religiously heterodox, at least in his native Savoy. More importantly, Maistre eventually interpreted the revolutionary events of his time as evidence of a divine purpose rather than any human design, and so showed scant interest in Barruel's (to him) crude conspiracy theory. The second half of the eighteenth century revealed something much deeper and more profound to Maistre than the naïve machinations of mere individuals. He thought that Barruel was looking in the wrong place for an explanation of the revolutionary events of the age; he mistook the effects for the cause.

Maistre's reaction to Burke's *Reflections* was very different.[94] He admired its author as a 'great writer who discerned the French Revolution', although he was not greatly influenced by his work.[95] Although the Revolution also had an enormous impact on Burke's thought, it did not affect him as directly as it did Maistre, who spent over two decades in exile after the armies of revolutionary France annexed his homeland in 1792. In addition, Burke was a generation older than Maistre, whose first major work appeared around the time of the former's death. Unlike Burke, Maistre was not given to waxing nostalgic about the natural harmony of human beings living in the quiet repose of their 'little platoons'. It is difficult to imagine him, for whom the 'entire earth, continually steeped in blood, is only an immense altar on which every living thing must be immolated without end',[96] writing *A Philosophical Inquiry Into the Origins of our Ideas on the Sublime and the Beautiful* (1756). As Isaiah Berlin writes in his study of Maistre, his 'violent preoccupation with blood and death belongs to another world from the rich and tranquil England of Burke's imagination'.[97] Maistre had too much in common with Thomas Hobbes to find Burke's outlook entirely congenial to his way of seeing things.

Like Burke, and unlike Barruel, Maistre's opposition to the Enlightenment did not develop fully until the 1790s, by which time he was in his forties. Indeed, like Hamann, he had been '[n]ourished in the thought of the Enlightenment',[98] elements of which he retained throughout his life: he was familiar with the important ideas of his age, had a natural curiosity about modern science, owned a large and diverse library, was an enthusiastic reader of contemporary periodical literature, and enjoyed the intellectual stimulation he received in the salons of Lausanne and St Petersburg, at which he was a frequent and popular guest while living in exile. As his books, notes and correspondence abundantly demonstrate, he was always a man of unusually broad and eclectic tastes and interests, if reactionary politics.

It was in the crucible of the French Revolution that Maistre's moderate 'enlightened conservatism' was transformed into a reactionary Counter-Enlightenment conservatism. The works for which he is now best known were all written after 1789 and bear the direct imprint of the Revolution.[99] Although he had initially supported the French *Parlementaires* and endorsed their campaign to force the calling of an *Etats-Généraux*, he soon became disillusioned with the course that events took after 1790, just as Burke had.[100] Like Barruel, he was eventually forced to flee from his native Savoy as the advancing army of revolutionary France annexed his homeland and confiscated his property. In addition, by the middle of the decade, Louis XVI had been executed and the Terror had begun. Maistre's mature outlook was formed in response to these events, which accentuated the dark, misanthropic dimension of his outlook and stirred his deep horror of disorder and fear of anarchy.

Although Maistre is now best known for his opposition to the French Revolution, he first interpreted it as a necessary consequence of the Enlightenment and, accordingly, held the *philosophes* to be much more culpable for the excesses of the 1790s than the revolutionaries themselves, who were little more than pawns of the overwhelming forces unleashed in the salons of Paris by men such as Voltaire, Diderot and Rousseau. In the first half of the 1790s he was much closer to the outlook of Burke and Barruel than he was after 1795. He depicted the *philosophes* as sorcerer's apprentices who released a monstrous genie that devoured Europe. He too regarded Rousseau in particular as a symbol of the close relationship between the Enlightenment and the Revolution.[101] Around the time of the Terror he wrote that it was Rousseau who 'posed the disastrous principles of which the horrors we have seen are only the immediate consequences'.[102] Like so many others, he lumped Rousseau in with the *philosophes* and blamed them collectively for the horrors of the Revolution:

> Philosophes! Having produced the cause, never will you be able to exonerate yourselves by expressing pity for the effect. *You detest the crimes*, you say. *You have not slaughtered anyone.* Well! *You have not slaughtered anyone*; that is the sole praise that you can be accorded. But you have caused the slaughter ... 'I *carried out terrible laws*', he [Ghislain-François-Joseph Lebon, Revolutionary Mayor of Arras] said, '*laws that have frightened you. I was wrong ... I can be treated as I treated others. When I met men of principle, I let myself be led by them.* IT IS ABOVE ALL THE PRINCIPLES OF J.-J. ROUSSEAU THAT HAVE KILLED ME'. He was right. The tiger that kills is following its nature; the real criminal is the one who unmuzzles him and launches him on society. Do not believe that you are absolved by your affected *threnodies* on Marat and Robespierre. Listen to a truth: wherever you are and wherever anyone has the misfortune to believe you, there will be similar monsters, for every society contains scoundrels who are only waiting to tear it apart and to be unleashed from the restraint of the laws. But without you, Marat and Robespierre would have caused no harm, because they would have been contained by the restraint that you have broken.[103]

In *Considerations on France* (1797), Maistre's first major published work and his counterpart to Burke's *Reflections*, and the *St. Petersburg Dialogues* (1821), the last major work published during his lifetime, he adopts a new, providential account of the Revolution that is much closer to his German contemporary Hegel (1770–1831) than it is to Barruel's or Burke's explanations. Like Hegel, Maistre now read the epochal events in France as a theodicy, a perspective that led them both to affirm *everything*, even violent revolution, to the degree that it is a consequence of some divine plan. Hence his view of the Revolution as a work of God's will rather than human design, an approach quite unlike that of Burke, for whom it had more to do with human folly than with divine justice, which may explain why Maistre had so little to say about Burke's revolutionary writings and felt the need to offer his own interpretation. In this sense Burke and Barruel were much more counter-revolutionary than Maistre, for whom violence and bloodshed are in some sense sanctified by their incorporation within a scheme of Christian providence. This explains how he could often write about the Revolution with an apparent calm, unlike Burke's rage, noting (in the mid-1790s) that 'it is gratifying amid the general upheaval to have a presentiment of the plans of Divinity'.[104] For Maistre, human affairs can only be properly understood in the context of a divine plan, complete knowledge of which is forever beyond human understanding. It is precisely this larger framework, he thought, that was missing from the prevalent interpretations of contemporary revolutionary events, including Burke's, which makes no

attempt to situate them in such a providential scheme. One of the fundamental objectives of his *Considerations on France* is to fill in this missing 'big
picture', thereby explaining the violent events of the 1790s in terms of a
divine logic in which the crimes of the French revolutionaries are punished
by the 'invisible hand' of God operating through them. (Invisible to non-
believers.) The chaotic events of the Revolution are explicable only in terms
of such a framework. Maistre had an even more radically circumscribed conception of human agency than Burke, a view no doubt greatly influenced by
the revolutionary juggernaut he experienced crashing through Europe and
the titanic forces unleashed by it, which seemed to overwhelm the wills and
intentions of human beings. 'The more we examine the influence of human
agency in the formation of political constitutions,' he writes in his *Essay on
the Generative Principle of Political Constitutions* (written in 1807, published in
1814), 'the greater will be our conviction that it enters there only in a
manner infinitely subordinate, or as a simple instrument.'[105] That is why the
revolutionaries were merely passive 'instruments of God' rather than effective agents responsible for their actions, since the Revolution was the work of
God rather than men. 'We cannot repeat too often,' he wrote in his *Considerations*, 'that men do not lead the Revolution; it is the Revolution that uses
men.'[106] However, Maistre did not regard this powerlessness of human
beings as a cause for despair, because he interpreted the violence and bloodshed of the French Revolution as a form of divine punishment meted out on
humanity for the 'crimes' of the eighteenth century. As such, it was salutary
and therefore welcome, however shocking and terrible to mortal eyes.

Most of Maistre's major works were written during his tenure as King
Victor-Emmanuel I's representative at the Court of Tsar Alexander I in St
Petersburg (1803–1817). He considered Russia's position in the opening
years of the nineteenth century to be broadly analogous to that of France
before the Revolution, and feared that it was about to repeat the same mis-
takes by embarking on an ill-considered process of liberalisation and
'enlightenment' that would lead it down the same path to violent revolution. Russia was then a country not only untouched by revolution but still
quite remote from the Enlightenment. However, Alexander was experiment-
ing with a programme of liberalisation and reform during this period; as a
result, 'the ideas of the Englightenment were ascendant in Russian domestic
politics' while Maistre was there.[107] If, as he argues in his *Considerations on
France* and in the works that followed it, the Revolution was a punishment
imposed by God on Europe for the sins of the eighteenth century, then it
must have been both necessary and good, in the same way that the sacrifice
of Jesus on the cross was necessary to redeem humanity for its sins. Russia,
Maistre thought, was still relatively innocent; it had not yet sinned in the
way that eighteenth-century Europe had, although he feared that it was
about to do so. He therefore allied himself closely with the leaders of the
conservative 'old Russian, anti-French' faction opposed to the Tsar's liberal-
ising policies, in the hope of influencing the Russians not to follow the path

of sin, and thereby revolution.[108] If revolution is the work of God, enlightenment (as understood by the *philosophes* of the eighteenth century) is the work of man.

Of particular concern to Maistre was the programme of educational reform being considered in Russia, a central aspect of which was to give greater prominence to science in the curriculum at the expense of religion, evidence, to his mind, of the ominous parallels between Russia during this period and pre-revolutionary France. By arresting enlightenment, he hoped to 'arrest the revolutionary spirit [in Russia], which enters at all doors, but above all through public education'.[109] Maistre believed that it was the eighteenth-century popularisers of modern science and philosophy, epitomised by the *encyclopédistes*, rather than the true philosophical and scientific innovators of the sixteenth and seventeenth centuries themselves or the revolutionaries of the 1790s, who destroyed 'the salutary wall with which the divine wisdom has surrounded us'.[110] God, he argued, 'has placed certain objects beyond the limits of our vision' which it would be 'dangerous for us to perceive'.[111] That is why he thought that the popular dissemination of useful knowledge, which was at the heart of the Enlightenment project in France, had had such a catastrophic effect in the second half of the eighteenth century.

Maistre's aversion to popular enlightenment derives from his belief that reason is, at best, a weak and unreliable human faculty, the power and importance of which was disastrously overestimated in the eighteenth century. He did not actually denigrate reason per se. Almost none of the Enlightenment's enemies did. He affirmed the Thomistic synthesis of reason and revelation, which had endured, more or less, until the eighteenth century, when reason was elevated to the role of an all-powerful tyrant by the *philosophes*, he believed. Maistre stressed the limitations of reason against this inflation, and interpreted the Revolution as the inevitable outcome of the attempt to construct social and political institutions and practices on the weak and precarious foundation of human rationality. In his unfinished essay 'On the Sovereignty of the People' (written 1794–1795), for example, he writes that 'I only wanted to demonstrate that human reason, or what is called philosophy, is as useless for the happiness of states as for that of individuals, that all great institutions have their origins and their conservation elsewhere, and that when human reason is mingled with such institutions, it only perverts or destroys them'.[112] Later in the same essay Maistre stresses that his *real* objection is not to reason as such, but only to 'human reason reduced to its own resources' without the guidance of tradition, authority, prejudice or faith:

> The more human reason trusts itself, the more it seeks all its resources from within itself, the more absurd it is and the more it reveals its impotence. This is why, in every century, the world's greatest scourge has always been what is called *Philosophy*, for Philosophy is nothing but

human reason acting alone, and human reason reduced to its own resources is nothing but a brute, all of whose power is restricted to destruction.[113]

Maistre regarded religion, not reason, as the proper foundation for durable social and political institutions. He argued that '[t]he more one studies history, the more one will be convinced of this indispensable alliance between politics and religion'.[114] This was a central theme in his critique of the Enlightenment, which he complained had sought to keep the two apart. 'The present generation', he wrote in terms that Hegel would echo a decade later in his own dark portrait of the Enlightenment in the *Phenomenology of Spirit* (1807), 'is witnessing one of the greatest spectacles ever beheld by human eyes; it is the fight to death between Christianity and philosophism. . . . Philosophy having corroded the cement that united men, there are no longer any moral bonds.'[115] Newton and Condorcet are then condemned, not Robespierre or the Committee of Public Safety. It is hardly surprising, therefore, that a recurring theme of Maistre's writings from the mid-1790s is what he regards as the predictably disastrous social and political effects that this 'extraordinary persecution stirred up against the national religion and its ministers' had throughout Europe in the 1790s.

During the Terror, Maistre wrote of 'individual reason' as the greatest threat to social and political peace. He dismissed it as pathetically weak with an infallible disposition towards error, unlike 'national reason' which, like Burke, he took to be the expression of the collective wisdom of a people, gradually built up over many generations. By submerging its individual members in the collective body, curbing 'individual reason' and proscribing philosophical enquiry, he believed that nations could check the wayward tendencies of their citizens, whose fallen natures are forever trying to break free of the bonds of society.

> [R]eligious and political dogmas must be merged and mingled together to form a complete *common* or *national reason* strong enough to repress the aberrations of individual reason, which of its nature is the mortal enemy of any association whatever because it produces only divergent opinions. All known nations have been happy and powerful to the extent that they have very faithfully obeyed this national reason, which is nothing other than the annihilation of individual dogmas and the absolute and general reign of national dogmas, that is to say, of useful prejudices. Let each man call upon his individual reason in the matter of religion, and immediately you will see the birth of an anarchy of belief or the annihilation of religious sovereignty. . . . Man's first need is that his nascent reason be curbed under a double yoke, that it be abased and lose itself in the national reason, so that it changes its individual existence into another common existence, just as a river that flows into the ocean always continues to exist in the mass of water, but without a name and

without a distinct reality. What is *patriotism*? It is this national reason of which I am speaking, it is individual *abnegation*.[116]

Maistre believed that our destructive passions are as powerful as our reason is weak. He conceived of humans as incorrigibly violent beings, and he dismissed the common Enlightenment belief in the 'natural goodness' of the species with impatient contempt. '[M]an's strongest inclinations,' he writes, 'are vicious to the point of obviously tending towards the destruction of society.'[117] His first major work contains a chapter on 'the Violent Destruction of the Human Species', noting that Buffon (1707–1788) 'has proven quite clearly that a large percentage of animals are destined to die a violent death'. Maistre then adds that Buffon 'could apparently have extended the demonstration to man', which is precisely what he proceeds to do, beginning with a long catalogue of the wars of recorded history. 'There is nothing but violence in the universe', he concludes from his knowledge of history and nature. '[B]ut we are spoiled by the modern philosophy that tells us that *all is good*, whereas evil has tainted everything, and in a very real sense, *all is evil*, since nothing is in its place.'[118] Perhaps his most uncompromisingly pessimistic account of the violence of the natural and social worlds occurs in the *St. Petersburg Dialogues*, published in the year of his death (1821). In it, he writes:

> from the maggot up to man, the universal law of violent destruction of living things is unceasingly fulfilled. The entire earth, continually steeped in blood, is only an immense altar on which every living thing must be immolated without end, without restraint, without respite until the consummation of the world, until the extinction of evil, until the death of death.[119]

4 The return of faith and feeling

No longer was the Light the seat of the gods or their heavenly sign – over themselves they drew the veil of Night. Night became the mighty womb of revelations – the gods drew back into it.[1]

(Friedrich von Hardenberg)

Introduction

The seismic shift in the intellectual life of Europe that led to what has since become known as 'Romanticism' occurred slowly and began to reveal itself well before the nineteenth century. There was no sudden break between one era and the next, although the pace of change quickened significantly in the last quarter of the eighteenth century. This is most apparent in the case of Germany, where the *'Sturm und Drang'* movement questioned some of the key assumptions and implications (as they saw it) of the *Aufklärung* in the 1770s. It was there that the term 'Romanticism' was first coined at the close of the eighteenth century. In France, virtually everything that came to pre-occupy Romantic writers was a matter of at least some interest and attention throughout the eighteenth century, even among the *philosophes*. However, the 'Other' of the Enlightenment began to receive an attention and central-ity in the closing decades of the eighteenth century that it had not received in an age when reason, empiricism, science and anti-clericalism were intel-lectually dominant. This was at least in part a backlash against the growing popularity of atheism and materialism in the quarter century before 1800, which caused increasing alarm in some quarters and made the question of the limits of enlightenment a matter of pressing concern for many. In addi-tion, as we saw in Chapter 3, the Revolution galvanised opposition to the *philosophes* and their (alleged) beliefs, which were 'tainted with the blood of the guillotine' in the eyes of many.[2] Thus by the time the first generation of Romantic writers were entering their late adolescence and early adulthood, the Enlightenment was already in a serious crisis.

Most notable among these early Romantics were Samuel Taylor Coleridge in England, Friedrich von Hardenberg ('Novalis') in Germany and François-René, vicomte de Chateaubriand, the 'Father of Romanticism', in France.[3]

Although all three eventually reacted against both the Enlightenment and the Revolution, they did not simply rally to the defence of the *ancien régime* or call for a return to the status quo ante. They propounded a radically new sensibility and outlook distinct not only from the eighteenth-century Enlightenment but also from that of orthodox conservatives of the preceding generation such as Burke, Barruel and Maistre, despite considerable overlap with the latter. One thing that distinguished these Romantic critics of the Enlightenment from conventional conservatives is the stress they placed on the importance of beauty in their critique of the eighteenth century. The *philosophes* portrayed the world, many Romantics believed, as ugly and disenchanted, like an impersonal machine devoid of humanity and empty of mystery, making beauty impossible. This is the view of Hardenberg, who rhapsodised the Catholic Middle Ages for its beauty and spirituality. He prophecied the arrival of a new age of religiosity, beauty and re-enchantment that would succeed the ugly, debased and spiritually arid eighteenth century. Chateaubriand also sang the praises of pre-modern Christendom and predicted a religious Renaissance in Europe, which he welcomed no less than his German contemporary. However, neither imagined that this new age of faith would simply be the same as before. Coleridge, one of the most traditional of these early Romantics, also came to see the eighteenth century as a time when faith slept and an impoverished, secular conception of man and nature was in the ascendant. Like Chateaubriand and Hardenberg, he made a virtue out of the mysteriousness and irrationality of faith, which he regarded as the key to its power and beauty. They had been tragically sacrificed to a degrading and reductionistic conception of man and nature that dominated the eighteenth century.

The mighty womb of revelations

The *Aufklärung* died in Germany in the 1790s.[4] The sun began to set on it in 1786 (if not before) with the death of the enlightened despot Frederick II of Prussia, after a reign of more than forty years. His unenlightened successor Frederick William II (1744–1797), with his reactionary minister of spiritual affairs Johann Christoph Wöllner (1732–1800) – a 'treacherous and intriguing priest', according to Frederick II – soon began to implement a regime of censorship and religious control that was abhorrent to the admirers of Frederick William's predecessor, who had for decades actively supported and encouraged the *Aufklärer* in Prussia and abroad. While the rising generation of Romantic writers like Friedrich von Hardenberg far from welcomed the reactionary regime of Frederick William II, they did hail the demise of what they saw as the soulless 'factory state' of his famous uncle.

The Enlightenment in Germany also suffered a major intellectual setback around the time of Frederick's death in 1786. At the centre of the so-called 'Pantheism controversy' were the prominent *Aufkärer* Moses Mendelssohn (1729–1786) and the anti-rationalist Friedrich Heinrich Jacobi. Jacobi, a neo-Humean sceptic of the type increasingly common in Germany in the 1780s,[5] was strongly influenced by Pietism, as had been his friend Hamann. Like Hamann, he despised what he branded the 'morgue berlinoise' of rationalist *Aufklärer* that Frederick II had gathered around him.[6] Following an in-depth study of Spinoza (1632–1677), which helped Jacobi 'to formalise his opposition to the philosophy of the Enlightenment', he led a campaign against moderate *Aufklärer* such as Mendelssohn for refusing to admit that the ultimate consequences of the rational enquiry they promoted were atheism, determinism and eventually nihilism. (Jacobi introduced the term *nihilismus* into the German language.[7]) Jacobi accused the *Aufklärer* of wanting to have both faith and reason when we must choose between them. (Like Hamann, he took his stand with faith.) Things came to a head in 1785 when Jacobi revealed that the celebrated *Aufklärer* Gotthold Ephraim Lessing (1729–1781) had confessed to him in private that he was a Spinozist, which at the time was tantamount to an admission of atheism. The unfortunate dénouement to this clash came in early January 1786 when Mendelssohn died after catching a cold while on his way to his publisher with the manuscript of his account of his debate with Jacobi over Lessing's alleged 'Spinozism', leading Frederick Beiser to conclude that 'Jacobi's "murder" of Mendelssohn is a fitting metaphor for his destruction of the *Aufklärung* itself'.[8]

The ground for this clash had been laid in Germany by the '*Sturm und Drang*' movement as early as the 1770s, when writers such as J. G. Herder – another friend of Hamann – raised questions about some of the basic values and beliefs of the *Aufklärung*. Herder, like Hamann and Jacobi from a Pietist family, was a key transitional figure in the shift from the *Aufklärung* to Romanticism in Germany and had an enormous influence on Hardenberg's generation. Although his attitude towards the *Aufklärung* was deeply ambivalent, and he is better described as a critic rather than as an enemy of the Enlightenment, his criticisms of some of the assumptions of the enlightened world of the eighteenth century would be taken up, developed and extended by his Romantic successors in the early nineteenth century.[9] However, it was not until the death of Frederick II that the Romantic movement really took off in Germany.

The German nobleman Georg Friedrich Philip von Hardenberg (1772–1801), a friend of both Jacobi and Hamann, wrote several influential works under the pseudonym 'Novalis' that gave perfect expression to the early Romantic outlook in Germany at the turn of the century. Like Jacobi and Hamann, he came from a Pietist family. By the time Hardenberg became a student in Jena early in the 1790s, Frederick II and virtually all of the leading French *philosophes* were dead, the German *Aufklärung* had passed its peak, and the French Revolution was shortly to enter its most extreme phase. In addition, philosophical idealism, which rejected the simple Lockean conception of the mind as a *tabula rasa* in favour of a more active and dynamic conception, was in the ascendant in Jena, where Hardenberg studied under the prominent idealist philosopher Carl Leonhold Reinhold (1758–1823). The influence of idealism was vast in Germany at the time. Reacting to the popular Enlightenment view of the mind as a blank screen on to which sense impressions were imprinted, many writers influenced by idealism began to favour a more active and creative conception of the mind. Although close to the *Aufklärer* in many ways, the 'transcendental idealist' Immanuel Kant (1724–1804) – the son of Pietist parents – was crucial in paving the way for this new, post-Enlightenment understanding of the mind. In his path-breaking *Critique of Pure Reason* (*Kritik der reinen Vernunft*, 1781), he argues that the mind brings innate 'categories' to the impressions of the senses which, when combined with the latter, gives us knowledge. This was a giant step away from the *carte blanche* view of the mind that the *philosophes* took (and radicalised) from Locke. Kant had been strongly influenced by Rousseau, particularly his *Emile*, where he first developed his views on the indispensable role of the 'inner voice' of conscience in our moral life (where God and soul meet).[10] Other philosophers of the period, such as Schelling and Fichte, offered versions of this idealist view of the mind, which impressed many of the young German Romantics like Hardenberg whose works they studied and whose lectures they attended in Jena in the mid-1790s.[11]

Among Hardenberg's favourite writers at this time was the 'Dutch Plato' François Hemsterhuis (1721–1790), who also counted Jacobi and Hamann among his admirers and Diderot among his critics. In the autumn of 1797 Hardenberg studied his work intensively and made copious notes that reveal his admiration for the Dutch philosopher. In his most important work, *Lettre sur l'homme et ses rapports* (1772), Hemsterhuis not only set out to combat 'the fashionable philosophy of the day: scepticism, materialism and atheism', but argued that intuition, feeling and an innate 'organe moral' had been neglected during the eighteenth century. The appeal of these ideas to the Pietistic Hardenberg is obvious, as is their congruence with the idealist rejection of empiricism. In the closing years of the century Hardenberg joined the so-called 'new school' in Jena, a circle of Romantic writers led by Friedrich Schlegel (1772–1829), another admirer of Hamann's, that took as its headquarters the home of his brother, the critic August Wilhelm Schlegel (1767–1845).[12] This circle also included Friedrich Schlegel's close friend Ernst Daniel Schleiermacher (1768–1834), yet another early Romantic writer influenced by Pietism, having been raised in a Pietist community established by Count von Zinzendorf in Moravia. The members of the Jena circle had all come to maturity in the waning years of the enlightened despotism of Frederick II, and all were under 30 years old when the Revolution erupted in 1789. Many of their writings appeared in the short-lived journal *Athenaeum*, the first issue of which was printed in May 1798. It was in this journal that Hardenberg published his celebrated *Hymns to the Night* (*Hymen die Nacht*) in 1800, one of the masterpieces of the 'Jena phase' of early German Romanticism. As its title implies, it is a dionysian panegyric to the inspirational power of the night, that 'quiet messenger of infinite mysteries' which alone can 'raise up the soul's heavy wings' to inspire great art and ideas.[13] Although the *Athenaeum* gave Hardenberg his greatest literary success with the *Hymns*, it also inflicted the greatest literary setback of his life when it refused to publish a polemic he wrote in favour of Christianity, which appeared posthumously as *Christendom or Europe* (*Die Christenheit oder Europa*, 1826).[14] When he read the essay aloud during the second 'Meeting of the Romantics' in Jena in November 1799, he had already achieved some notoriety for a controversial set of aphorisms, *Faith and Love or the King and the Queen* (*Glauben und Liebe oder der König und die Königin*, 1798), which had created a sensation in Berlin when they appeared the year before. Friedrich Wilhelm III (1770–1840) read them with disapproval and prohibited the publication of the third instalment, even though they had been written to celebrate his accession to the throne in 1797.

When Hardenberg read *Christendom* to his friends at August Wilhelm Schlegel's house in November 1799, their response was uniformly negative. Although the Schlegels had originally encouraged Hardenberg to write the essay, they soon distanced themselves from it. The same is true of Goethe, who also advised against publication, and Schelling, who wrote an amusing parody of it entitled *Epikurisches Glaubensbekenntnis Heinz Widerporstens* (*Heinz Widerporsten's Epicurean Confession of Faith*, 1799). Although the essay appeared the year after Hardenberg's death, it was later withdrawn and disowned by its editors. It did not appear in its entirety until the fourth edition of the *Novalis Writings* in 1826, with the title *Die Christenheit oder Europa*.

Schleiermacher was among those who disliked Hardenberg's essay on Christianity, even though it had been inspired by his own, recently published book *On Religion: Speeches to its Cultured Despisers* (*Über die Religion: Reden an Gebildeten unter ihren Verächtern*, 1799), which had made a deep impression on Hardenberg. He described himself as 'completely taken, penetrated, enthused, and enflamed' by Schleiermacher's work when he read it in September 1799 and promised Schlegel that he would write a kindred piece on Catholicism, which became *Christendom or Europe*. In *On Religion*, Schleiermacher attacks the 'enlightened religions' fashionable in his day for failing to understand that the essence of faith is 'neither thinking nor acting, but intuition and feeling'.[15] 'Everything must proceed from intuition', he insists.[16] This is especially true of religion, which 'stops with the immediate experience of the existence and action of the universe, with the individual intuitions and feelings'.[17] That is why belief in God depends on the imagination, which Schleiermacher called 'the highest and most original element in us'.[18] He believed that truly religious minds have been distinguished through the ages by a 'mystical tinge'.[19] Hardenberg eagerly devoured these ideas immediately before he began to write *Christendom or Europe*.

Christendom was written in the shadow of immediate events that stirred its Pietist author's sympathies for the beleaguered Catholic Church in an anti-Christian age. The papacy 'lay in its grave', as Hardenberg saw it, following

Napoleon's attack on the papal states and the death in exile of Pope Pius VI in 1799. Ironically, it was the Protestant Hardenberg's controversial essay that became one of the first sympathetic reappraisals of Catholicism at the end of the eighteenth century – the first of many. Hardenberg shared with almost all of the early Romantic writers a deep disillusionment with mainstream German Protestantism at this time, which they regarded as little more than an arm of the bureaucratic state epitomised by Frederick's enlightened despotism. They also protested against the elimination of beauty from the life of faith which 'natural religion' represented. That is why he praises the enchantment and beauty of medieval Catholicism, and criticises Martin Luther, the Enlightenment and philosophy. *Christenheit* also refers sympathetically to the Jesuits and the Counter-Reformation, and portrays the French Revolution as the climax of a 'history of modern disbelief' that Hardenberg saw as a prelude to a new religious epoch to come.

Although Hardenberg eulogises the 'old Catholic faith' in *Christendom*, he never became a Catholic and never advocated Catholicism. He remained faithful to his Pietist roots and its commitment to an inner faith based on feeling, like Rousseau. His sympathetic portrait of the Catholic Middle Ages – the 'infamous thing' that Voltaire campaigned to crush – has led many of his readers to regard *Christenheit* as reactionary, a call for a return to those 'beautiful splendid times' before the Reformation. He writes in poignantly nostalgic terms of the religion of the Middle Ages that once dominated Europe as 'a faith that had come alive. Its presence in all aspects of life, its love of art, its deep humanity, the indissolubility of its marriages, its generous openness, its joy in poverty, obedience, and fidelity make it unmistakably the true religion.'[20] Hardenberg's lyrical portrait of a world of simple beauty and deep piety contrasts strikingly with his forbidding account of the sterile secular age that succeeded it, an ugly, divided world made up of 'rigid seas, dead cliffs, fog instead of the starry heavens'.[21]

But it would be a mistake to label *Christendom* as reactionary in the ordinary sense of wanting to return to the pre-Reformation status quo ante. Hardenberg's essay presents a triadic conception of history that starts with the harmony and enchantment of the Catholic Middle Ages, moves on to the disruption and disenchantment of secular modernity and ends in prophesying a new, post-Revolutionary world of harmony and faith. Far from being 'reactionary', it is 'progressive' in the sense of looking forward to a new era that will restore the unity which prevailed in the pre-modern age without reverting to the Catholic Middle Ages, which are irretrievably gone. In this respect, it has something in common with Hemsterhuis, whose *Alexis ou de l'âge d'or* (*Alexis or the Golden Age*, 1787) situates the golden age of humanity at the end of history rather than at its beginning – a 'truly prophetic' insight, Hardenberg thought, and one that he readily adopted.[22]

The modern, secular age that Hardenberg portrays in *Christendom* began with the Protestant Reformation and extended to the French Revolution, a period that constitutes a 'history of modern disbelief'. He traces the decline of Christianity to the Protestant churches, and depicts the Enlightenment and the Revolution as manifestations of the same, essentially anti-religious spirit that began with Luther's rebellion against the Church. Hardenberg, like Coleridge, was an admirer of the German mystic Jakob Boehme (1575–1624), and he indicted Protestantism for its superficial emphasis on the visible world and the letter, rather than the spirit, of Christianity, in contrast to medieval Catholicism, which understood and reflected the impenetrable mysteriousness of faith. The Medieval Catholic priest was a true 'man of spirit', unlike the cold, lifeless 'scholar' of Protestantism and the negative, vacuous eighteenth-century 'man of letters'.

Hardenberg also attacked the Protestant churches for permitting themselves to be dominated by the state. He condemned their Erastianism and argued that the principal institutional vehicle for *Bildung* in the future must be religion because only it 'can awaken Europe again and make the peoples secure, and with new splendour install Christendom visibly on earth once more in its old peace-bringing office'.[23] According to Hardenberg, Protestantism's 'personal hatred of the Catholic faith' led naturally in the eighteenth century to the *philosophes*' 'hatred of the Bible' and Christianity, which then burgeoned into a general 'hatred of religion' among the French revolutionaries. Finally, this antipathy towards religion 'extended itself very naturally and consequentially to all the objects of enthusiasm, made heretics of imagination and feeling, rectitude and love of art, the past and the future . . . and turned the infinite, creative music of the universe into the uniform clattering of a monstrous mill, driven by the stream of chance and floating on it, a mill of itself without builder or miller and really a true *perpetuum mobile*, a mill grinding itself'.[24] According to Hardenberg, this great revolt against the sacred led directly to the heartless, barren, ugly world of post-Christian modernity, epitomised by the materialism of the Enlightenment, which has made nature 'look ever more impoverished'.[25] This theme of desacralisation and religious disenchantment in modernity is a common one among the Romantic critics of the eighteenth century, particularly in Germany. As we shall see, it was taken up again in the early twentieth century by Max Weber, who influenced many later Enlightenment critics on the left and the right with his concept of modern disenchantment (*entzauberung*).

Hardenberg paints a very stark and unflattering picture of the Enlightenment in *Christendom*. It falls within Europe's 'monstrous' anti-religious middle period, sandwiched between medieval Christianity on the one hand, and the new, post-revolutionary religious epoch he prophesied on the other. In this context, it is a deviation from the norm of religiosity. Not surprisingly, its chief characteristic is its hostility to faith and to all of those things that Hardenberg associated with it. He accuses it of:

> rooting out every trace of the sacred, spoiling the memory of all uplifting incidents and people by sarcastic remarks, and stripping the world of all bright ornament. Because of its mathematical obedience and its

boldness, light had become their darling. ... they named their great task after it, Enlightenment [*Aufklärung*]. In Germany, this task was pursued more thoroughly, the system of education was reformed, an attempt was made to give the old religion a newer, rational, more common meaning, by carefully washing away from it all the wonder and mystery; all available learning was summoned to cut off the flight to history, while it was attempting to refine history so that it might become a portrait of domestic and bourgeois moral and family life. God was turned into an idle spectator of the great, moving spectacle performed by scholars.[26]

Hardenberg writes sneeringly in his essay of 'all you philanthropists and encyclopedists' whose 'clever enlightenment plans' (*die klugen Aufklärungs-Pläne*) even the 'supernatural fire' of faith proved powerless to stop.[27] He also laments the effects of the popular dissemination of this secular outlook among ordinary, pious folk, a trend that has given rise to a disastrous new form of what he calls 'cultivated enthusiasm':

> [A]nd thus there arose a new guild of Europeans: the philanthropists and enlighteners [*die Philantropen und Aufklärer*]. What a shame that nature remained so marvellous and incomprehensible, so poetic and infinite, in spite of all efforts to modernise it. If somewhere an old superstitious belief in a higher world and suchlike reared its head, the alarm was sounded at once on all sides, and whenever possible the dangerous spark was suffocated in the ashes by philosophy and wit; nonetheless tolerance was the slogan of the educated, and particularly in France was equated with philosophy. This history of modern unbelief is extremely strange, and is the key to all the monstrous phenomena of recent times. It does not begin until this century and especially during its second half, then it grows in a short time to immeasurable size and diversity; a second Reformation.[28]

According to Hardenberg, the campaign against organised religion that began in Protestant Europe shifted in the eighteenth century to Catholic France, where the *philosophes* became the champions of 'secular Protestantism'.[29] Religion was progressively stripped of its rights and status there, leaving it a 'strange unprepossessing orphan'. Yet what eventually replaced it was not, as might have been expected, an irreligious void but a perverted new secular religion with its own 'priests and mystagogues' in the form of zealous *philosophes* and fanatical revolutionaries. Like Hamann, Hardenberg subscribed to a version of the 'iron law of religiosity', as I shall call it – the belief that religion in *some* form (however 'perverted') is inevitable because humans are essentially religious beings. He found evidence for this in the anti-Christian policies of the Jacobins, who made reason their God. 'The attempt of that great iron mask, which under the name of Robespierre sought in religion the centre and the strength of the republic,' he writes, 'remains historically remarkable; so also the coldness with which theophilanthropy, this mysticism of the later Enlightenment [*der neueren Aufklärung*], was taken up.'[30]

While France was the 'birthplace and the seat' of this new anti-religious faith, Hardenberg discerned signs of a properly religious spirit re-emerging in Germany in his day, and he believed that it was his country's historic mission to lead Europe back to its path, a view he shared with Hegel and a great many other German intellectuals of the period. In *On Religion*, for example, Schleiermacher had written to his compatriots of his deep conviction that 'you are the only ones capable, and thus also worthy, of having the sense for holy and divine things aroused in you'.[31] These sentiments are echoed in Hardenberg's essay, where he writes that 'Germany is treading a slow but sure path, ahead of the other European countries ... the German is educating himself with all diligence to participate in a higher cultural epoch. ... An infinite amount of intellectual spirit is being developed ... stirring a mighty sense of creative will, of limitlessness, of infinite diversity, of holy particularity, and the infinite capacity of the human spirit.'[32] Whereas France was the origin of the intellectual and political revolutions of the eighteenth century that led Europe away from faith, Germany was destined to lead a spiritual revolution that would lead it back to Christianity. Hardenberg never lived to see if his prophecy came true, since he died very soon after it was written, aged just 29.

Night, sacred night

Only a couple of months after the controversy stirred up in Prussia by the publication of Hardenberg's *Faith and Love*, his exact contemporary Samuel Taylor Coleridge arrived in Germany for a well-timed visit intended to complete his education. He and his friend William Wordsworth (1770–1850) were among the very few English Romantic writers who had any direct contact with Germany at this time.[33] Although Coleridge had originally planned to spend most of his time at Jena, he unfortunately ended up in Göttingen instead, and so never met Hardenberg and his small but influential circle of early German Romantics.[34] Even so, the months he spent in Germany proved immensely stimulating and important to him during the early spring of German Romanticism, and helped to shape his mature outlook. Like many Romantic writers, Coleridge was already keenly interested in German religious mysticism at this stage, particularly the 'reveries of Swedenborg' (1688–1772) and the writings of Jakob Boehme, in whom Hardenberg also shared a lively interest.

Coleridge's firsthand encounter with German intellectual and cultural life at this key juncture marked a crucial early stage in the gradual transition from his youthful 'Jacobin' works, such as *Conciones ad Populum* (1795) and the 'Pantisocracy project' (1794–1795), to his more religiously orthodox and politically conservative later writings, *The Statesman's Manual* (1816), *Lay Sermons* (1817), *Biographia Literaria* (1817), *Lectures 1808–19: On Literature, The Friend* (1818), *Lectures 1818–1819: On the History of Philosophy* and *On the Constitution of the Church and State* (1829). In addition, what he called 'the complete failure of the French Revolution',[35] the ascendancy of Napoleon, and the fact that, from the mid 1790s, Britain was continuously at war with France for two decades, had some influence on Coleridge's increasingly critical views about the course of events on the Continent.

The first clear signs of Coleridge's 'profound spiritual reaction against the rationalism of the French Enlightenment', as his biographer Richard Holmes has put it, began to emerge following his return from Germany.[36] Although he did not begin a systematic study of the ideas of 'the great German metaphysician' Kant until some time later, he came back from Germany deeply dissatisfied with the standard Lockean view of the mind as a passive *tabula rasa*.[37] Although Coleridge eventually found Kant wanting too, primarily for his neglect of the central role of feeling in our mental life, he regarded his more active conception of the mind as a major advance on Locke's. But even Kant's view of the mind was simply too narrow to accommodate the full breadth of human experience as Coleridge understood it. So he set about devising his own, alternative conception in which feeling and imagination were central.

Coleridge's strategy for restoring the centrality of feeling to mental life was not to repudiate reason or subordinate it to the emotions, but to redefine it so that the emotions lie at its heart. He rejected the conventional separation of reason from emotion, and in doing so believed that he was returning to an older, more profound conception of reason, which he depicted as a 'magical' faculty capable of immediate, intuitive perception of 'Truths above Sense', especially spiritual, aesthetic and moral truths.[38] Far from denigrating or marginalising reason, Coleridge regarded it as the highest of all human faculties – when properly understood.

> The REASON (not the abstract reason, not the reason as a mere *organ* of science, or as the faculty of scientific principles and schemes a priori) but reason as the integral *spirit* of the regenerated man, reason substantiated and vital, 'one only, yet manifold, overseeing all, and going through all understanding; the breadth of the power of God, and a pure influence from the glory of the Almighty; which remaining in itself regenerateth all other powers, and in all ages entering into holy souls maketh them friends of God and prophets' (*The Wisdom of Solomon*, c. vii), the REASON without being either the SENSE, the UNDERSTANDING or the IMAGINATION contains all three within itself.[39]

Only reason thus understood – capable of immediately apprehending 'invisible realities' and 'spiritual objects' – can guide the conduct of practical worldly affairs, but it was precisely this that was fatally neglected by 'the Illuminati and Constitution-manufacturers' of '"this *enlightened* age"', Coleridge believed.[40] Below reason he placed understanding, the faculty with which 'we reflect and generalise' on the experiences of our senses.[41] Sensation, which the *philosophes* regarded as the principal source of knowledge, was at the very bottom of his cognitive hierarchy. But the 'distinguishing characteristic of man as a progressive being',[42] and the key to all human creativity for Coleridge, is imagination – 'the living Power and prime Agent of all human Perception'.[43]

Although Coleridge's remarks on imagination are surprisingly few, given the importance that he attributes to it, and are scattered across his later works, he said more about it than any other Romantic writer. He claims that it is a 'synthetic and magical power' that gives unity, coherence and even beauty to the mind's varied and often discordant elements and the objects that it contemplates. It is a 'reconciling and mediatory power, which incorporating the Reason in Images of the Sense, and organising (as it were) the flux of the Senses by the permanence and self-circling energies of the Reason, gives birth to a system of symbols, harmonious in themselves, and consubstantial with the truths, of which they are the *conductors*'.[44]

According to Coleridge, poets are blessed with an unusually acute and well-developed ability to interpret and express the 'system of symbols' to which the imagination gives rise. With the aid of an active imagination, the poet 'diffuses a tone and spirit of unity, that blends, and (as it were) *fuses*, each into each, by that synthetic and magic power, to which we have exclusively appropriated the name of imagination'.[45] For Coleridge, there was a special affinity between the poetic imagination and the human receptivity to religion. Imagination was for him an essentially religious faculty, and therefore beyond the limits of reason, since religion 'passes out of the ken of Reason only where the eye of Reason has reached its own Horizon; and that Faith is then but its continuation: even as the Day softens away into the sweet Twilight, and Twilight, hushed and breathless, steals into the Darkness. It is Night, sacred Night! the upraised Eye views only the starry Heaven which manifests itself alone.'[46]

The 'general Irreligion' characteristic of what Coleridge referred to scoffingly as 'this enlightened age' was a great concern to him because he listed 'the predominance of a presumptuous and irreligious philosophy' among the principal causes of the French Revolution.[47] In the *Statesman's Manual*, he inveighs against the *philosophes*' irresponsible dissemination of their sceptical doctrines among the decent, pious, law-abiding public:

> The teeth of the old serpent sowed by the Cadmuses of French literature under Lewis XV produced a plenteous crop of such philosophers and truth-trumpeters in the reign of his ill-fated successor. They taught many *facts*, historical, political, physiological, and ecclesiastical, diffusing their notions so widely that the very ladies and hair-dressers of Paris

became fluent encyclopaedists; and the sole price, which their scholars paid for these treasures of new light, was to believe Christianity an imposture, the Scriptures a forgery, the worship of God superstition, hell a fable, heaven a dream, our life without Providence, and our death without hope.[48]

Coleridge's philosophical writings are very fragmentary, unsystematic and quite often inconsistent. He was not a philosopher per se and, like Burke, never engaged with the *philosophes* in any sustained or very philosophically serious way. He did not regard them as substantial enough to warrant much more than polemical put-downs and personal jibes. However, the increasingly conservative, religious and Francophobic Coleridge filled many of his later works with polemics against particular *philosophes*, above all Rousseau, Voltaire and Condillac, and he regularly denounced them collectively with epithets such as 'the Parisian Philosophers',[49] 'French *Philosophers*',[50] 'these City Philosophers',[51] 'the teachers of physiocratic science, demagogues of this "enlightened age"',[52] 'the Hospital of Cosmopolites at Paris',[53] the 'No-thinking Free-thinkers throughout Europe',[54] 'the so-called Encyclopaedists',[55] and 'French Encyclopaedists and the other great Anti-Christian wits of the last century'.[56] This aversion to what his friend Wordsworth called the 'pestilential philosophism of France' was quite typical of English Romantics of their generation. Wordsworth, who had accompanied Coleridge to Germany in 1798–1799, came to share his friend's hostility to 'the paradoxical reveries of Rousseau, and the flippancies of Voltaire',[57] as did William Blake (1757–1827), who waxed poetical about these philosophical heroes of the French Revolution:

> Mock on, mock on, Voltaire, Rousseau;
> Mock on, mock on: 'tis all in vain!
> You throw the sand against the wind,
> And the wind blows it back again.[58]

Like so many other opponents of the Enlightenment, Coleridge singled out the much calumnated Voltaire for special abuse and blamed him personally for many of the disasters of the eighteenth century. '[S]carcely anyone has a larger share of my aversion than Voltaire', he declared in an essay in 1809.[59] Voltaire's knowledge, although extensive, was superficial and his writing is full of 'lies' and 'exaggeration'.[60] Even his celebrated wit has been overrated, being entirely 'without imagery, without character, and without that pathos which gives the magic charm to genuine humour'.[61] Coleridge attacked Voltaire's *Philosophical Dictionary* (1734) as a worthless 'jumble of Ignorance, Wickedness, & Folly' that had done incalculable damage by popularising the idea that Lockean sensationalism was just a 'modest commonsense system' rather than a dehumanising philosophy that undermined faith.[62] Voltaire bore specific responsibility for helping to lead the 'enlightened despots' of Europe (for example, Frederick II of Prussia and Catherine II of Russia) disastrously astray under 'the banner of Antichrist':

> But though the growing alienation and self-sufficiency of the under-standing was perceptible at an earlier period, yet it seems to have been about the middle of the last century, under the influence of Voltaire, D'Alembert, Diderot, say generally of the so-called Encyclopaedists, and alas! – of their crowned proselytes and disciples, Frederick, Joseph, and Catharine, that the Human Understanding, and this too in its narrowest form, was tempted to throw off all show of reverence to the spiritual and even to the moral powers and impulses of the soul; and usurping the name of reason openly joined the banner of Antichrist, at once the pander and the prostitute of sensuality, and whether in the cabinet, lab-oratory, the dissecting room, or the brothel, alike busy in the schemes of vice and irreligion.[63]

Coleridge was no less savage in his comments on 'the crazy Rousseau', whom he viewed as a typical *philosophe* and Voltaire's 'twin'. Together they were 'the Alpha and Omega of Continental Genius',[64] a view common to several generations of intellectuals (starting with Burke, who was still enormously influential at this time[65]) who compressed them into 'one ideological bogey-man' symbolising the worst aspects of the Enlightenment and its corrosive effects.[66] The revolutionary 'pantheonisation' of Voltaire and Rousseau did not escape the notice of Coleridge any more than it did Burke, Barruel or Maistre, all of whom demonised them both as *philosophes* and fathers of the French Revolution. The 'proud', 'vain', 'suspicious' and 'ignorant' Rousseau abandoned his faith and allowed himself to be steered 'by the compass of unaided reason', which inevitably led him into intellectual folly and led Europe into political calamity through disciples such as Robespierre.[67] Rousseau, Voltaire, and the Revolution were bound together in a tight causal knot in Coleridge's mind. Echoing Barruel, Burke and Maistre, Coleridge depicts Voltaire and Rousseau as 'the two modern Conspirators' against the authority of revealed religion in the eighteenth century, whom he contrasted unfavourably with Erasmus and Luther – the two great 'Puri-fiers of revealed Religion'.[68] In a note in his essay *On the Constitution of the Church and State* Coleridge muses about the effects of Rousseau's *Social Con-tract* during the Revolution: 'I am not indeed certain that some operatical farce, under the name of a Social Contract or Compact, might not have been acted by the Illuminati and Constitution-manufacturers, at the close of the eighteenth century; a period which how far it deserved the name, so compla-cently affixed to it by the contemporaries of "this *enlightened* age", may be doubted. That it was an age of *Enlighteners*, no man will deny'.[69]

Although the Enlightenment was essentially a French affair for Coleridge, as it was for most of its enemies, he acknowledged two important exceptions. One was David Hume, who belonged with the 'French

Encyclopaedists and the other great Anti-Christian wits of the last century' rather than, as Hamann and Jacobi believed, with their German critics. In his *Biographia Literaria* (1817), Coleridge complains that thinkers of the high calibre of Bacon, Harrington, Machiavelli and Spinoza are no longer read because thinkers of the low calibre of Hume, Condillac and Voltaire are.[70] However, it does not appear that Coleridge actually read Hume's philosophical works very closely, if he read them at all. By contrast, he knew those of William Godwin (1756–1836), the atheist author of *An Enquiry Concerning Political Justice* (1793), very well, since they were close friends and drinking companions. Coleridge included him among 'the demagogues of this "enlightened age"' and constantly chastised him for his atheism and rationalism. Although he wrote relatively little about Godwin directly, it is very likely that he had his non-believing friend in mind (among others) in his assaults on the 'No-thinking Free-thinkers throughout Europe'.

Midnight of the soul

The Romantic movement in France started out as conservative, religious and monarchical, and gradually became liberal and reformist, the reverse of Coleridge's ideological trajectory.[71] It emerged in reaction to violent revolution that had overturned throne and altar and cast all tradition and hierarchy aside in France in the name of freedom, equality and reason. Typical of this early phase is François-René, vicomte de Chateaubriand, the most famous and influential of the early Romantics in France and author of *Atala* (1801), the first 'Romantic' novel in French. Although he never became 'reactionary' or politically absolutist like his contemporary and fellow *émigré* Joseph de Maistre, he was a moderate conservative with 'liberal' tendencies, whose views were decisively and directly shaped by the Revolution. Although no Jacobin, the aristocratic Chateaubriand was still quite anti-clerical and not wholly unsympathetic to aspects of the Revolution while living in exile in London (like Barruel) between 1793 and 1800, as his *Essai historique* (1797) makes apparent. Given its anti-clericalism, it is surprising how harsh the *Essai* is in its attacks on the *encyclopédistes* for having helped to create the atmosphere which led to the Revolution. It is a work that is simultaneously anti-Christian and anti-*philosophe*, an awkward stance which Chateaubriand would soon abandon. In it he compares the *philosophes* to the Sophists of ancient Greece, rather than to its genuine philosophers, and concludes that most of their philosophy is already forgotten – 'all that remains is the French Revolution'. Like so many Romantics of his generation, he too supported the 'continuity thesis':

> Be it understood that they [the *philosophes*] were not the *only* cause of the Revolution, but a *great* cause. The French concussion did not proceed from this or that man, from this or that book. ... It was principally caused by the progress of society towards knowledge and corruption.

Hence it was that so many excellent principles were attended with such disastrous consequences. The former were derived from an enlightened theory, the latter from the corruption of morals; so that an incomprehensible mixture of crimes was grafted on a philosophic trunk, as I have endeavoured to show throughout this essay.[72]

It was above all an 'alteration in the religious ideas of the people that overturned the government of France', according to Chateaubriand's diagnosis in the *Essai*.[73] And it was the 'atheistic sect' of the *philosophes*, led by Voltaire – who 'wrote witty couplets, and instilled immorality'[74] – that was principally responsible for this dramatic change in the beliefs of ordinary people in France. Their self-appointed mission was to exterminate Christianity and thereby 'destroy the morality of France' by the power of ideas rather than by the force of arms, and in this they succeeded beyond their wildest dreams. Under the 'reign of the Encyclopedists',[75] a torrent of new ideas rushed into people's heads, subverting their faith and eroding their morals.[76] It became so fashionable to be a non-believer in France during this 'siècle incrédule' that Rousseau – a man 'of a superior stamp to the Encyclopedists'[77] – was ruthlessly persecuted by 'the sect' and driven out of the country when he valiantly defended religion. Under these circumstances, morals were relaxed and a 'rage for systems' combined to bring about a popular revolution in France.[78] What was the real spirit of this zealous atheistic sect, Chateaubriand asks? Destruction. And what did they wish to erect on the ruins of what they had so thoroughly destroyed? Nothing.

> The spirit of innovation and doubt, which arose under the Regent, soon made rapid progress. During the reign of Louis XV an association was formed, consisting of the most brilliant men that France has produced, viz. Diderot, D'Alembert, Voltaire & c. Only two great persons refused to become members of it, J. J. Rousseau and Montesquieu. Hence the aversion to them felt by Voltaire; and particularly to the former, because he was the champion of God and morality. This society stated its object to be the diffusion of knowledge and the destruction of tyranny. Undoubtedly no object could be more noble; but the true spirit of the Encyclopedists was a persecuting fury and intolerance of opinions, which aimed at destroying all other systems than their own, and even preventing the freedom of thought. In fine, it was a rage against what they called *l'infâme*, or the Christian religion, which they had resolved to exterminate.[79]

Although Chateaubriand's family was saved from the guillotine at the last minute by the amnesty following Robespierre's fall from power in 1794, his pious mother soon died as a result of the treatment she had received in prison, but not before she told her son that his anti-clerical *Essai* had saddened her last days, and her dying wish was that he return to the Catholic fold.[80] In a guilt-induced crisis caused by this, he granted her wish, and *The Genius of Christianity* is the literary expression of his return to the faith of his youth and the fulfilment of his promise to his mother. In addition, Chateaubriand came into greater contact with French *émigré* intellectuals such as Barruel in London when he moved there in 1793, and this undoubtedly coloured his perception of events on the Continent. It also meant that he was exposed to English counter-revolutionary writings and ideas, such as Burke's still-influential *Reflections*, the same milieu in which Coleridge and Barruel were immersed during these years.

As is obvious from its title, *The Genius of Christianity* is a work of Christian apologetics made necessary, he believed, by the total denigration of faith in his 'impious age'. In it he undertakes to 'summon all the charms of the imagination, and all the interests of the heart' in defence of religion in general and Christianity in particular.[81] Like most Romantic writers, he campaigned to end the eighteenth-century 'sleep of religion', as Hardenberg called it, and heralded the imminent arrival of a new religious epoch.[82] Like Hardenberg's *Christendom or Europe*, his Romantic defence of religion became an early and enormously influential part of a broader Catholic renaissance in Europe in the opening years of the nineteenth century after many decades on the defensive from the 'fanaticisme philosophique' of the *encyclopédistes* and the aggressive anti-clericalism of the French revolutionaries. In addition, the French Army had invaded the papal states and forced the Pope into exile, where he died in captivity in France. It was from these depths that the pendulum began to swing back towards religion, which Napoleon made 'official' when he signed a Concordat with the Vatican in April 1801, restoring some of the powers it had lost during the Revolution. The publication of Chateaubriand's *Genius* less than a week later could not have been more propitious and was a major factor in its instant success; part of the genius of *Genius* was its timing.

A central feature of Chateaubriand's book is its 'aesthetic' defence of religion. A significant portion of it is taken up with descriptions of the surpassing beauty of the medieval church, which is a 'kind of poetry'.[83] Religion is valuable (in part) because it is beautiful, and its eclipse is as much a crime against beauty as it is against faith. He shared Hardenberg's admiration for the sublime beauty of the old Catholic faith of the Middle Ages, a period despised by most *philosophes*. He also argues that Christianity has always been unusually sympathetic to and supportive of the fine arts because it knows that '[w]ithout religion the heart is insensible and dead to beauty'.[84] In this, Christianity is in fundamental agreement with the legislators of antiquity, since both wisely 'discouraged philosophers', 'protected the arts' and 'lavished honours upon artists'.[85] Atheism, by contrast, is necessarily crude, ugly and incompatible with the flourishing of artistic creativity.

Like Coleridge, Hamann, Hardenberg and Maistre, Chateaubriand made a virtue out of what he saw as the essential mystery of faith. He believed that it was folly for Christians even to try to reconcile their religious beliefs with reason and modern science. Like Maistre, he was influenced by the religious mystic Louis Claude de Saint-Martin (1743–1803) and believed that Christianity is of an essentially 'spiritual and mystic nature'[86] whose core doctrines do not have their seat 'in the head, but in the heart'.[87] For the Romantic defenders of faith like Chateaubriand this was a strength, not a weakness, the key to its bewitching power and the mysterious beauty of medieval Christianity.

Most Romantics associated this powerful inner feeling with an 'infinite beyond'. As we have already seen, Rousseau was a pioneer in forging the inner path to the '[d]ivine instinct, immortal and celestial voice, certain guide' of conscience,[88] which he regarded as infallible, prior to reason and linked directly to the divine. By associating conscience to God and morality and making it intuitive rather than rational, Rousseau had been a lone voice in the wilderness of the eighteenth century for many early Romantics, pointing the way to a revival of both feeling and faith. Chateaubriand was not alone in Romantic circles in his respect for Rousseau's unorthodox religiosity, and many saw him as a kindred 'man of feeling'. His own account of conscience in *The Genius* seems to come straight from the pages of Rousseau's *Emile*: 'Each individual has within his own heart a tribunal,' he waxes, 'where he sits in judgement on himself till the Supreme Arbiter shall confirm the sentence. . . . I hear a voice in the recesses of my soul, protesting so loudly against the mere idea of such a superstition, that I cannot for one moment doubt the reality of conscience.'[89]

Many followed Hamann and viewed the attempts by eighteenth-century deists to reconcile faith and reason as both a practical disaster, since it failed to prevent the French revolutionary attack on religion, and a theoretical failure, since it could not withstand the sceptical arguments of writers such as Hume. An increasingly stark choice seemed to present itself between a rationalistic atheism on the one hand, and a non-rational religiosity rooted in feeling and intuition on the other. This led to a radical reinterpretation of the very nature of religion, which was to become 'a main feature of romanticist thought with the dawn of the new century'.[90]

Not surprisingly, in religious ages (such as the Middle Ages) it is to the heart that people turn and prosper, whereas in irreligious ages (such as the eighteenth century) they turn to the head and suffer, according to Chateaubriand. Since 'the natural propensity of man is to the mysterious', we find ourselves drawn instinctively to the shadowy regions where religion naturally dwells in enchanting obscurity.[91] The dark forest, 'full of wonders', is the real 'cradle of religion'.[92] Echoing Hardenberg's *Hymns to the Night*, Chateaubriand claims that nothing could be more fatal to this magic, and therefore destructive of both beauty and belief, than to enlighten the darkness that is religion's natural habitat.

> Far from sullying the imagination by allowing it to indulge in unbounded curiosity, it [religion] has drawn the veil of doubt and

obscurity over things which it is useless for us to know; and in this it
has shown its superiority over that false philosophy which is too eager to
penetrate into the nature of man and to fathom the bottom of everything. We should not be continually sounding the abysses of the heart;
the truths which it contains belong to the number of those that require
half light and perspective. It is highly imprudent to be incessantly
applying our judgement to the loving part of our being, to transfer the
reasoning spirit to the passions. This curiosity gradually leads us to
doubt of everything generous and noble; it extinguishes the sensibili-
ties, and, as it were, murders the soul. The mysteries of the heart
are like those of ancient Egypt; every profane person who strives to penetrate into their secrets without being initiated by religion, as a just
punishment for his audacity is suddenly struck dead.[93]

According to Chateaubriand, modern science is the antithesis of the mysterious spirit of religion, which is why it 'necessarily produce[s] irreligious ages'
and is also the necessary consequence of such ages – both the cause and effect
of disbelief.[94] It is to the vanity of science, he warns his readers, echoing
Rousseau's *Discourse on the Sciences and the Arts*, that 'we owe almost all of our
calamities', and he points out that 'the ages of science have always bordered
on the ages of destruction', as the biblical story of Adam and Eve attests no
less than the tragic history of France in the second half of the eighteenth
century.[95] Whereas the fine arts which religions support 'impart a magic
colouring to life, melt the soul, fill us with faith in the Divinity, and
conduct us by religion to the practice of every virtue', science by contrast
'contracts the heart, robs nature of her charms, leads weak minds to atheism,
and from atheism to crimes of every kind'.[96] It is hardly surprising that
Chateaubriand, like so many Romantics, admired Rousseau (Coleridge was
an exception), and why Maistre solicited Chateaubriand's assistance in
arranging the publication of his book *Du Pape*.[97]

It is not only science that poses a grave threat to the order of society,
according to Chateaubriand. Philosophy can also be extremely dangerous, as
Rousseau, Hamann, Maistre and Coleridge had warned, which is why, just
like the ages of science, those of philosophy 'have invariably bordered upon
the ages of destruction'.[98] The wisest men in history have all agreed that
philosophy is 'fraught with extreme danger for the multitude'[99] and that it
is best for it to 'dwell in the mansions of the rich, and leave the people in
general to the care of religion'.[100] This is something that the writers of the
eighteenth century (Rousseau excepted) never understood, since they 'owe
most of their defects to a delusive system of philosophy'.[101] Coleridge
thought so too, observing in 1809 that there is a 'natural affinity' between
despotism and modern philosophy.[102]

The scorn with which Chateaubriand treated the *philosophes* in his *Essai* is
even more pronounced in the *Genius*. This is most apparent in his remarks
on Voltaire, 'le patriarche de l'incredulité' and the man he held chiefly

responsible for the 'impious rage' of the eighteenth century. According to Chateaubriand, Voltaire possessed 'the baneful art of making infidelity fashionable'. His 'destructive system' spread so far, wide and deep in eighteenth-century France, as Coleridge had already noticed, that '[w]omen of fashion and grave philosophers alike read lectures on infidelity', inevitably undermining their morals and their respect for institutions and thereby paving the way into the 'abyss' of violent revolution.[103]

As a masterful stylist himself, Chateaubriand was well able to appreciate Voltaire's genius as a writer, and he professed his admiration for some of his personal attributes as well – the 'elegance of his manners, the urbanity of his demeanour, his love of society, and, above all, his humanity'.[104] The tragedy is that Voltaire directed his considerable gifts against religion, and this alone prevented his attaining the height for which nature qualified him.[105] Like Maistre, Chateaubriand rated the literature and philosophy of the eighteenth century far below those of the seventeenth century, principally because of the former's antipathy towards Christianity.[106] If only Voltaire had been a devout Christian his works 'would have acquired that moral tint without which nothing is perfect'[107] and he would have produced an effect comparable to that of his illustrious seventeenth-century predecessors.[108] By writing against his faith, however, he 'broke with his own hand the most harmonious string of his lyre', as a consequence of which he never attained the highest peaks of literary greatness.[109] Even so, Chateaubriand was only too happy to quote approvingly Voltaire's criticisms of the *Encyclopédie* – that 'Babel of the sciences and of reason', as Voltaire once sneeringly referred to it in private – and delighted in mentioning occasional, unflattering comments on the 'wretched work' by its own editors.

Chateaubriand rated Rousseau much higher than Voltaire as a stylist entirely because 'he believed in something'.[110] This is in direct contradiction to Coleridge, who attributed Rousseau's shortcomings to his abandonment of his faith in favour of reason. Chateaubriand thought the same of Montesquieu, one of 'the truly great man of the eighteenth century' whose genius 'rested upon religion alone', despite the occasional anti-clerical remark.[111] That Chateaubriand made an exception of Rousseau in his assaults on the *philosophes* is not surprising, although it was by no means inevitable, as we have seen in his treatment at the hands of Burke, Maistre and Coleridge.

5 The strange case of Friedrich Nietzsche and the Enlightenment

> The revolutionary spirit has for a long time banished *the spirit of the Enlightenment {der Geist der Aufklärung} and of progressive evolution*: let us see – each of us within himself – whether it is possible to call it back![1]
>
> (Nietzsche)

> [A]t bottom, we good Europeans wage a war against the eighteenth century.[2]
>
> (Nietzsche)

We children of the Enlightenment[3]

If there is a thinker whom one would expect more than any other to have come out all guns blazing against the Enlightenment, it is Friedrich Nietzsche (1844–1900), the Dionysian 'prophet of extremity' who has given inspiration to generations of opponents of modernity, progress, reason, truth and morality. Yet things are not as straightforward as they may seem at first glance here. His thought underwent a significant transformation in the late 1870s and early 1880s, corresponding to major changes in his life. This was the period of transition to his mature works, starting with *Also Spoke Zarathustra*, published between 1882 and 1885. During these 'middle' years he abandoned his academic career as Professor of Classical Philology at Basel University, from which he resigned in 1879, and was crippled by chronic and debilitating physical and mental ailments that would torment him until the full onset of insanity in 1889, from which he never recovered.[4] Nietzsche also broke with his hero Richard Wagner at this time, partly to preserve his own independence and partly from revulsion at his mentor's nationalism, anti-Semitism and embrace of Christianity in his final opera, *Parsifal* (premiered at Bayreuth in 1882) in which a disgusted Nietzsche smelled 'the spirit of the Counter-Reformation'. In reaction to the Romantic Bayreuth cult to which Nietzsche had subscribed until then, the writings of his 'middle period' – *Human, All Too Human* (1878), 'Assorted Opinions and Maxims' (1879), 'The Wanderer and His Shadow' (1880), *Daybreak* (1881) and *The Gay Science* (1882) – represent a turn 'from German romanticism to the French enlightenment, and from Wagner to independence', as he felt his way towards his own philosophy.[5] Nietzsche's embrace of the Enlightenment at this stage was a key aspect of his rejection of Wagnerian Romanticism. It was a necessary step in the formation of his own intellectual identity, which he had to assert against 'the Master'. He picked up the Enlightenment and used it to help free himself from what he came to see as just another herd mentality, and he turned violently against it just as quickly when it had served this intellectual purpose. After all, Nietzsche believed that philosophy is always 'a confession on the part of its author and a kind of involuntary and unconscious memoir'.[6]

In his 'middle' works, Nietzsche sharply opposed the Enlightenment to the French Revolution, taking his stand with the former. This is most apparent in *Human, All Too Human*, the first edition of which he dedicated to Voltaire, 'one of the greatest liberators of the human spirit'. It is an acerbically witty book in the style of Voltaire in which the French rather than the Germans are depicted as the true heirs of ancient Greek culture. It is a work that seems designed to annoy the nationalistic Wagner and the Bayreuth cult. Nietzsche argues that the French Revolutionaries, inspired by the utopian dreams of 'political and social fantasists' such as Rousseau, undertook 'a revolutionary overturning of all social orders' in the naïve belief that this would liberate the supposed natural goodness of human beings from corrupt and repressive social and political institutions and practices. In reality, it merely brought about 'the resurrection of the most savage energies in the shape of the long-buried dreadfulness and excesses of the most distant ages'.[7] It was not, on Nietzsche's view, Voltaire's essentially moderate nature but Rousseau's 'passionate follies and half-lies' that called forth the destructive force of the Terror. He concludes by noting that the revolutionary spirit 'has for a long time banished *the spirit of the Enlightenment and of progressive evolution*: let us see – each of us within himself – whether it is possible to call it back!'[8]

In this epic clash, Nietzsche stood foursquare behind the Enlightenment and called for it to be rescued from the revolutionary cause with which it had become erroneously and disastrously associated. In fact, as Nietzsche later claimed, the 'semi-insanity, histrionicism, bestial cruelty, voluptuousness, and especially sentimentality and self-intoxication, which taken together constitutes the actual *substance of the Revolution*' actually set the Enlightenment on its head.[9] It was Voltaire's arch-enemy Rousseau who diverted the Enlightenment in a fanatical direction, leading to revolution; otherwise, the eighteenth century would have ended on a tranquil note, rather than in a terrible fury of destruction.

> [T]he Enlightenment [*die Aufklärung*], which is fundamentally so alien to the Revolution and, left to itself, would have passed quietly along like a gleam in the clouds and for long been content to address itself only to the individual: so that it would have transformed the customs and institutions of nations only very slowly. Now, however, tied to a

violent and impulsive companion, the Enlightenment itself became violent and impulsive. Its perilousness has thereby become almost greater than the liberating illumination it brought to the great revolutionary movement. He who grasps this will also know out of what compound it has to be extracted, of what impurity it has to be cleansed: so as then to *continue* the work of the Enlightenment *in himself,* and to strangle the Revolution at birth, to make it not happen.[10]

This is as complete a rejection of the 'continuity thesis' as it is possible to find, one that Nietzsche would soon completely disown when he turned violently against the Enlightenment in his later works.

In his next book, *Daybreak*, Nietzsche depicts Germany as fundamentally hostile to the Enlightenment; even its natural scientists 'paid homage to romanticism and had renounced the spirit of the Enlightenment'.[11] As a consequence, a 'cult of feeling' replaced the Enlightenment's 'cult of reason' in Germany. Fortunately, the very spirits that the Germans invoked in the name of Counter-Enlightenment obscurantism and reaction actually thwarted their intentions to the benefit of *'that very Enlightenment [eben jener Aufklärung]* against which they were first conjured up'.[12] As in *Human, All Too Human*, Nietzsche ends with a call to his readers by claiming that it is the 'Enlightenment we must now carry further forward'.[13]

In *The Gay Science*, the last major work of Nietzsche's 'middle period', he claims that Christianity unintentionally 'made a great contribution to the enlightenment *[einen grossen Beitrag zur Aufklärung]',*[14] even though he argues elsewhere that the 'growth of the Enlightenment *[die wachsende Aufklärung]* undermined the dogmas of religion and inspired a fundamental distrust of them'.[15] This inadvertent, self-destructive Christian promotion of enlightenment was caused by the moral scepticism it released when it sought to destroy other faiths. Fortunately, Nietzsche thought, the 'worm' of Christian scepticism eventually spread 'to all *religious* states and procedures', undermining Christianity itself and thereby promoting secular enlightenment.[16] He here associates the Enlightenment with a healthy scepticism that is actually supportive of powerful institutions, such as the medieval Church. He had earlier expressed his grudging admiration for the strength, tactical skill and self-discipline of the Jesuits, whose methods and outlook 'we children of the Enlightenment' would do well to emulate.[17]

Although Nietzsche does make some critical comments on the Enlightenment during this 'middle' period, they are few and relatively minor. In *Human, All Too Human*, for example, he complains that 'in the period of the Enlightenment *[In der Periode der Aufklärung]* the significance of religion was not adequately appreciated', just as in the reaction that followed it religion was appreciated much too highly.[18] And in *Daybreak*, he remarks in passing that truth by itself is utterly powerless, 'whatever its flatterers of the Enlightenment may be accustomed to say to the contrary!'[19]

Even when Nietzsche was a partisan of the Enlightenment (as he understood it) during his 'middle period', he was extremely hostile to Kant, who stood in his 'great divide' with Rousseau and the French Revolution against Voltaire and the Enlightenment. He writes in *Daybreak* that Kant was an essentially religious man, with a fanatic's temperament, who had been 'bitten by the moral tarantula Rousseau', as a consequence of which he came to harbour in his soul 'the idea of that moral fanaticism whose executor another disciple of Rousseau felt and confessed himself to be, namely Robespierre, *"de fonder sur la terre l'empire de la sagesse, de la justice et de la vertu"* [to establish the empire of wisdom, justice and virtue on earth]'.[20] This view is echoed often in Nietzsche's later works as well, such as the *Nachlass* – unfinished notes that were published posthumously – in which Kant is derided as a 'moral fanatic à la Rousseau; a subterranean Christianity in his values; a dogmatist through and through' who was heir to Luther and the antithesis of Voltaire's light, joyous, sceptical spirit.[21] Nietzsche's Kant was an enemy of the Enlightenment, like Rousseau.

Volte-face

Nietzsche underwent a complete volte-face on the Enlightenment in his later works, where he depicts it in quite conventionally conservative terms reminiscent of Burke, Maistre and Barruel. This is not at all surprising given his radical turn against all notions of truth, reason, progress and happiness. Whereas previously he had portrayed the Enlightenment as the antithesis of the Revolution that he always abominated, he later called for Europe to 'wage war' against the *entire* eighteenth century. In these later works he writes in terms of the eighteenth century in general, encompassing both the Enlightenment *and* the Revolution, which he had earlier contrasted in the starkest possible terms. He now claims that disgust for the Enlightenment is 'noble'[22] and declares that his goal is 'to overcome the eighteenth century'[23] as a whole.[24] The French Revolution, which Rousseau inspired, is 'the last great slave revolt'[25] and 'the daughter and continuation of Christianity – its instincts are against caste, against the noble, against the last privilege'.[26] After *The Gay Science*, Nietzsche embraced what I have called the 'continuity thesis' so common to the enemies of the Enlightenment. This later tendency is most apparent in a passage from *Beyond Good and Evil*, where Nietzsche claims that 'there have already been two grand attempts to relax the bow [of spirit], once by means of Jesuitism, the second time by means of democratic enlightenment'.[27] Nowhere in his earlier works does he refer to the Enlightenment as 'democratic', an attribute he had previously assigned to its antithesis: the Revolution. In his eyes, the Enlightenment has now lost its aristocratic character, to its detriment. This clearly indicates a significant darkening of Nietzsche's view of the Enlightenment and marks a major step in the direction of earlier conservative critics of the Revolution who linked it to the *philosophes*.

In his *Nachlass* Nietzsche depicts the nineteenth century as a major improvement on the eighteenth century for three reasons. First, he claims that it represents a return to nature 'understood more and more decisively in the opposite sense from Rousseau's idiotically benign conception.[28] His own view of nature is more Maistrean than Rousseauian. Second, he compares the spirit of the nineteenth century favourably to the eighteenth for being 'anti-idealistic, more concrete, more fearless, industrious, moderate, suspicious against sudden changes, *antirevolutionary*'.[29] Finally, Nietzsche enthusiastically welcomed the new priority that the nineteenth century gave to the health of the body over that of the soul, which he identified with both Christianity and democratic moralism, to which it is inextricably linked in his mind.[30]

Nietzsche indulges his taste for sweeping and indiscriminate generalisations of entire centuries in his unfinished *Nachlass* more than anywhere else. Here he speaks approvingly of the seventeenth century, as Maistre and Chateaubriand had done, for being rational and aristocratic (epitomised for Nietzsche by Descartes and the French *moralistes* such as the Duc de la Rochefoucauld, whom he greatly admired), depicts the eighteenth century as feminine, moralistic and soft (represented by Rousseau), and describes the nineteenth century as animalistic and gloomy (symbolised by Schopenhauer). 'The eighteenth century,' he explains with a breezy assurance, 'is dominated by woman, given to enthusiasm, full of *esprit*, shallow, but with a spirit in the service of what is desirable, of the heart, libertine in the enjoyment of what is most spiritual, and undermines all authorities; intoxicated, cheerful, clear, humane, false before itself, much canaille *au fond*, sociable.'[31] In a section 'Against Rousseau', Nietzsche compares the 'domineering will' of the great Renaissance man, epitomised by Cesare Borgia, with the 'tender and moralised' spirit of the effeminate man of the eighteenth century.[32] At times, he emphasises the Enlightenment dimension of the eighteenth century. For example, he refers to how 'the feeble-optimistic eighteenth century had prettified and rationalised man'.[33] At other times its revolutionary side is stressed, with no less contempt. Surprisingly, Nietzsche's high regard for Voltaire survived his later turn against the Enlightenment. In his writings after the mid-1880s he not only continued to oppose the vulgar plebian Rousseau to that aristocratic *'grandseigneur* of the spirit' Voltaire,[34] but actually intensified his identification with the latter. He did this by simply removing Voltaire from the eighteenth century. Voltaire's positive image was preserved by distancing him from the age in which he actually lived, so that in *Beyond Good and Evil* he becomes the 'dying echo' of the 'noble culture' of seventeenth-century France that Nietzsche admired, just as Rousseau heralded the coming of the 'bloody farce' of the French Revolution that Nietszche detested.[35] Voltaire still stands for the spirit of elite, anti-clerical libertinism Nietzsche had previously associated with the Enlightenment, in contrast to Rousseau, who represents the fanatical moralism of the herd that he associated with the Revolution which destroyed the aristocratic free spirit of *philosophes* like Voltaire. Nietzsche praises Voltaire for his moderation, tolerance and anti-clericalism, calling him in his *Nachlass* a '*Missionary of culture*, aristocrat, representative of the victorious, ruling classes and their valuations'.[36]

In the *Nachlass*, Nietzsche traces what he calls the still unresolved 'problem of civilisation' back to the 'fight between Rousseau and Voltaire' that began in the mid-eighteenth century.[37] He paints an apocalyptic picture on a vast canvass pitting Christianity, Luther, Rousseau, Kant, the French Revolution, Romanticism, democratic egalitarianism, nationalism, morality and the Enlightenment against the seventeenth century, religious scepticism, nobility, Voltaire and all other 'free spirits' on the other. According to Nietzsche, the 'aristocratic' Voltaire defended civilisation as a victory over the barbarism of nature and man's innate bestiality, whereas the plebeian Rousseau – 'beyond a doubt mentally disturbed' – inspired the revolutionary overthrow of all social orders in the name of the natural goodness of man. He thought that Voltaire had correctly realised that man is a 'beast of prey' and that civilisation is a 'tremendous triumph' over his bestial nature. That is why Voltaire felt 'the mitigation, the subtleties, the spiritual joys of the civilised state', unlike Rousseau, whose idealised conception of nature led him to cast a 'curse upon society and civilisation'.[38] This clash was decisive not only for Voltaire personally, but for European civilisation as a whole. From that moment, Voltaire ceased to be a mere 'bel esprit' and became 'the man of his century' whose intense envy and hatred of Rousseau drove him on to the heights of greatness.[39] This bold reading of Rousseau clearly owes much to the *philosophes*, particularly Voltaire, whose famous quip about Rousseau's *Discourse on the Origins of Inequality* was the first in a very long line of depictions of him as an antisocial primitivist. 'I have just received your book against the human race,' Voltaire famously wrote to Rousseau in 1755. 'Never has so much wit been used in an attempt to make us like animals. The desire to walk on all fours seizes one when one reads your work.'[40]

For Nietzsche, the Enlightenment was a French affair, as it was for Hegel. With the exception of Kant, he completely ignores the German *Aufklärung* in his attacks on the eighteenth century, which he looked upon as essentially French, unlike the nineteenth, which was basically German. And as we have already seen, Nietzsche initially associated Kant with Rousseau and the Revolution *against* the spirit of the Enlightenment. Nietzsche's later turn against the Enlightenment was not motivated by either German nationalism, which he attacked with a passionate intensity, or Francophobia, since he often professed to admire the French for their wit, aristocratic sense of style and *savoir vivre* with much to teach other Europeans, above all his vulgar compatriots (as he saw them). However, under Rousseau's malign influence, the French revolutionaries destroyed the civilisation that made these aristocratic virtues possible.

6   Enlightened totalitarianism

> [T]he great eighteenth-century philosophers were ultimately responsible for
> a lot of intellectual tyranny, ending in the Soviet Union, in the *gulag* ...
> these good men, who were against superstition, falsification, authority, and
> were great liberators, had nevertheless preached doctrine which led, albeit in
> a somewhat perverted form, to tragic consequences.[1]
>
> (Isaiah Berlin)

Introduction

Two concepts emerged more or less simultaneously in the intellectual discourse of the mid-twentieth-century West: totalitarianism and enlightenment. The first of these concepts has been 'the signal contribution of
the twentieth century to the history of political thought' in the eyes of
many.[2] Although the term had occasionally been used since the 1920s, it
did not become widely used until the earliest years of the Cold War, just
as communism was replacing fascism as the liberal democratic West's
principal ideological adversary.[3] In this context, totalitarianism proved to
be an irresistibly convenient and highly serviceable concept for combining –
and anathemising – twentieth-century liberalism's two great ideological
foes, which many came to see as forms of a single new species of regime.
Several books published around this time played a decisive part in the
scholarly adoption and routinisation of the concept of totalitarianism,
most notably Friedrich Hayek's *The Road to Serfdom* (1944), Karl Popper's *The
Open Society and Its Enemies* (1945), Arthur Schlesinger, Jr.'s *The Vital
Center* (1948), George Orwell's *1984* (1949), Hannah Arendt's *The Origins of
Totalitarianism* (1951), Czeslaw Milosz's *The Captive Mind* (1951), Jacob
Talmon's *The Origins of Totalitarian Democracy* (1952), and Carl Friedrich's
Totalitarianism (1954).

It was during this same period that 'enlightenment' emerged as a key
organising concept in social and political thought. Although the word had
long existed in English, its use took off in the postwar period when the
expression 'the Enlightenment' (definite article, capital 'e') first started to be
widely employed to designate a particular period in Western history, associ-

ated in particular with eighteenth-century Parisian intellectuals such as Voltaire, Rousseau, Diderot, Condorcet and d'Alembert.

Not surprisingly, many writers at this time combined these two concepts and accused the Enlightenment of having been a (if not *the*) major contributing factor in the emergence of twentieth-century totalitarianism. In the late 1940s and 1950s versions of this charge began to spring up on virtually all points of the ideological compass in the works of a generation that had been born around the turn of the century, thereby producing a point of generational consensus among many ideological enemies. Max Horkheimer (born in 1895) and Theodor Adorno (born in 1903) led the charge from the left with *Dialectic of Enlightenment* (1947), which defends the proposition that 'enlightenment is totalitarian'; Counter-Enlightenment liberals like Jacob Talmon (born in 1916) and Isaiah Berlin (born in 1909) believed that the Enlightenment had unintentionally played a key part in helping to bring about the horrors of twentieth-century totalitarianism; and conservatives such as Eric Voegelin (born in 1901) and Michael Oakeshott (born in 1901) traced many of the pathologies of twentieth-century politics back to the ideas of the eighteenth-century *philosophes*, just as their ideological ancestors Edmund Burke and Joseph de Maistre had done with the French Revolution.

From Marx to Max Weber

Max Horkheimer and Theodor Adorno were foremost among those on the left in the 1940s who became increasingly convinced that the disastrous events of the age were rooted in a single process of enlightenment that had dominated the whole development of Western civilisation since antiquity. Their interests and language shifted during these years away from Karl Marx towards Max Weber. This shift is not surprising given the enormous influence of Weber's work at this time among Horkheimer and Adorno's generation. This is most apparent in the case of the early Frankfurt School, for whom the influence of Weber rivalled that of Marx himself. This can readily be seen in the five public lectures that Horkheimer gave on 'Society and Reason' at Columbia University in February and March 1944, which were published the same year as *Dialectic of Enlightenment*, with the Weberian title *The Eclipse of Reason*. He described these lectures as a 'more or less popular version of the philosophy of enlightenment as far as it has taken shape in the chapters of the book we have so far completed [*Dialectic*]'.[4] They are organised around a distinction between 'objective' and 'subjective' reason that echoes Weber's famous distinction between instrumental or formal rationality (*zweckrationalität*) and substantive or value rationality (*wertrationalität*).[5] According to the latter, an action is rational only if it is consistent with a particular belief 'independently of its prospects of success'.[6] Formal rationality, by contrast, is oriented towards practical mastery of the world which knowledge of the natural and social sciences makes possible. Such knowledge enables individuals to judge the most effective means to their desired ends without questioning those ends.

Weber argued that the process which has led to the hegemony of instrumental rationality in the modern West began with the disenchantment and rationalisation of the self, which was a necessary condition for the subsequent mastery of the external world. He believed that the Puritans led the way in this process in the West when they demanded that individuals suppress their emotions and defer the gratification of their desires through rigorous self-discipline and control. Such self-control eventually made possible the unprecedented technological advances and great material prosperity characteristic of the modern West. But this has come at a great price, according to Weber, since the same process has facilitated the development of sophisticated techniques for the 'political, social, educational, and propagandistic manipulation and domination of human beings',[7] which have turned the modern age into an 'iron cage'. Rationalisation and disenchantment have simultaneously liberated human power over nature while diminishing the importance of individual action;[8] the individual has become a 'small cog in a ceaselessly moving mechanism' of his own creation.[9] According to Weber, capitalism and bureaucracy – the two most powerful and important manifestations of instrumental rationality in modernity – have together been manufacturing a 'shell of bondage' that threatens to leave modern human beings 'as powerless as the fellahs of ancient Egypt'.[10] Even the vitalistic power of charisma can do little to break the vice-like grip of the instrumentally rationalised modern world.

Max Horkheimer's *The Eclipse of Reason* is basically a restatement of Weber's account of the dominance of instrumental reason in the modern West, which in our time is 'triumphing everywhere with fatal results'.[11] What Horkheimer terms 'subjective rationality' is a 'neutralised impotent' faculty concerned exclusively with means and utterly indifferent to the question of whether the particular ends it advances are just. Like Weber's instrumental rationality, this reason is merely a 'dull apparatus for registering facts', calculating probabilities and matching the most efficient means to our preferred ends.[12] Once, Horkheimer argues, reason was 'inherent in reality', providing insight not only into means, but into the essential nature of things and the substantive ends of life as well. Even the rationalist philosophers of the seventeenth century and their Catholic opponents were in agreement on this, whatever their other differences, but since the eighteenth century reason has 'liquidated itself as an agency of ethical, moral, and religious insight'.[13] Subjective and objective reason have been pried apart, with the former being equated with reason per se while the latter has withered away. That is why Horkheimer depicts modern reason as 'diseased', 'deranged' and 'irrational'. In the clash between the *philosophes* and the Church, Horkheimer was far from unsympathetic to the latter. The 'philosophers of the Enlightenment attacked religion in the name of reason', he writes, but in the end what they killed was 'the objective concept of reason itself.[14] The *philosophes* threw out the baby of objective reason with the bath water of clerical oppression, for which the twentieth century has paid a terrible price.

Although Weber's name appears only once in Horkheimer and Adorno's *Dialectic of Enlightenment*[15] – their most sustained and influential treatment of Western enlightenment (*westlichen Aufklärung*) – he is an invisible presence throughout. The book is a very loose collection of essays on the various manifestations of Western enlightenment from Homer to Hitler. It is essentially an application and extension of Weber's analysis of instrumental rationality to the concept of enlightenment. Only one chapter – of which Horkheimer was the principal author[16] – deals directly with the eighteenth century, when Western enlightenment received its 'classical formulation'.[17] One of the most distinctive features of Horkheimer and Adorno's account of Western enlightenment is their claim that it is dialectically entwined with myth, that just as 'myths already entail enlightenment, with every step enlightenment entangles itself more deeply in mythology'.[18] Horkheimer had claimed in his earlier essay 'Reason Against Itself' (written in 1940) that the 'French Enlightenment ... tried to attack mythology' because it laboured under the delusion that enlightenment and myth are mutually exclusive.[19] In fact, it was out of the mythic world of antiquity that 'the unending process of enlightenment' emerged, while the myths which 'fell victim to the Enlightenment were themselves its products'.[20] Horkheimer and Adorno found the earliest evidence of Western enlightenment in Homer's mythic epic *The Odyssey*, whose hero is a 'technically enlightened man', the prototype of the modern man of science idolised by the *philosophes* who seeks mastery of disenchanted nature through rational understanding and control.

Odysseus' direct modern descendant is the Marquis de Sade's (1740–1814) 'enlightened Juliette', the principal subject of the chapter of *Dialectic of Enlightenment* that focuses on the eighteenth century. The true nature of the eighteenth-century Enlightenment was revealed by this 'child of the aggressive Enlightenment' (much more so than by Voltaire, Rousseau or Diderot, none of whom are even mentioned) with a truly terrifying honesty, Horkheimer and Adorno thought. Her 'enlightened reason' is an extreme manifestation of 'value-neutral' instrumental reason which 'arranges the world for the purposes of self-preservation and recognises no function other than that of working on the object as mere sense material in order to make it the material of subjugation'.[21] Far from being lost in a sadistic frenzy of sexual passion and violence, she is always 'efficient, enlightened' and 'cool and reflective' like a scientist.[22] Her mind is free from the 'bite of conscience' and her face displays the greatest calm even as she commits the most horrendous atrocities. Like her ancient ancestor she is a 'proficient manipulator of the organ of rational thought' whose scandalous transgressions of conventional values are undertaken with the rational organisation and efficiency of a production-line. Juliette is Western enlightenment turned against itself, like Frankenstein's monster come back to destroy the very society that produced it. 'The instrument by means of which the bourgeoisie came to power, the liberation of forces, universal freedom, self-determination – in short, the Enlightenment,' Horkheimer and Adorno grimly conclude, itself 'turned against the bourgeoisie as soon as that class, as a system of rule, was forced to suppress those it ruled.'[23]

According to Horkheimer and Adorno, Juliette's immediate descendants are positivists, the 'epigoni of eighteenth-century Enlightenment'[24] who reduce all thought to a 'mathematical apparatus' capable of easy manipulation. Positivism is a form of what Adorno would later label 'identity thinking', which reduces all qualitative differences to quantitative differences in order to facilitate the 'universal interchangeability' and manipulability of all things.[25] The uniqueness of each particular is thereby sacrificed to the utility of exchange and control through a single abstract medium such as money. Perhaps its most important manifestation is modern science, which discriminates against 'any kind of thought that does not conform perfectly' to its postulates.[26] Although Horkheimer and Adorno grant that science is 'an element of truth', positivists mistakenly equate it with the whole truth. This procrustean outlook is symptomatic of the totalitarian mentality that is so prevalent in twentieth-century modernity. The two forms of 'total society' on which Horkheimer and Adorno focus in *Dialectic* are fascism and capitalism, both bitter fruits of the same seed of Western enlightenment originally planted by Homer's Odysseus.[27] Their surface differences obscure the fact that both are really manifestations of a single basic conception of enlightenment run amok.

The process of Western enlightenment that began with Odysseus' rational assertion of his individuality has ended with the final dissolution of individuality in the twentieth century, according to Horkheimer and Adorno. At an earlier stage of modernity, before the arrival of mass technocratic society, individuals could at least preserve some sense of their own dignity and integrity. Now even this has been obliterated, as individuals are completely absorbed by the overwhelming forces unleashed by Western enlightenment that now determine our civilisation. In the twentieth century, the individual has become 'fictitious', an 'illusion', a mere 'pseudo-individual' drained of all substance and inner life, leaving only a one-dimensional being emptied of everything with which to resist complete absorption into the social and cultural mainstream of modern mass society.

Given the grim picture that Horkheimer and Adorno paint of the dialectical development of Western enlightenment and the belief that, as Horkheimer put it, the 'hopes of mankind seem to be farther from fulfilment today than they were even in the groping epochs when they were first formulated by humanists',[28] their impatience with the modern 'idolisation of progress' is understandable. The contemporary compulsion to arrive at a cheerful conclusion only obscures the fact that the advent of 'enlightened' technological civilisation 'threatens at every stage to transform progress into its opposite, complete barbarism'.[29] To offset their relentless pessimism, Horkheimer and Adorno planned to write a sequel to *Dialectic of Enlightenment* that would be a 'positive theory of dialectics' in which the 'liberating elements in enlightenment and pragmatism are to be brought out just as much as the repressive ones';[30] it would prepare the way for a 'positive concept of enlightenment which liberates it from its entanglement in blind domination'.[31] According to James Schmitt, this counts as evidence that Horkheimer and Adorno 'somehow remain loyal to the enlightenment's hopes. Hence the importance of the book's unwritten sequel. ... The unwritten *Rettung der Aufklärung* [Rescuing the Enlightenment] would awaken the enlightenment from its nightmare, restore it to consciousness, and set it back on its path.'[32] Yet the planned sequel never saw the light of day, which suggests that Horkheimer and Adorno were unable to conceive of a form of enlightenment not prone to the self-destructive tendencies outlined in *Dialectic*. It points to an impasse which they were never able to overcome and explains why the hope they had expressed in the earlier edition of *Dialectic* about a more optimistic enlightenment project was left out of the final edition.[33]

Counter-Enlightenment liberalism

Most liberals have seen themselves as the natural heirs of the Enlightenment, which is commonly held to be either the origin of liberalism or one of the most decisive moments in its development. But not all forms of liberalism derive either historically or logically from the Enlightenment. Indeed, one form actually associates the Enlightenment with assumptions that led to deeply sinister consequences in the twentieth century. One of the best examples of this is Jacob Talmon's book *The Origins of Totalitarian Democracy* (1952), a work intended, in the words of Yehoshua Arieli, 'to account for the emergence of a messianic totalitarian democratic ideology out of the universalistic background of the radical Enlightenment'.[34] It originated in an undergraduate seminar on the Jacobin dictatorship in France that Talmon attended during the 1938 Moscow trials. It was there that a connection between eighteenth-century Jacobinism and twentieth-century Bolshevism first dawned on him.[35] He was already an enthusiastic admirer of Alexis de Tocqueville and regarded his own work as 'an extension of Tocqueville's quest to explicate the threat of "democratic despotism"'.[36] In *The Old Regime and the French Revolution* (1856) Tocqueville had claimed that the spread of letters and philosophy in eighteenth-century France played a key role in undermining the *ancien régime* and thereby helped to bring about the French Revolution and the Napoleonic wars.[37] Talmon likewise emphasised the influence of Enlightenment ideas on what he regarded as the Jacobins' direct twentieth-century totalitarian descendants.

Although Talmon does not specifically refer to 'the Enlightenment' in his account of the emergence of twentieth-century totalitarianism – the expression was still uncommon in English at the time – he focuses on the role of 'the *philosophes*' and 'eighteenth-century thinkers' such as Morelly, Baron d'Holbach, Mably, Voltaire, Rousseau, Helvétius, Diderot and Condorcet in the genesis of modern totalitarianism. Indeed, he writes that the object of the book is 'to examine the stages through which the social ideals of the eighteenth century were transformed – on one side – into totalitarian democracy'.[38] What for Talmon began with the *philosophes* as a form of 'extreme individualism' was eventually transformed into 'a collective pattern of coercion before the eighteenth century was out'.[39] The 'tragic paradox' of eighteenth-century utopianism, he claims, is that, 'instead of bringing about, as it promised, a system of final and permanent stability, it gave rise to utter restlessness, and in place of a reconciliation between human freedom and social cohesion, it brought totalitarian coercion'.[40] While the *philosophes* spoke the language of individual freedom and human happiness, 'their preoccupation with the general interest, the general good and the natural system led to collectivism' that ultimately betrayed that commitment.[41] Liberty, spontaneity and the revolt against traditional restrictions in the eighteenth century eventually lost out in the Terror – and later under Bolshevism – to the pursuit of equality, virtue and social harmony imposed by the state.

According to Talmon, at the root of the conflict between liberalism and totalitarianism is a fundamental epistemological opposition between empiricism and rationalism, the former of which he calls 'the ally of freedom' and the latter 'the friend of totalitarianism'. Rationalism affirms a belief in a single, naturally correct pattern to which social and political life should conform as closely as possible, and denies certain incontrovertible facts of history and nature, such as 'the inveterate irrationality of man's ways'.[42] The lessons of nature and history, Talmon tells us, echoing Edmund Burke, show civilisations to be 'the evolution of a multiplicity of historically and pragmatically formed clusters of social existence and social endeavour, and not as the achievement of the abstract individual men on a single level of existence'.[43] By contrast, rationalists view human nature to be absolutely uniform rather than as something that varies from time to time and place to place. They look upon the diversity and messy irregularity of the human world as a regrettable and corrigible deviation from the perfection and uniformity of the natural order, and seek to eliminate all 'imperfections' and 'errors' through the application of 'deliberately planned uniform patterns' on social and political life that replicate nature's perfection. On this view, which came to dominate French thought in the second half of the eighteenth century, our happiness is advanced by adjusting the human world to the 'necessary order of things', while all misery 'is the outcome of a vain attempt to kick against the natural order'.[44] Individual behaviour, political institutions and social practices should therefore conform to this natural order, by force if necessary. That is why Talmon believes that the eighteenth-century idea of the natural order 'found its expression in the totalitarian democratic tradition'.[45] Freedom and individuality are sacrificed in the name of happiness, understood as conformity to the perfect order of nature. This radical 'eighteenth-century restrictionist attitude' required that all 'the existing traditions, established institutions, and social arrangements were to be overthrown and remade. ... It envisaged man per se, stripped of all those attributes which are not comprised in his common humanity ... to the exclusion of all groups and traditional interests.'[46]

Talmon argues that the Jacobins of revolutionary France translated this 'all-explaining and all-determining principle of the *philosophes*' into a form of democratic totalitarianism, just as the twentieth-century Russian Bolsheviks would translate it into the Marxist idea of class warfare.[47] The *philosophes* were the intellectual ancestors of Jacobins, Babouvists, Blanquists, Communists, Socialists and Anarchists, all of whom 'belong to one religion'. Talmon describes Morelly's *Code de la Nature* (1755) as the first work in a line of thought that led first to the French revolutionary Reign of Terror, and later to twentieth-century totalitarianism.

Talmon's work is structured around a series of binary oppositions – liberalism versus collectivism, empiricism versus rationalism, pluralism versus totalitarianism, realism versus utopianism – that he traces back to the eighteenth century. All grew from a common Enlightenment root that did not diverge until the French Revolution, 'the absolute turning point' of modern history. Some *philosophes* had a modest, fallibilistic, trial-and-error conception of truth that Talmon associates with empiricism, liberalism and pluralism, in contrast to the dogmatic rationalist conception of truth common to their proto-totalitarian opponents. These two views co-existed uneasily until the French Revolution, when the rationalist pursuit of virtue clashed directly with the empiricist pursuit of liberty. They have been locked in unremitting combat ever since, the Cold War clash between the liberal West and the communist East being only its most recent manifestation.

One day in 1947 Jacob Talmon visited Oxford to interview the 'sage of English liberalism', Isaiah Berlin. They spent much of the day, Berlin later recalled, 'discussing what afterwards became the central theme of his most famous book, *Totalitarian Democracy* [*sic*], and since my ideas were tending in the same direction, I found that talking with him was highly stimulating and intellectually delightful'.[48] Talmon found a receptive audience because Berlin already shared many of his views about the relationship between eighteenth-century ideas and twentieth-century politics. Berlin devoted much of his scholarly career to exploring the ideas of a rogues' gallery of Counter-Enlightenment figures such as Joseph de Maistre, J. G. Hamann and Georges Sorel. His interest in such figures was not merely the morbid curiosity of a liberal wishing to provide his enlightened readers with a *frisson* of excitement in the face of reactionary madness. He genuinely believed that we have something to learn from these losers in the struggle of ideas. For example, he described Maistre as 'a violent antidote to the over-blown, over-optimistic and altogether too superficial social doctrines of the eighteenth century'.[49] Berlin thought that this Catholic reactionary's grim portrait of the natural world stood up surprisingly well next to the Panglossian optimism of Condorcet. '[W]hen, against him [Condorcet], Maistre says we are told to follow Nature, but that this leads to curious consequences, what he says is not absurd', Berlin states.[50] He believed that simplistic Enlightenment assumptions about human nature have been superseded in the nineteenth and twentieth centuries by 'an increasingly complicated and unstable picture as new and disturbing hypotheses about the springs of action were advanced by psychologists and anthropologists'.[51] In this respect – if in few others – the conservative Edmund Burke was a man ahead of, rather than behind, his times, as was Maistre:

> Burke said some very wise things. He said that the idea that there can be discovered such an entity as pure human nature if one strips away all the layers of civilisation and art, that you can penetrate to 'the natural man,' i.e. a creature who embodies what is common and true of all men everywhere, at all times, and nothing beside this, that this idea is false. To make a revolution in the name of true human nature . . . is absurd and wicked. There is for Burke no such thing as a universal human nature.[52]

Berlin looked upon the Enlightenment 'as one of the best and most hopeful episodes in the life of mankind'[53] and described its values as 'deeply sympathetic to me'.[54] The *philosophes*, he thought, 'liberated people from horrors, obscurantism, fanaticism, monstrous views. They were against cruelty, they were agianst oppression, they fought the good fight against superstition and ignorance and against a great many things which ruined people's lives. So I am on their side.'[55] Yet Berlin also perceived what he thought was a very dark side to this well-intentioned project, as revealed in the sinister phrase of Rousseau's *Social Contract* that individuals must sometimes be 'forced to be free'. Many of the political disasters of the past two centuries, beginning with the revolutionary Reign of Terror and including Soviet communism, originate in this Enlightenment project to unbend 'the crooked timber of humanity' to make it conform to a single monistic ideal, 'to bring the many into a coherent, systematic unity'.[56] Berlin attributes to the Enlightenment the belief that the world possesses a single, unalterable structure governed by universal laws. These laws are discoverable by a combination of reason – when unclouded by myth, prejudice, religious dogma and emotion – and disinterested empirical observation. The ultimate goal of the Enlightenment was the eradication of error by the removal of impediments to knowledge. Hence its emancipatory drive to free the minds of human beings by attacking all forms of authority that impede progress towards this goal. Societies will tend to converge to the extent that they are based on the universal truths of science, thereby reducing, if not eliminating, a major source of human conflict and suffering. 'In this way the rationalist argument', Berlin writes, 'with its assumption of the single true solution, has led by steps which, if not logically valid, are historically and psychologically intelligible, from an ethical doctrine of individual responsibility and individual self-perfection to an authoritarian state obedient to the directives of an *élite* of Platonic guardians.'[57] For Berlin, the rational reorganisation of the human world according to nature resonates with a deeply sinister – if ultimately well-intentioned – undertone born of a naïve and misplaced confidence in human rationality and a simplistic view of reality. His own version of the 'dialectic of Enlightenment' is scarcely less pessimistic than that of Horkheimer and Adorno.

Having defined the Enlightenment as essentially monistic, a drive to, if not completely eradicate the diversity of the world, then at least subordinate it to a universal standard of truth, morality and civilisation, Berlin characterised the Counter-Enlightenment as a movement that arose in opposition to this project. Indeed, its most important influence on European thought was 'the belief that science and reason do not have all the answers, that to some central questions of value – ethical, aesthetic, social, political – there can be more than one valid answer'.[58] Just as an unintended political consequence of the eighteenth-century Enlightenment has been twentieth-century totalitarianism, a view shared by Talmon, so an unintended consequence of Counter-Enlightenment thought has been pluralism, which ironically owes more to Machiavelli, Hamann and Maistre than it does to Voltaire, Condorcet or Helvétius.

The epigones of Burke

The ethical and religious concerns of many of the early critics of the Enlightenment have resurfaced in the twentieth century with the revival of serious conservative thought in the postwar West.[59] In the USA these concerns were expressed most systematically by the German *émigré* Eric Voegelin, a Christian conservative who believed that the 'great dream' of the eighteenth-century *encyclopédistes* had become the lived nightmare of the twentieth century. Although he employed arguments that had first been raised against the Enlightenment by men such as Burke, Maistre and Barruel, his analysis of the 'crisis' of Western modernity in the twentieth century appears to have owed most to Max Weber.

In his *Autobiographical Reflections* (1989) Voegelin is more forthcoming than his contemporaries Horkheimer and Adorno were about the decisive importance of Weber to his early intellectual formation. He writes that Weber's *Sociology of Religion* (1920) and *Economy and Society* (1922) came out during these early years and were 'devoured by us students'.[60] He also singles out Weber's 'Science as a Vocation' (1919) for revealing to him something crucially important about the nature of values that became 'the great problem with which I have dealt during the 50 years since I got acquainted with his ideas'.[61] Like Nietzsche, Weber held that values are rationally groundless because, according to Voegelin, he was blind to the 'experiences that would have supplied the criteria for existential order and responsible action', the evidence for which is the absence of any significant treatment of early Christianity or of classical philosophy in his work.[62] Weber only avoided falling into Nietzschean relativism because of his 'staunch ethical character', but his unflinching ethical commitments – however admirable – lacked any rational foundations.[63] For Voegelin this is both dangerous and unsatisfactory, since it carries with it the risk that emotions will 'carry you away into all sorts of ideological and idealistic adventures'.[64] He also faults Weber for failing to perceive the existence of genuine answers to the question of the grounds of ethical belief that are furnished by Christianity.

In his book *From Enlightenment to Revolution*, Voegelin links the totalitarian ideologies of the twentieth century directly to a spiritual and intellectual crisis that originated in the second half of the eighteenth century, when a new attitude 'radically incompatible' with the values of classical and Christian civilisation arose in the minds of *philosophes* such as Voltaire and Helvétius.[65] Although not published until 1975, this work is part of an aborted history of political ideas that Voegelin worked on in the 1940s and early 1950s,[66] described by its editor as 'a contribution to the revisionary assessment of the Enlightenment then underway'.[67] Substantial progress had already been made on it by the time Voegelin took up an appointment at Louisiana State University in 1942.[68] He argues that the 'de-divination' of the world (the process Weber had labelled *'entzauberung'* – disenchantment) that led to the present crisis of Western civilisation originated in 'the rational dissolution of the Christian mystery through the eighteenth-century movement toward deism and atheism'.[69] The Enlightenment assault on Christianity unhinged the West from the 'transcendental anchorage' of faith, a necessary condition for the later emergence of secular ideological substitutes in the nineteenth and twentieth centuries. Totalitarianism has its roots in this secularising trend, evidence of which is apparent to Voegelin in Voltaire's *Essai sur les moeurs* (1753), which he read as the first in a long series of profane histories that sought to provide a secular substitute for the meaning found in Christian 'sacred history'. In the latter, meaning is given to human affairs and the world by God, whereas Voltaire's secular version of history can provide only the meaningless ideal of 'empirical completeness'.[70]

Worse, as attention shifted in modernity from the sacred to the profane, a reductionistic model of man as a purely material being, devoid of any spiritual substance, replaced the more elevated model on which Christianity was based. According to Voegelin, humans came to be defined exclusively by their animal nature, as creatures whose behaviour could be entirely explained 'by the operations of physical sensibility or of a pleasure–pain mechanism' rather than by any transcendental aims and capacities.[71] We were reduced to a mere 'crippled, utilitarian fragment' of our former selves, ripe for manipulation by a 'pragmatically planning will'.[72] The destruction of our spiritual life in modernity is simultaneously the 'last consequence of the scandal of the *Encyclopedistes*'[73] and the 'first in a series of totalitarian, sec-tarian movements to be followed later by Positivism, Communism and National Socialism'.[74]

According to Voegelin, twentieth-century 'political religions' such as communism and national socialism have replaced the true religion of Chris-tianity undermined by the *philosophes*. Since humans are essentially religious beings, he reasons, the secularisation begun in the eighteenth century opened the door to a 'respiritualisation of the public sphere from other sources, in the forms of nationalism, humanitarianism, economism both liberal and socialist, biologism and psychologism'.[75] These profane 'collect-ive religions' have inherited the materialistic conception of man first sketched by the *philosophes*, with politically disastrous consequences.

In *From Enlightenment to Revolution* Voltaire, d'Alembert, Helvétius, Turgot, Condorcet and Bentham are all indicted by name for helping to create a situation that eventually made the 'wrecking operations of the present' possible.[76] Although Voltaire is praised for his tolerance, common sense, and advocacy of free speech and thought, Voegelin charges him with doing more than anybody else 'to make the darkness of enlightened reason descend on the Western world'.[77] Helvétius is described as a 'radical social Satanist' whose diabolical vision had offshoots in Soviet communism.[78] Turgot and Condorcet are denounced as totalitarians, although the evil of the former was 'not yet more than a spark' whereas the latter gave the world 'the first systematic project elaborated by a Western totalitarian for the radical destruction of all civilisations of mankind' which would transform the surface of the globe 'into the habitat of a standardised mankind which is formed by the ideology of a handful of megalomaniac intellectuals. There is hardly any discernible difference on this point between the totalitarian Progressivist and his Communist and National Socialist successors.'[79] Even the views of the relatively moderate and humane d'Alembert betray 'the profound antihuman-ism underlying the Enlightenment'.[80] As in Foucault's *Discipline and Punish*, also first published in 1975, *From Enlightenment to Revolution* depicts Jeremy Bentham as a man ahead of his time, with a 'Gestapo dream of complete physical and mental control over a group of human beings'.[81] He was born 'one hundred years too early – a century later, circumstances would prove more favourable for the realisation of his dream. . . . In Lenin, as in Bentham, we see at work the sadistic imagination devising circumstances that will leave to the victim only the choice between submission and suicide.'[82]

Bentham plays a no less diabolical role in the work of the English conservative philosopher Michael Oakeshott. Bentham is the thread con-necting the eighteenth-century 'philosophisme' that Oakeshott denounced in his 1932 essay on 'The New Bentham' to the rationalism that he attacked in his famous 1947 article on 'Rationalism in Politics'. Although he never used the term 'the Enlightenment' in these essays (or elsewhere, for that matter), it is clear enough that what he calls 'philosophisme' (as distinct from genuine philosophy) is what we would now call 'the French

Enlightenment'. In the earlier essay, he contrasts his own view of Bentham –
'the *philosophe*, the creature of the eighteenth century, the native of France
rather than England, the companion in thought of Helvétius, Diderot,
Voltaire, and d'Alembert' – with the standard image of Bentham as a typical
nineteenth-century English utilitarian.[83] When restored to his proper eighteenth-century context, Oakeshott believed, it is easy to see why Bentham
was regarded so highly in Europe and so poorly in England, where
'philosophisme' was utterly alien. The general tone of Oakeshott's description of the *philosophes* here is sneeringly contemptuous. He portrays them as
too narrow-minded to appreciate anything beyond the immediate present,
with an outlook on life intended to make themselves comfortably at home in
the world but lacking all depth or profundity. The *philosophe*, he asserts, is
'entirely ignorant of the senseless depredation his lack of discrimination
involves' and is completely 'unconscious of his vulgarity'.[84] Men such as
Voltaire and Helvétius, whose minds were 'replete with half-conceived
ideas', made no serious contribution to our store of knowledge, and the
'philosophisme' of the eighteenth century was a mere 'backwater so far as the
mainstream of European scholarship, philosophy and scientific research is
concerned'.[85] According to Oakeshott, the character of the *philosophes* is distinguished by three attributes: a limitless and indiscriminate thirst for and
confidence in knowledge, a confidence that the sceptical Oakeshott thought
was not only completely misplaced but dangerous; a naïve credulity about
knowledge which their 'tough hide of self-confidence' obstinately shielded
from doubt; and a rationalist belief that 'what is made is better than what
merely grows, that neatness is better than profusion and vitality'.[86] Indeed,
the particular 'genius' of *philosophes* such as Bentham is their 'genius for
rationalisation, for *making* life and the business of life rational rather than for
seeing the reason for it'.[87]

There are strong echoes of Weber in Oakeshott's account of rationalisation, although there is little direct evidence in his published writings that
he was influenced by, or even familiar with, Weber's work. In his 1950 essay
on 'Rational Conduct', for example, he attacks the conception of the mind as
a 'neutral instrument' which 'attracts truth, repels superstition and is alone
the spring of "rational" judgment and "rational" conduct' without once
mentioning Weber.[88] This 'rational' mind is devoid of content and unencumbered by acquired dispositions of any sort. It is also purposive, with the
power of 'first imagining and choosing a purpose to pursue, of defining that
purpose clearly and selecting fit means to achieve it'.[89] The rationalist is
someone who stands above all 'for independence of mind on all occasions, for
thought free from obligation to any authority save the authority of
"reason"'.[90] In his essay on 'Rationalism in Politics', published the same year
as Horkheimer and Adorno's *Dialectic of Enlightenment* (1947), Oakeshott
claims that modern rationalism equates all knowledge with one particular
form of it, which he calls 'technical knowledge'. This reductionistic view
refuses to admit the value, or even the possibility, of 'practical knowledge,'

which is acquired, like language, slowly and unselfconsciously by experience and imitation and is passed on by tradition and custom. Rationality is never abstract and external to such traditions; it is simply 'the certificate we give to any conduct which can maintain a place in the flow of sympathy, the coherence of activity, which composes a way of living'.[91] Activity is only rational when it preserves and enhances the internal coherence of the particular form of life within which it is situated. Thus, while Oakeshott shared the hostility of many of his contemporaries towards the modern hegemony of what Weber had called 'instrumental rationality', his own relativistic conception of rationality diverged markedly not only from that of fellow critics such as Horkheimer and Adorno but also from many natural law and natural right conservatives such as Voegelin and Leo Strauss.

Oakeshott's well-known 1947 essay is an analysis and critique of rationalism in politics. It is an attack on that 'enemy of authority, of prejudice, of the merely traditional, customary or habitual', the political rationalist, whose unencumbered mind is supposedly completely free and open. Like Weber's 'specialists without spirit, sensualists without heart', he is a single-minded technocrat and perfectionist obsessed with certainty and technique, with no use or respect for inherited wisdom or tradition. His knowledge is acquired easily and abstractly from books, rather than gradually and concretely through hard-won experience. Like Voegelin, Oakeshott portrays the political rationalist as someone who typically relies on an abstract ideology to fill the void left by the traditions he has eradicated. Like Berlin and Talmon, he also depicts political rationalism as a 'politics of perfection and uniformity' forever seeking to impose a single, rationally perfect pattern on the natural imperfection and diversity of human life. The political rationalist lacks any sense for, or appreciation of, the different local traditions, customs and practices that spontaneously emerge among people when left alone by the state. Instead, he judges everything against a universal standard of abstract perfection and then undertakes to adjust the messy irregularity of life to it, to 'unbend the crooked timber of humanity', as Berlin put it, quoting Kant. That is why political rationalism is necessarily a politics of 'destruction and creation' rather than of preservation and repair. This is apparent in the case of Voltaire who, Oakeshott claims, believed that the only way to have good government is 'to burn all existing laws and to start afresh'.[92] Ambitious and self-confident central planning is the natural corollary of this outlook, according to Oakeshott, just as a sceptical, conservative politics of caution and restraint follow from his much more modest conception of reason.

Conclusion

For a generation of intellectuals born in *fin-de-siècle* Europe – writing in the shadow of Nietzsche and Weber, educated in an intellectual milieu saturated with angst and *kulturpessimismus*, emotionally scarred by the traumas of twentieth-century European history – the dreams of the eighteenth-century Enlightenment seemed as remote as could be. While others interpreted this dark age as a betrayal of the values and beliefs of the *philosophes*, they saw it as their outcome. For them it was not the absence of reason that best explained the political tragedies of twentieth-century Europe, but its perversion by the Enlightenment. They favoured a more modest conception of the nature, scope and limits of human rationality than the totalising or unitary ideas of reason of the kind each associated with totalitarianism and which they traced back to the Enlightenment. The emergence of the concept of totalitarianism in the early years of the Cold War not only coincided with this major reconceptualisation and reassessment of the legacy of the Enlightenment, but also provided a crucial link between the two, resulting in a form of Counter-Englightenment thought distinctive of the mid-twentieth-century West. Unfortunately, it has been eclipsed by both earlier Enlightenment criticism, usually associated with late eighteenth- and early nineteenth-century reactionaries, particularly in Germany (an approach typified by Berlin), and by the prominence of more recent postmodern critics. As a result, it has become something of a lost chapter in the history of Enlightenment criticism. This is perhaps not so surprising given that it anticipated so many of the criticisms of the Enlightenment among its postmodern critics, who have been wary (to say the least) of acknowledging any such intellectual patrimony.

7 The postmodern challenge

Couldn't it be concluded that the Enlightenment's promise [*la promesse de l'Aufklärung*] of attaining freedom through the exercise of reason has been turned upside down, resulting in a domination by reason itself, which increasingly usurps the place of freedom? This is a fundamental problem we're all struggling with, which many people have in common, whether they are communist or not. And as we know, this problem was isolated, pointed out by Horkheimer before all the others; and it was the Frankfurt School that questioned the reference to Marx in terms of that hypothesis.[1]

(Michel Foucault)

Introduction

A basic axiom of postmodernism in the English-speaking world is that the end of the modern era that it heralds also marks the end of the 'Enlightenment project' that is allegedly its consummate expression. Indeed, many regard hostility to the Enlightenment as 'the pathognomonic sign of the postmodern', in the words of Arthur Goldhammer.[2] 'And what is postmodernity,' asks Slavoj Žižek, 'if not the ultimate defeat of the Enlightenment in its very triumph.'[3] One of the more striking features of the 'postmodern turn' for Johnson Wright is 'the extent to which its leading proponents have been willing to focus their critical energies on a single polemical target – the European Enlightenment, held to be the first source of the illusions of modernity from which postmodernism promises to release us'.[4] For Hugo Meynell, a writer is postmodern to the extent that 'she repudiates the norms of cognition and evaluation that were propounded and applied by thinkers of the Old Enlightenment, and inveighs against the abuses to which they may be supposed to have given rise'.[5] Claims of this sort pervade English-language commentary on postmodernism.[6]

Such overt hostility to the Enlightenment is much less apparent among French writers normally associated with postmodernism. Even Jean-François Lyotard (1924–), one of the few prominent French 'postmodernists' who refers directly and critically to the Enlightenment with any regularity, nowhere singles it out for special attention or criticism; it is just one of many forms of Western 'meta-narrative' that has now become 'obsolete', along with Christianity and Marxism.[7] The final goal of the Enlightenment, he claims, had been the establishment of a rational unanimity among all people in favour of universal peace.[8] But the 'grand narrative of the Enlightenment' (*le grand récit des Lumières*[9]) is now defunct, its 'project' ended, which Lyotard welcomes, since the obsolescence of universalism can free us from its 'totalising obsessions'.[10] He says relatively little about the Enlightenment beyond this, and makes virtually no direct reference to any particular *philosophe*, a tendency he shares with many other postmodern critics of the Enlightenment.[11]

Although French postmodernists have tended to be more circumspect in their views on the Enlightenment than their English-speaking cousins, clear echoes of earlier accounts of the Enlightenment and totalitarianism may none the less be heard in the writings of many postmodernists such as Michel Foucault. He was rarely forthcoming about what, if anything, he was opposing in his account of what he called *l'âge classique* ('the classical age'). In his scholarly work, he usually preferred subtlely to suggest his views by means of selective descriptions and language rather than attacking issues head-on. He bristled when pressed to declare himself either for or against the Enlightenment, and denounced the insistence on taking sides on it as a form of blackmail (*chantage*) to which he refused to submit.[12]

While Michel Foucault is often depicted in the English-speaking world as 'the prime progenitor of anti-Enlightenment thinking',[13] he only occasionally referred to 'l'âge des Lumières'[14] and used expressions like 'the rationality of the Enlightenment [*la rationalité de l'âge des Lumières*]' quite sparingly,[15] preferring the more ambiguous term *l'âge classique*. He used this latter expression idiosyncratically, to cover the period from 1660 to 1800, which more or less coincides with the period we now call 'the Enlightenment' in English and 'l'âge des Lumières' in French. Although his use of the term is clear and consistent, it does not coincide with the normal usage of literary critics, art scholars, philosophers and historians, who commonly use it to refer to the literature and arts of the seventeenth century, from about 1630 (following 'l'âge baroque') to 1685, a period that produced many of the 'classics' of French literature and thought (e.g. Descartes, Pascal, Corneille, Racine, Molière), when the influence of the Greek and Roman classics was very strong. Foucault, by contrast, uses 'l'âge classique' to cover the period between 1650 and 1800, which (more or less) encompasses the period of what is called 'the Enlightenment' in English.[16]

Several of Foucault's books elaborate how a new type of society – what he called 'the disciplinary society' – arose during this period,[17] and he describes in detail the new order of concepts, disciplines, and institutions that correspond to it, which together constituted a vast, interconnecting and enveloping 'web' or 'network'.[18] His account of its emergence in books such as *Madness and Civilisation* (*Folie et déraison*, 1961), *The Birth of the Clinic* (*Naissance de la clinique*, 1963) and *Discipline and Punish* (*Surveiller et punir: nais-*

sance de la prison, 1975) is highly subversive of the 'humanitarian' and 'progressive' self-image of the age. There is something deeply sinister about this new society that Foucault associated with the reformist movements of the eighteenth century. One of his principal objectives is to show how, during this period, the emergence of the 'human sciences' and the 'reform' movement that he associates with them corresponded to and helped rationalise and justify a major trend towards a new form of social discipline and control that left human beings constrained in subtle new ways and to an unprecedented degree. His depiction of this society strongly echoes both Weber's account of modernity as an 'iron cage' and the 'enlightened' totalitarian society that Horkheimer and Adorno sketched in *Dialectic of Enlightenment*. Towards the end of his life Foucault acknowledged in an interview that the Frankfurt School 'had tried, earlier than I, to say things I had also been trying to say for years':

> the philosophers of that school raised problems we're still labouring over today – in particular, that of the effects of power in their relation to a rationality that was defined historically and geographically, in the West, from the sixteenth century onward .... And, in fact, how can that rationality be separated from the mechanisms, procedures, techniques, and effects of power that accompany it and for which we express our distaste by describing them as the typical form of oppression of capitalist societies – and perhaps socialist societies as well?[19]

Foucault shares Horkheimer's and Adorno's concerns about the political power of reason in modernity, which threatened to crush individuals and usurp their freedom. He writes of this particular kind of modern rationality that it 'originates in the Enlightenment? [*remonte aux Lumières*]'.[20] Elsewhere Foucault claims that '[o]ne of the Enlightenment's tasks [*l'une des tâches des Lumières*] has been to multiply reason's political powers'.[21] It was only in the nineteenth century that this nexus between reason (narrowly understood) and power began to be seen as a grave threat that had to be checked. Indeed, according to Foucault post-Kantian philosophy set itself the tasks of 'prevent[ing] reason from going beyond the limits of what is given in experience' and 'keeping watch over the excessive powers of political rationality'. For Foucault the 'relationship between rationalisation and the excesses of political power is evident. And we should not need to wait for bureaucracy or concentration camps to recognise the existence of such relations.'[22] In *Discipline and Punish*, he argues that the ideal society dreamt of by the philosophers and reformers of the eighteenth century was actually a 'military dream of society' resembling 'the meticulously subordinated cogs of a machine'.[23] Most of what Foucault wrote about the eighteenth century employs such military and machine-like metaphors, and focuses on this dark side that he claims lay hidden beneath the rhetorical surface of the 'perfect society' of the reformers. In this way he hoped to unmask the dystopic reality underlying the utopian discourse and self-image of the 'classical age' in a manner similar to that of Horkheimer and Adorno in *Dialectic of Enlightenment*.

However, Foucault's approach is more subtle than that of Frankfurt School writers like Horkheimer and Adorno, who painted on a vast canvass with broad brush strokes, in stark contrast to his carefully detailed and intimate portraits of oppression. He usually investigated the links between reason (as it was conceived in the 'classical age') and power at the micro level of specific institutions and practices, rather than at the macro level of society or culture as a whole, as did Horkheimer and Adorno.[24]

Foucault does this by means of an 'archaeological analysis of knowledge', as distinct from a study of abstract concepts and theories.[25] At this subterranean level, below the surface squalls of ideas and rhetoric, Foucault discerned what he took to be the truth of the momentous changes that occurred in the West during the period from 1660 to 1800, and in doing so exposed the great (and growing) gap between the real and the ideal. It is at this subrosa level that he believed he had unearthed the systematic marginalisation of the 'Other' of the Enlightenment during the classical age – those social groups and individuals that were perceived as a threat to the hegemony of reason. A whole range of new institutions – hospitals, workshops, barracks, schools, asylums, prisons – were established during this period to enable 'classical rationalism' ('le rationalisme classique', as Foucault calls it) to 'watch out for and guard against the subterranean danger of unreason'.[26] The Hôpital Général of Paris (founded by Royal decree in 1656) was among the first such 'houses of confinement' designed to shut up the 'enormous reservoir of the fantastic, a dormant world of monsters supposedly engulfed in the darkness of Hieronymous Bosch which had once spewed them forth' who marred what might otherwise have been the 'perfect society'.[27] Its institution marked the start of what would become an ambitious project of social hygiene to 'purify' Western civilisation of all these wild, atavistic elements, to clean it up, as Hamann had complained two centuries earlier.

The disciplinary society of the eighteenth century

Foucault's first major book, *Madness and Civilisation*, focuses on one such instance of the clash between the real and the ideal in the eighteenth century – its conception and treatment of madness. He argues that madness is one particular form of 'unreason' that was split off and segregated from other forms during this period. It had been at the heart of things during the Renaissance, 'present everywhere and mingled with every experience by its images or its dangers'.[28] Early modern society had allowed unreason to 'come into the light of day',[29] where it engaged in dialogue with mainstream civilisation. It was still generally believed that something important, even profound, could be learned from madness, since it was a 'sign of another world', linked to, and revealing, a mysterious realm of hidden forces and insights that eluded ordinary human perception.

However, a much less tolerant attitude emerged during the classical age, when madness came to be seen as an aspect of our own inner 'weaknesses, dreams, and illusions' rather than as something linked to another world.[30] It came to be viewed as a disease of the mind, something wild and bestial within us that 'could be mastered only by *discipline* and *brutalising*'.[31] Having internalised this disorderly 'beast', it now threatened the rational self-image of Western man. This change brought with it a mounting sense of fear and shame about madness, particularly in the second half of the eighteenth century, leading to its isolation and confinement 'under the eyes of a reason that no longer felt any relation to it and that would not compromise itself by too close a resemblance'.[32] An alienation had occurred between madness and reason; their 'dialogue' was broken off, madness was 'silenced' and stigmatised as bestial, and it was redefined in terms of a 'mental illness' that had to be constrained and repressed, if not cured.

Foucault argues that there was a moralistic impulse behind the movement to segregate and order disordered 'unreason' during the classical age. The institutions constructed to contain madness were miniature 'cities of pure morality'[33] and 'prisons of moral order'.[34] The public philanthropic and reforming justification for confinement obscured what was in reality just another 'instrument of moral uniformity and of social denunciation' conceived to impose 'a morality that will prevail from within upon those who are strangers to it'.[35] Indeed, Foucault depicts the entire reform movement of the second half of the eighteenth century as part of a sinister compulsion to cleanse the world so that 'reason reigned in the pure state'.[36] This obsessive drive to erect a 'perfect city' was eventually extended beyond the confines of the asylums and hospitals to the entire social world of the classical age.[37]

Foucault perceived the same controlling and purifying trend in the treatment of crime during the classical age. *Discipline and Punish* is his account of this process, analogous to his earlier treatment of madness. As before, he undertakes to reveal the deeper meaning and implications of the apparent 'humanisation' and 'reform' that became so pronounced during this age, especially after 1750. His subversive intention is signalled throughout by his constant use of quotation marks around words like 'humane', 'humanisation', 'reform', 'great reformers' and 'leniency', a tactic obviously intended to question the progressive self-image of these professed 'reformers'. What Foucault perceived in this great eighteenth-century 'humanitarian' movement was a *redefinition* of punishment rather than a reduction. Its real goal was actually to punish *better*, not to punish less, and while the amount of physical pain was significantly reduced, the amount of actual punishment increased massively. The target of punishment shifted from the body, which was treated more humanely, to the soul, which was tortured and manipulated as never before;[38] punishment now struck at the inner person, at 'the heart, the thoughts, the will, the inclinations' of the criminal without leaving so much as a mark on his body.[39]

According to Foucault, the role and status of the public executioner diminished dramatically during the eighteenth century as a consequence of this trend, replaced by an army of reform-minded technicians who went to work with a moralistic zeal on the inner life and mind of the criminal to shape him into an obedient and compliant subject. The blunt instruments of the executioner – his pincers, knives and axe, designed to torment the body of the criminal – were replaced by a 'more finely tuned justice' intended to manipulate his thoughts, perceptions and self-image.[40] The violent, theatrical, spectacular, public face of punishment gradually faded away, replaced by 'a subtle, calculated technology of subjection' that went on discretely in institutions carefully shielded from the public gaze.[41] There, the criminal was subjected to new forms of coercion and constraint with a relentless and demoralising regime of 'time-tables, compulsory movements, regular activities, solitary meditation, work in common, silence, application, respect, good habits'.[42]

Within the modern prison – the 'penalty of civilised societies' – this new regime took the form of constant surveillance of the inmates. The ideal form of surveillance was Jeremy Bentham's 'Panopticon', a large circular tower situated in the centre of a round, inward-looking prison enabling the surveyor to scrutinise every inmate in his open cell around the clock, the perfect form of discipline and power that underlay the surface rhetoric of eighteenth-century penal 'reformers'. This perfect disciplinary apparatus could illuminate everything within its purview; it was 'a perfect eye that nothing would escape and a centre towards which all gazes would be turned'.[43]

The real complaint of the 'humanists' and judicial 'reformers' of the classical age, Foucault alleged, was not so much against the cruelty of the methods hitherto employed against criminals, but against their inefficiency. The old system was sporadic and uneconomical, even if it *looked* spectacular. A more subtle but persistent and extensive approach to punishment would be more effective at controlling the criminal elements not only in society at large, but in all of us. 'The true objective of the reform movement,' Foucault reveals, 'was not so much to establish a new right to punish based on more equitable principles, as to set up a new "economy" of the power to punish, to assure its better distribution ... so that it should be distributed in homogeneous circuits capable of operating everywhere, in a continuous way, down to the finest grain of the social body.'[44]

The ultimate goal of this new form of punishment was 'normalisation' – the process of taming the wayward, 'unreasonable', unruly elements of society by subjecting them to the 'power of the Norm'.[45] The messy and erratic penalties of the public executioner were gradually replaced during the eighteenth century by the clean and efficient 'penality of the norm'.[46] Foucault describes 'normalisation' as 'one of the great instruments of power at the end of the classical age' that operated pervasively, inside and outside of prisons, 'down to the finest grain of the social body'.[47] While the criminal was subjected to a systematic and unrelenting regime of normalisation and discipline inside the prison – a 'machine for altering minds'[48] – the entire non-criminal population was subjected to incessant scrutiny, judgement and normalisation too, albeit in a less systematic and overt manner than the prison population. In the 'disciplinary society' of the classical age, the 'judges of normality' are omnipresent in the form of teachers, doctors, educators and social workers.[49] There was a 'disciplinary generalisation' during this period, in which the new mechanisms of discipline 'spread throughout the whole social body',[50] giving rise to the 'panopticisms of every day'.[51] By the end of the eighteenth century the power to punish ran the whole length of the social network, acting at each of its points so that, in the end, it 'would no longer be perceived as a power of certain individuals over others, but as an immediate reaction of all in relation to the individual'.[52] This entire ensemble of techniques of control and normalisation were aspects of a new tactics of power and a '"new micro-physics" of power' that emerged during the classical age. Foucault's argument in *Discipline and Punish* – to the extent that he may be said to be arguing *for* anything at all – extends far beyond just prisons. He is also describing the advent of 'a whole type of society'[53] in general that emerged in the eighteenth century – the 'disciplinary society' that is 'penetrated through and through with disciplinary mechanisms', established in the name of Enlightenment ideals of humanitarianism, reform and reason.[54]

Corresponding to the social institutions and practices of the classical age is what Foucault calls 'the classical *episteme*', the distinctive way in which knowledge was conceived, ordered and constituted in the eighteenth century. In *The Order of Things* (*Les mots et les choses*, 1966), he takes as his subject the cognitive status of the modern 'sciences of man' such as biology, philology and economics during the classical age, corresponding to the social institutions that he examines in *Madness and Civilisation* and *Discipline and Punish*.[55] He believed that what counts as knowledge varies from one period to another, and that each epoch's conception of knowledge is ultimately grounded in what he calls its 'experience of order', the particular way in which it sees things as connected to one another. According to Foucault, during the classical age the dominant principle of ordering knowledge was representation, based on relations of identity and difference according to which the elements of reality are arranged in series by precise criteria, as in a table. In the classical episteme these properties were seen as essentially quantitative and hence expressible in terms of a common unit of measurement. On this view, both the natural and social worlds form a mathematical system, a 'universal calculus',[56] that may be measured precisely and studied scientifically.

Androcentic Enlightenment

It should be apparent by now that opposition to the Enlightenment can make strange bedfellows. Two of the most improbable of these are the American postmodern feminist Jane Flax and the eighteenth-century

German pietist J. G. Hamann, even though she was not at all influenced by him.[57] Both single out Kant's famous essay 'Was ist Aufklärung?' for particular criticism and both strongly object to the 'purity' of reason that it allegedly propounds.[58] Echoing Hamann in her essay 'Is Enlightenment Emancipatory?' (1992), Flax treats Kant as a spokesman for the Enlightenment in general, so that the shortcomings in his conception of 'pure' reason are applicable to the Enlightenment as a whole. Like Hamann, she flatly rejects the idea of reason as 'pure', 'transparent' and 'neutral', a view which she argues is based on a specious mind–body dualism that has been persuasively called into question by radical thinkers such as Michel Foucault, Richard Rorty and Luce Irigaray.[59] In fact, Kant's entire essay is pervaded by 'gendered dichotomies' like this.[60] According to Flax, he tried to keep reason 'pure' from merely contingent bodily and social influences, to which he accorded no significant status or value. He segregated the subordinate, domestic, 'feminine' sphere of the body – 'the locus of passion, tutelage, feeling, the concrete and particular, the subjective, the mortal, the familial and kinship' – from the superior, dominant, public, 'masculine' sphere of 'reason, the abstract, autonomy, maturity, and universal, objective, immortal (reason and knowledge) and the productive (value producing) employment of labour or thought'.[61] Nor does Flax believe that a clear line can be drawn between the public sphere of the state and the private sphere of the family that Kant's divisions presuppose in a way that serves male interests by depoliticising domestic life.

According to Flax, without the essential support provided by these now discredited assumptions about reason, the optimistic conclusion that the Enlightenment drew from them – that 'ordering our selves and our practices according to its dictates is emancipatory' – is groundless.[62] 'The Enlightenment hope', she writes, was that 'utilising truthful knowledge in the service of legitimate power will assure both freedom and progress', provided that knowledge is 'grounded in and warranted by a universal reason, not particular "interests"'.[63] On this optimistic view, rational power does not produce new forms of domination, which means that it may be used by a neutral instrument to promote human well-being independently of particular interests that might distort the impartial pursuit of truth or the fair application of justice.[64] But according to the sceptical Flax, this set of assumptions rests on a number of wishes which are impossible to fulfil, such as the belief that reason, power and interest can be disentangled. In this she agrees with Hamann, Nietzsche and Foucault, for whom power and truth can never be 'innocent'.[65]

Apart from Kant, the only other writers whom Flax discusses at any length in her essay are 'neo-Kantians' John Rawls (1921–2002) and Jürgen Habermas, whose theories she flatly rejects as 'inadequate for feminist purposes' because they do not address 'the structural limitations of Enlightenment concepts of the public and the domination of a certain form of reason within them'.[66] For example, both are guilty of privileging rational discourse and argument over other qualities such as 'nurturance and caretaking (traditionally female activities) or a commitment to beauty or pleasure'.[67] By conflating discourse and reason in their accounts of the ideal public sphere, Rawls and Habermas have effectively excluded many other qualities which are often necessary to a full public life, as Flax sees it – for example 'loyalty, empathy, fantasy, courage, a sense of righteous rage', qualities that she associates with the feminine.[68] The feminine is therefore another example of the 'Other' of the Enlightenment that has been denigrated and marginalised like the criminal and the insane in Foucault's classical age.

In an essay on feminist epistemology, Sandra Harding presents a much more ambivalent view of the Enlightenment than Flax, although her reservations appear to go very deep. Of the feminist theories of knowledge she considers, the two 'mainstream epistemologies' that are still within the Enlightenment fold (what she calls 'objectivism' and 'interpretationism') are found to be inadequate from a feminist point of view. Both exclude some forms of knowledge and its acquisition in an effort to rationalise the beliefs of the most powerful members of society, who are, of course, overwhelmingly male. According to Harding, objectivism is the 'official dogma of the age' and the closest to mainstream eighteenth-century empiricism. It prescribes only one legitimate method for establishing valid claims to truth: 'dispassionate, disinterested, value-free, point-of-viewless, objective inquiry.'[69] This narrowly circumscribed approach leaves the knowledge claims of women outside its 'tightly defended barricade', where they lack all value and legitimacy. It is also based on 'the Enlightenment's transhistorical, unitary individual' who is entirely denuded of gender.[70] Interpretationism, the other mainstream epistemology, is the 'loyal opposition' to objectivism. It silences women no less effectively than its 'twin' objectivism does by 'refusing to recognise existing power relations of male dominance'.[71] These two epistemologies within the Enlightenment fold are simply blind to the realities of gender, and are therefore incapable of unbiased perception of the truth.

Harding is much more sympathetic to the epistemology of 'feminist empiricism', which at least acknowledges the pervasive problem of gender bias that distorts the findings of modern Western science, unlike the more mainstream objectivism and interpretationism. Although it hardly differs from them at the level of the basic scientific norms and principles of research, feminist empiricism is much more radical at the level of actual scientific practice, where it stresses the degree to which sexism distorts the application of scientific method, leading to bad science and biased results. The advantage of feminist empiricism over more moderate theories of knowledge is that it rejects the Enlightenment myth of the transhistorical 'ideal knower' who supposedly stands outside of any particular context. Unlike mainstream empiricism, feminist empiricism has a contextualist view of knowledge, in which the scientist necessarily observes from within a specific situation, including a gender situation. It is the frank acknowledgement of the particular location of the researcher that permits him or her to provide a less biased account of science than Enlightenment empiricism ever could.

For some, even feminist empiricism is not sufficiently receptive to issues of race, class and cultural difference, unlike standpoint theory, which 'explicitly articulates, develops, and pushes to more radical conclusions the anti-Enlightenment tendencies that were only implicit in feminist empiricism'.[72] This theory not only denies that *any* method (least of all the 'scientific method') is sufficient to eliminate social biases in scientific research, but affirms that science is unavoidably permeated by politics.[73]

Harding claims that these two, more radical approaches to knowledge are 'in tension with' and 'uncongenial' to Enlightenment science,[74] and that 'a case can be made' that feminist empiricism and standpoint theory 'begin to undermine Enlightenment assumptions in significant ways'.[75] Unfortunately, Harding's evasive language makes it very difficult to discern the extent to which she believes that feminist empiricism and standpoint theory really part company with the Enlightenment. This seems to be because she is not at all sure herself. On the one hand, she says of these radical epistemologies that, while they are more congenial to feminism, 'each begins to move out of the terrain of the Enlightenment'.[76] On the other hand, Harding argues that, however a 'feminist alternative to Enlightenment projects may develop, it is not clear how it could completely take leave of Enlightenment assumptions and still remain feminist. The critics are right that feminism (also) stands on Enlightenment ground.'[77]

The curious Enlightenment of Professor Rorty[78]

According to the American 'postmodern bourgeois liberal' Richard Rorty, the 'Enlightenment Project' has been only a partial failure, and we are better off without the part that has failed. As a philosophical project, he believes that the Enlightenment has failed comprehensively, and that this is an entirely good thing. As a political project, however, Rorty believes that it is alive and well, and that this is also a good thing. The political values he associates with the Enlightenment are, basically, liberal. He uses 'liberalism' and 'Enlightenment' more or less interchangeably and frequently refers to 'Enlightenment liberalism', a view, he claims, that favours the maximisation of individual freedom and decency and the minimisation of cruelty, humiliation and suffering. Rorty is unqualified in his endorsement of this political Enlightenment. The fears of those who believe that it is unsustainable in the absence of universal philosophical foundations are, he argues, completely misplaced. All that is needed to sustain such commitments – all that *can* sustain them – are shared historical narratives or traditions about the way in which the practices and institutions of our 'enlightened' civilisation have made it more free and tolerant than other societies. In other words, we can throw the philosophical ladder away from the Enlightenment without fear of falling into political disaster as a consequence, since our political commitments are philosophically free-floating.[79] Indeed, Rorty agrees with Joseph Schumpeter's claim that to 'realise the relative validity of one's convictions and yet stand for them unflinchingly is what distinguishes a civilised man from a barbarian', a view endorsed by Isaiah Berlin.[80]

One view of the relationship between the political values of the Enlightenment and its philosophical foundations holds that the status of the latter is directly relevant to the strength of our commitment to the former. A leading contemporary proponent of this view is John Gray. 'We live today,' he writes with apocalyptic relish, 'amid the dim ruins of the Enlightenment project'. Since liberal cultures 'depend on the Enlightenment project, and its illusions, for their very identity', we are bound to see it as 'unreasonable to expect the institutions and practices of liberal society to survive unaltered the cultural mutation encompassed in abandoning the Enlightenment project'.[81]

Against this is the view that the realisation of the groundless contingency of one's values in no way affects the degree of one's commitment to them. On this side of the fence Rorty places Isaiah Berlin,[82] Joseph Schumpeter, John Rawls, Michael Oakeshott and John Dewey,[83] all of whom, he claims, 'helped to undermine the idea of a transhistorical "absolute validity" set of concepts which would serve as "philosophical foundations" of liberalism' in the belief that this would strengthen, rather than weaken, liberal institutions.[84] This view of 'Enlightenment rationalism' as antithetical to 'Enlightenment liberalism' provides a basis – upon which Rorty himself seeks to build – for constructing what he calls 'a mature (de-scientised, de-philosophised) Enlightenment liberalism'.[85]

According to Rorty, the philosophical discourse of the Enlightenment is merely one particular narrative which emerged in the seventeenth and eighteenth centuries as part of a 'deep metaphysical need'[86] – inherited from Christianity – to 'have human projects underwritten by a nonhuman authority'[87] such as God or nature or reason. In fact, he argues, Enlightenment values do not supervene on such facts. The persistent belief that the liberal values of the Enlightenment ought to draw their justification from universal philosophical foundations is just a cultural habit which we can, and should, kick.

Rorty concedes that this lingering philosophical vocabulary of the Enlightenment, based on metaphysical notions of truth, reason and nature, is 'a powerful piece of rhetoric' that was instrumentally necessary to the original establishment of liberal democratic societies. However, he asserts that the Enlightenment's search for objective truth has long since 'gone sour' and now does more harm than good. Rorty therefore calls on us to disengage Enlightenment politics from Enlightenment philosophy, jettisoning the latter and retaining the former.[88] The value of the Enlightenment for Rorty is 'just the value of some of the institutions and practices which [it has] created. ... I have sought to distinguish these institutions and practices from the philosophical justifications for them provided by partisans of objectivity, and to suggest an alternative justification'.[89]

Although the Enlightenment discourse of tolerance, civility, respect and decency is Rorty's preferred *political* vocabulary for ethnocentric reasons, the Enlightenment language of reason, nature and science is part of a universal philosophical vocabulary that he claims should be dispensed with altogether. He writes that the Enlightenment's philosophical assumptions about human nature, reason, science, epistemology and history do not have the status of 'truths', as the *philosophes* imagined them to have. Rather, they are part of a contingent, Western, modernist vocabulary that is no closer to a correspondence with the true nature of reality than any other vocabulary. This is not because he knows for certain that the Enlightenment is wrong. Rather, it is because he believes that no vocabulary may be said to be 'true' in this sense, including his own, which he admits does not 'correspond to the nature of things' any more than do other vocabularies.[90]

Rorty believes that an impenetrable wall should be erected between Enlightenment philosophy and Enlightenment politics comparable to that which the *philosophes* sought to build between politics and religion. He commends Thomas Jefferson for helping to 'make respectable the idea that politics can be separated from beliefs about matters of ultimate importance – that shared beliefs among citizens on such matters are not essential to a democratic society'.[91] If this were not the case, if philosophy and politics really were linked, then John Gray would indeed be right that the liberal political values of the Enlightenment are doomed by the collapse of the philosophical project in which they are supposedly grounded. Rorty's composure arises from the fact that he believes that this Jeffersonian separation between our shared public political world and our private philosophical beliefs both can and should be upheld.

Unfortunately, Rorty claims, the dominant public culture of the West is, like its dominant intellectual culture, 'still metaphysical'.[92] Enlightened liberal societies should, he thinks, finally admit to themselves that their cherished values are just part of one particular form of life among others with no more claim to be 'true' philosophically than any other. For Rorty, the ideal citizen is someone who is sufficiently historicist and nominalist to have abandoned the idea that his or her fundamental beliefs refer to something beyond the reach of time and chance. The Enlightenment values that unite us should no longer be thought of as anchored to any universal philosophical substrate such as nature or truth. Rather, such a philosophically post-Enlightenment culture 'would regard the justification of liberal society simply as a matter of historical comparison with other attempts at social organisation'.[93]

While Rorty believes that both the public realm of political values and the private realm of philosophy should be historicised and nominalised, eschewing universal metaphysical assumptions about their supposed 'truth', he argues that irony should be restricted to the private realm. In *Contingency,*

Irony and Solidarity, he specifies three conditions that define an 'ironist': 'She has radical and continuing doubts about the final vocabulary that she currently uses . . . she realises that argument phrased in her present vocabulary can neither underwrite nor dissolve these doubts . . . she does not think that her vocabulary is closer to reality than others'.[94] The effect of irony, he thinks, is to destabilise our beliefs, inducing a chronic state of flux and experimentation, so that individuals would 'never quite [be] able to take themselves seriously because always aware that the terms in which they describe themselves are subject to change, always aware of the contingency and fragility of their final vocabularies'.[95] Rorty labels such a state 'metastable', and associates it with doubt, detachment and lack of commitment.

Rorty is insistent that our commitment to shared Enlightenment political values would be unsustainable if ironised, and that this is undesirable. While we should see them, like our private beliefs, as 'contingent through and through', we should not feel 'any particular doubts about the contingencies they happen to be'.[96] The light-hearted, light-minded, ironic detachment characteristic of our private, post-Enlightenment worlds would thereby co-exist with a robust, if historicised, public commitment to the Enlightenment as a political project, free of ironic doubt and characterised as much by the 'spirit of gravity' as our attitude towards philosophy, religion and other 'matters of ultimate importance' would be characterised by the 'spirit of lightness'. This point is often overlooked – or at least obscured – by Rorty's critics. For example, John Gray attacks what he believes to be Rorty's call for a comprehensive 'ironisation' of our civilisation. 'The recurring theme in Rorty's work', he writes, 'is that liberal cultures whose relationship with their most central and fundamental practices is ironic will be better . . . than liberal cultures which seek "foundations" for themselves in "universal principles". . . . Irony is the negation of the spirit of seriousness, a playful engagement in world-making'.[97] Yet, for Rorty, the element of doubt that he associates with irony should have no place in our historicised public culture, which would remain unflinchingly committed to our Enlightenment political values. In this way, public solidarity and commitment can be combined with private irony, doubt and detachment. Rorty is unambiguous on this point.

> But even if I am right in thinking that a liberal culture whose public rhetoric is nominalist and historicist is both possible and desirable, I cannot go on to claim that there could or ought to be a culture whose public rhetoric is ironist. I cannot imagine a culture which socialised its youth in such a way as to make them continually dubious about their own process of socialisation. *Irony seems inherently a private matter.* On my definition, an ironist cannot get along without the contrast between the final vocabulary she inherited and the one she is trying to create for herself.[98]

Rorty categorically rejects the view that one cannot combine 'commitment with a sense of the contingency of . . . [one's] own commitment'.[99] Although our common convictions are based on 'nothing more profound than the historical facts' and not metaphysical beliefs about nature, reason or truth,[100] he argues that 'a belief can still regulate action, can still be thought worth dying for among people who are quite aware that this belief is caused by nothing deeper than contingent historical circumstance'.[101] This is because political life is, for Rorty, independent of intellectual life. What happens within the former has little or no bearing on the latter. Our shared, first-order, affirmed political commitments are not sustained by reflective, second-order philosophical assumptions and arguments. The very idea that they are, or should be, Rorty professes to find 'ludicrous'.[102]

Even if this is the case, what reasons do we have for remaining unflinchingly loyal to the particular political values of the Enlightenment? For Rorty, the cement that holds Western societies together and binds them to the Enlightenment is ethnic, not philosophical. The inculcation of values is a social and cultural process, not a conscious rational process, and these values are supported by a shared, non-rational sense of ethnic solidarity that binds individuals together in a common commitment to particular values.[103] It is good socialisation, particularly in the form of shared narratives and common vocabularies and experiences, that sustains our commitments. This 'mild ethnocentrism' reflects Rorty's view of the basically non-rational, non-philosophical way in which our political commitments are instilled and maintained.[104] He interprets his own 'anti-anti-ethnocentrism' as a 'protest against the persistence of Enlightenment rhetoric'.[105] The liberal political values of the Enlightenment will persist as the 'final vocabulary' of our common public world long after Enlightenment philosophy has died. Rorty's arguments about the Enlightenment are really an elaboration of Hans Blumenberg's claim that 'the "historicist" criticism of the optimism of the Enlightenment, criticism which began with the Romantics' turn back to the Middle Ages, undermines self-foundation but not self-assertion'.[106] The ethnic self-assertion of Western liberal democracies is benign, according to Rorty, because it is detached from metaphysical assumptions which would allow us to assert that our form of life is *intrinsically* superior to or truer than any other. But if, as Rorty claims, 'a belief can still regulate action, can still be thought worth dying for among people who are quite aware that this belief is caused by nothing deeper than contingent historical circumstance', then it cannot be assumed that even such self-aware societies will refrain from asserting themselves against others.

8 From Enlightenment to nothingness

> For, within Western cultures, the Enlightenment project of promoting autonomous human reason and of according to science a privileged status in relation to all other forms of understanding has successfully eroded and destroyed local and traditional forms of moral and social knowledge; it has not issued in anything resembling a new civilisation, however, but instead in nihilism.[1]
>
> (John Gray)

Introduction

It became a common complaint early on that the Enlightenment was better at destroying than creating. Among its early opponents it is not at all difficult to find examples of the claim that the *philosophes* contributed to the collapse of the moral and political order of Europe in the eighteenth century by attacking Christianity and encouraging scepticism towards traditional beliefs and institutions without putting anything positive in their place. It was Jacobi, Hamann's friend and ally, who first coined the term *nihilismus* in German in the early nineteenth century to refer to the ultimate consequences of rational enquiry when taken too far, particularly in matters of faith, as he believed had occurred in Frederick II's enlightened state.[2] In the wake of the French Revolution, Hegel's 'darkest and deepest work',[3] the *Phenomenology of Spirit*, portrayed the Enlightenment as pervaded by negativity, wholly incapable of constructing anything positive of its own to replace the faith that it destroyed with such ruthless efficiency. What began in the eighteenth century as 'a glorious mental dawn' heralding human emancipation ended for Hegel in the 'sheer terror of the negative that contains nothing positive' during the Reign of Terror.[4] Nietzsche's dramatic and highly influential account of the nihilistic collapse of meaning in modern Europe following the 'death of God' belongs to this same Germanic current of thought.[5]

In the second half of the twentieth century, a variation on this theme has appeared in the claim that the 'Enlightenment project' of rationally justifying morality has failed and that the ethical nihilism that has allegedly haunted Western civilisation ever since is a direct consequence of this failure. Among those in the postwar West who have stressed the nihilistic effects of 'the Enlightenment project' are Lester Crocker, Alasdair MacIntyre and John Gray, all of whom have acknowledged the importance of Nietzsche in particular to their thinking about it. All three argue that the Enlightenment was doomed to fail because of its mistaken assumptions about reason, nature and morality, and that this failure has led directly to a moral crisis in the West that remains unresolved.

Lester Crocker offers an account of the Enlightenment in which its central project of finding a naturalistic substitute for Christian ethics not only failed completely, but was destined to fail because the *philosophes* were searching for something that, he believes, does not exist.[6] The Enlightenment attempt to justify morality in terms of nature was necessarily 'self-defeating and supererogatory' because moral concepts are meaningless in nature.[7] Having thus unwittingly 'loosed the metaphysical moorings and set him [man] adrift'[8] with this realisation, the *philosophes* opened the way to 'the contrary but related extremes of nihilism and social tyranny'.[9] That is why the Marquis de Sade is such a pivotal figure for Crocker, as he was for Horkheimer and Adorno, since his writings 'crystallised' the moral crisis into which the eighteenth century had unintentionally strayed and indicated the dark path down which the West would head in the century and a half to come as a direct consequence. According to Crocker, Sade was the first to see clearly the total futility of the *philosophes'* efforts to reconcile nature and culture and fatefully to set off in a radically new direction that would eventually lead through nihilism to totalitarianism.

In *After Virtue* (1981), the neo-Aristotelian philosopher Alasdair MacIntyre outlines yet another version of the rise and tragic fall of the 'Enlightenment Project', in which the failure to provide a rational justification for morality – the essence of the project in his view – provides the 'historical background against which the predicaments of our own culture can become intelligible', as it does for Crocker.[10] Unlike Crocker though, MacIntyre holds that it was the *abandonment* of naturalistic ethics, not its embrace, that led to the Nietzschean predicament which currently grips Western civilisation. The Enlightenment project to justify morality was futile when, following David Hume, the *philosophes* of the eighteenth century rejected nature as a normative standard in favour of reason. For Crocker, by contrast, it was precisely their turn to nature that led them to run aground on the rocks of nihilism. Yet Crocker and MacIntyre agree that the Enlightenment path led, and could *only* lead, to a moral dead-end, where our civilisation languishes.

For John Gray Nietzsche was the supreme diagnostician of modernity whose writings 'accomplished the dissolution of the Enlightenment project'[11] which is the final phase of the modern age. He even took the title for his book *Enlightenment's Wake* (1995) from Nietzsche.[12] Like Crocker and MacIntyre, he sees the Enlightenment as a road leading ineluctably to nihilism, in the process bringing utter devastation to the traditional cultures of the West and threatening to decimate those beyond it.[13] This is because the Enlightenment is part of the futile search for an illusory universal civilisation based on reason which Western philosophers have been pursuing in vain since antiquity. Like Crocker, and unlike MacIntyre, Gray sees no obvious way out of this predicament and, following Nietzsche, he calls on Westerners to accept it unflinchingly as their tragic fate and non-Westerners to resist it as best they can.

The road to nowhere[14]

Although Lester Crocker counted himself a 'devoted admirer' of the Enlightenment, he argued that the *philosophes'* search for 'a secular and social system of ethics that would effectively steer between the equally odious poles of supernatural authoritarianism and anarchy' ended in total failure.[15] He conceded that their destructive work of clearing away obstacles to freedom and understanding was an enormous success, ruthlessly exposing the untenability of the whole structure of traditional religious beliefs and values in *ancien-régime* France. But the *philosophes* failed utterly to construct a naturalistic substitute for the religious order they had toppled so effectively. Their tragedy (and ours) is that they were only half-successful, destroying religious oppression and heteronomy, but failing to avoid the 'equally odious' pole of anarchy.

Echoing Jacob Talmon, Crocker argues that the ethical thought of the Enlightenment developed in two contradictory directions, one 'liberal-utilitarian', the other 'collectivist and prototoalitarian'.[16] Thus the eighteenth century, 'while advancing steadfastly toward liberalism and rights, also initiates moves toward the two extremes of anarchism and totalitarianism'.[17] Among the pluralistic, libertarian type of *philosophe* Crocker lists Montesquieu, Voltaire, d'Alembert, Condorcet and the early Diderot, who together 'laid the foundations of modern liberal societies'.[18] Those who 'verged toward a collectivist or totalitarian way, toward a monism' include Morelly, Mably, Rousseau and the later Diderot.[19] Given this latter tendency, Crocker concludes that, 'while lauding the Enlightenment, in traditional fashion, for its legacy of liberalism, we must recognise that nihilism and totalitarianism ... were also parts of its legacy'.[20]

Yet even the moderate, liberal-utilitarian *philosophes* inadvertently advanced the cause of anarchy, nihilism and, thereby, totalitarianism, according to Crocker. What really distinguishes his liberal *philosophes* from their 'prototoalitarian' cousins are their intentions rather than the actual consequences of their beliefs, since the principles of utility and natural right that the former promoted 'really led to opposite practical conclusions'.[21] Tragically, these would-be humanists did not see that they were opening a Pandora's box with their 'eighteenth-century re-evaluation of values', the disastrous effects of which only became fully apparent during the French Revolution, by which time it was much too late.[22] This is yet another example of 'the inversion thesis', in which the attempted implementation of Enlightened principles and ideals produces the very opposite effect to that intended by the *philosophes*, resulting in disaster. This explains how an 'unbroken line of thought leads from such eighteenth-century views to Hitler's *Mein Kampf* and the Nazi infamies'.[23]

In addition, a 'faint shadow of collectivist control' may be seen in the most humanistic writers of the eighteenth century, all of whom were led by their empiricist assumptions about the malleability of human nature towards collectivism 'as the necessary mechanism of man's reconditioning'.[24] Even they favoured a reductionistic and deterministic 'pleasure–pain' view of human psychology which, when combined with their utopian belief in the essential goodness of human nature, led to a perfectionist view of society that had an unmistakably 'totalitarian colour'.[25]

As with Horkheimer and Adorno, the Marquis de Sade plays a key role in Crocker's tragic story of the eighteenth-century Enlightenment, since it was in 'the incarnadine flowers of Sade's rebellion' against traditional moral restraints that the 'seeds of eighteenth-century nihilism blossom'.[26] He is a vital link between the 'crisis' of the Enlightenment and the 'crisis' of the twentieth century. On the one hand, Sade was 'the culmination of eighteenth-century radical thought',[27] the most extreme expression of the tragic ethical impasse that the *philosophes* had reached by the century's end. He was the first to recognise the revolutionary implications of the failure to bridge the nature–culture abyss that the *philosophes* had inadvertently exposed, and simply rejected reason and culture in favour of nature, which he conceived in the most violent terms reminiscent of Hobbes and Maistre – with more than a dash of Freud.[28] On the other hand, Sade's nihilism was also prophetic, since it 'foretold the course of the crisis of Western civilisation' in the nineteenth and twentieth centuries and he was the first in a long line of radical thinkers such as Stirner and Nietzsche who celebrated the overthrow of ethics as a great liberation for our long-suppressed instincts.[29] For Crocker, the works of Sade represent the Enlightenment's belated realisation of the futility of morality to constrain human nature and the nihilistic implications of this revolutionary idea.

In *Nature and Culture*, Crocker casts nihilism in Freudian terms as 'the rejection of the prevailing organisation of instincts which is imposed by any culture, and *ipso facto* of all moral restrictions to the id'.[30] In the absence of any moral laws or principles to constrain or guide the primitive id, it becomes a law unto itself and runs amok, as in the violent novels of Sade. Crocker believes that the *philosophes'* faith in their ability to impose limits on our selfish instincts was fatally misplaced, as Sade realised and as the dramatic 'upsurge of nihilism' and violence at the end of the eighteenth century amply demonstrates. Crocker interpreted totalitarianism as 'a defence of culture based on the acceptance of the truth of nihilism ... a tyrannical and arbitrary imposition of a superego and contemplates the remaking of the individual, through the pressures of total conditioning, so that the id is inhibited and the ego enslaved'.[31] In this way, the Enlightenment led to nihilistic anarchy, which was born of the moral crisis caused by the failure of the eighteenth century to solve the problem of ethics, and this intolerable situation eventually called forth totalitarianism, a form of collective super-ego that aimed to repress the unbounded natural desires that the *philosophes* had inadvertently unleashed. That is how the Enlightenment could have started with individualism and ended up with the opposite, how it could, 'by a slight turn of logic, lead to anarchism, to the cruelest totalitarianism, or to humanitarian democracy'.[32] Thus, while liberal assumptions about rights, liberty and rational self-interest arose out of the Enlightenment, it also produced 'theories of indoctrination, of conditioning and control, which compromised them'.[33] Crocker argues that the nihilistic impasse of the late eighteenth century contained 'the seed of modern irrational movements, such as Nazism';[34] the 'termini of nihilism' brought about by the Enlightenment, he tells us, are 'the holocaust and the apocalypse' of early twentieth-century Europe.[35]

Like so many of the early Counter-revolutionary conservatives, Crocker subscribed to the continuity thesis, linking what he saw as the ethical failure of the Enlightenment to the violence of the French Revolution – which was 'the culmination of the crisis that had been building up during the century'. However, he stressed that the Revolution was in no way *caused* by the ideas of the eighteenth century and dismissed as 'patently absurd' the attempt to blame the *philosophes* for the upheavals of the 1790s. Even so, he believed that, like Sade himself (most of whose writings were published during the Revolution), the violent events of the period cast a revelatory light on the 'weakness of Enlightenment ideas' because it was 'an attempt to implement ideas of the eighteenth century; and its failure reflects in some measure, at least, upon the inadequacies of those ideas and the outlook they embodied'.

> What had been in the realm of mind came to life in the realm of political events. The French Revolution was the logical crowning of a hundred years of struggle to free men's minds and institutions from a thousand years' dead weight of medievalism. The men of the Revolution tried to create the rational society of which the *philosophes* had dreamed.[36]

This is an almost verbatim restatement of Edmund Burke's version of the continuity thesis between the Enlightenment and the Revolution, and shows just how persistent it is.

Unfortunately, Crocker thought, the Revolution brutally exposed the fact that social life is fundamentally a Hobbesian struggle of self-interest and power, and human nature is neither benign nor predominantly rational. The rational society of which the *philosophes* dreamed was, for Crocker, really just a childish illusion. Like Isaiah Berlin and Joseph de Maistre, he is severely critical of the Enlightenment's simplistic conception of human nature, which was 'entirely wrong'.[37] Indeed, he claims that the chief weakness of the *philosophes* was their 'vague optimism and trust in man's natural moral impulses'.[38] Had they been more realistic about human nature, as Sade was, they would have seen how totally unsuitable it is as a foundation for ethics and how hopelessly impractical their ideals were in the real world. In this Crocker was on the side of Maistre against the Enlightenment, as was Berlin.

According to Crocker, the complete failure of the Enlightenment project to find a natural substitute for the religiously grounded ethics it destroyed has brought Western civilisation to a deep crisis of meaning which it has yet to overcome. Having failed to find a substitute for the moral system which the *philosophes* overthrew, the West has found itself 'lost in endless space and time'.[39] This is why Crocker believes that existentialism is a 'child of the Enlightenment'.[40] The crisis that the *philosophes* exposed us to is 'the crisis of man' in general and the 'unsolvable problem' of ethics itself, which the nineteenth and twentieth centuries have continued to wrestle with unsuccessfully. The groundlessness of ethical life was revealed during the eighteenth-century Enlightenment, which 'opened the consciousness of modern man . . . to the fact that he is lost among the stars, with no meaning to his existence except the meaning he creates; that he must therefore be his own guide, his happiness and well-being on earth his only lodestar'.[41] For Crocker the Enlightenment's principal function and significance resides less in its ideals and beliefs, many of which have not survived the terrible events of subsequent history, and more in the conservative, anti-utopian fact that 'basic problems cannot be solved in terms of political reforms or enlightenment'.[42]

The failure of the 'Enlightenment project'[43]

In his account of the failure of the 'Enlightenment project' in *After Virtue*, Alasdair MacIntyre agrees with Lester Crocker that the *philosophes* set out in search of a new foundation for ethical life, and ended up lost in an abyss of nihilism as a consequence. However, contrary to Crocker, MacIntyre claims that eighteenth-century moral philosophers adopted a conception of ethics in which moral ends are *not* naturally given. Whereas Crocker depicted the *philosophes* as turning *to* nature as the source of ethics and coming up empty, MacIntyre sees them as turning *away* from nature with the same disastrous result. In doing so the *philosphes* turned against the Aristotelian tradition, according to which human beings have a natural essence and ethics is understood as the prescriptive science of promoting the conditions necessary for the realisation of our nature. On this view, the virtues are those attributes of character that facilitate the realisation of our natural ends, the vices those that inhibit them. The facts of human nature are thereby imbued with a normative significance that is objective and universal.

According to MacIntyre, the moral philosophers of the eighteenth century flatly rejected this classical conception of ethics because they accepted as a 'timeless logical truth' David Hume's famous anti-Aristotelian claim in his *Treatise of Human Nature* (1739–1740) that purely factual premises (about human nature, for example) do not logically entail any moral or evaluative conclusions, that claims about what *ought* to be are not derivable from facts about what *is*.[44] To believe otherwise is to commit what is now branded the 'naturalistic fallacy',[45] which MacIntyre labels the 'epitaph to their entire project'.[46] The Enlightenment rejection of Aristotelian natural teleology not only marks a radical break with the classical tradition of ethics, but also signals 'the decisive breakdown of the eighteenth-century project of justifying morality'[47] because, according to MacIntyre, without a teleological framework 'the whole project of morality becomes unintelligible'.[48] This is apparent to him in contemporary moral discourse, which is made up of the residues of earlier ethical discourses, such as that of Christianity, which have lost the original context that gave them their coherence and meaning, leaving behind only 'incoherent fragments of a once coherent scheme of thought and action'.[49] Moral debate since the eighteenth century has been so interminable because morals have been viewed as matters of purely subjective preference with no universal applicability. There is no common framework (such as nature) to which appeal may be made to settle competing moral claims. In addition, having rejected the classical teleological conception of humans, the *philosophes* undertook to ground morality in reason rather than in nature, a project that was doomed from the outset because of their narrow conception of reason as purely 'calculative', incapable of discerning 'man's true end'.[50] Reason came to be seen as merely 'instrumental' in the Weberian sense, restricted to questions of means only, as Horkheimer and Adorno had earlier claimed, and was therefore incapable of leading us to knowledge about beauty, justice or the substantive ends of life.

In *Whose Justice? Which Rationality?* (1988), the second in a trilogy of books that began with *After Virtue*,[51] MacIntyre examines reason at length and defends a pluralistic conception of it that he calls the 'rationality of traditions', to which he claims the Enlightenment was blind. For the Enlightenment there was one universal rationality in terms of which everything needed to be justified. 'It was a central aspiration of the Enlightenment', he writes,

> to provide for debate in the public realm standards and methods of rational justification by which alternative courses of action in every sphere of life could be adjudged just or unjust, rational or irrational, enlightened or unenlightened. So, it was hoped, reason would displace authority and tradition. Rational justification was to appeal to principles undeniable by any rational person and therefore independent of all those social and cultural particularities which the Enlightenment thinkers took to be the mere accidental clothing of reason in particular

times and places. And that rational justification could be nothing other than what the thinkers of the Enlightenment had said that it was came to be accepted.[52]

Three Rival Versions of Moral Enquiry (1990), the final volume in MacIntyre's ethical trilogy, contrasts this strong Enlightenment view of reason, based on a single, substantive conception of rationality whose methods and standards, if followed correctly, would issue in 'a comprehensive, rationally incontestable scientific understanding of the whole',[53] with the weak conception that is prevalent in contemporary academic culture, which has been in the ascendant ever since the advent of Nietzschean genealogy in the late nineteenth century. The tragedy for the Enlightenment and for Western civilisation ever since, according to MacIntyre, is that it was unable actually to agree on the principles on which all rational persons were supposed to concur, a fact that has been disguised by a 'rhetoric of consensus'. The Enlightenment left the West with a monistic ideal of universal rational justification 'which it has proved impossible to attain'.[54]

MacIntyre's goal in *Whose Justice? Which Rationality?* is to explain and defend the idea that reason is plural rather than monistic – that there are rationalities rather than rationality – without lapsing into relativism, which he considers no less mistaken than monism. He claims that each tradition has its own particular standards of reasoning in terms of which its beliefs, texts and authorities find their justification. This is necessarily so because we are all inextricably embedded in a particular tradition, and there is no universal perspective or 'God's eye view' beyond all traditions from which to judge them.[55] MacIntyre holds that there is no alternative to rational enquiry on the basis of immanent, context-particular standards of reasoning. Rational justification comes from within – and can *only* come from within – the tradition from which it springs. The rationality of each tradition can be vindicated internally by means of critical self-reflection upon its existing beliefs and conceptions in light of beliefs and conceptions previously held within that tradition. Only if they transcend the limitations and shortcomings of their predecessors within that tradition can its prevalent beliefs and conceptions be deemed 'rationally' superior to them.[56] Those that fail this Darwinian competition of traditions will wither and die as 'less rational'. The rationality of a particular tradition can also be 'dialectically tested' externally, against the traditions of other contexts. In the ensuing argumentative contest the 'adequacy and the explanatory power of the histories which the resources of each of those traditions in conflict enable their adherents to write' will be tested and one will emerge as the victor.[57] In both of these ways, relativism is supposedly avoided, although it is not at all clear how MacIntyre can avoid presupposing a shared framework of rationality embraced by *all* traditions when judging these dialectical contests between them.[58] Of the traditions of rationality scrutinised in *Three Rival Versions of Moral Enquiry*, MacIntyre believes that Christian Thomism emerges as the provisional victor over Nietzschean genealogy and the encyclopaedic tradition to which the Enlightenment belonged.

According to *After Virtue*, the revolutionary eighteenth-century overthrow of ethical naturalism released the individual agent from the teleological framework that had bound him normatively to certain natural ends. Yet for MacIntryre this freedom has come at a terrible price: the loss of 'any authoritative content from the would-be moral utterances of the newly autonomous agent'.[59] The sovereign individual now floats about aimlessly in a void with no way of arbitrating moral disputes and no rational basis for his ethical judgements – a condition MacIntyre labels 'emotivism'. The emotivist self is caught in a Nietzschean clash of groundless, subjective preferences and values between which he is powerless to make any rational choices, an ethical *bellum omnium contra omnes*. The result is a form of groundless moral decisionism. Nineteenth-century utilitarianism and twentieth-century analytical moral philosophy have failed to rescue this autonomous moral agent from 'the predicament in which the failure of the Enlightenment project of providing him with a secular, rational justification for his moral allegiances had left him', according to MacIntyre.[60] The only real alternatives that now remain for individuals are to carry on down the apocalyptic post-Enlightenment road already taken by Western civilisation and marked out by Nietzsche, or to retreat to the pre-Enlightenment naturalism of Aristotle.

Gray's Elegy[61]

The Enlightenment has few more strident opponents today than John Gray. He has not only set himself against the whole of Western modernity, of which the Enlightenment is the 'final phase', but against the entire Western intellectual tradition as far back as the pre-Socratics. He offers a breathtakingly sweeping version of the continuity thesis, comparable in scope to that of Horkheimer and Adorno, according to which *all* of Western philosophy is but a series of variations on the same basic theme: the (in Gray's view futile) search for 'a universal consensus on the essential content of morality'.[62] Socrates, Christianity, the Enlightenment, the Revolution and everything in between are all manifestations of a single, basic outlook, which explains why Western moral philosophy has been a long succession of tragic failures, since no such universal consensus in matters of morality does, or ever could, exist, according to Gray. Although Western modernity rejected the particular metaphysical and religious beliefs of classical and Christian civilisations, the fundamental moral categories, logic and hopes which they presupposed have been 'secularised in humanist doctrines of autonomous reason, progress, romantic self-assertion and similar ideas' characteristic of the Enlightenment.[63]

The central theme of Gray's portrait of Voltaire – 'the Enlightenment thinker *par excellence*'[64] – in his short book *Voltaire* (1998) is the similarity between his 'secular faith' and that of the Christianity he despised and campaigned to destroy. This is essentially a restatement of Carl Becker's thesis in *The Heavenly City of the Eighteenth Century Philosophers* (1932) that 'there is more of Christian philosophy in the writings of the *Philosophes* than has yet been dreamt of in our histories'.[65] In Becker's eyes, the *philosophes* were religious fanatics, with a 'messianic enterprise' of reform which they pursued with 'an extraordinary amount of earnest conviction, of devotion, or enthusiasm', comparable to the Christian true-believers whom they attacked.[66] What he calls 'the essential articles of the religion of the Enlightenment' are a rejection of original sin, perfectibility, the belief that the end of life is life itself, and the necessity of freeing our minds of ignorance and superstition.

According to Gray, this was also 'Voltaire's religion', a 'new religion of universal enlightenment' which he devoted his life to propagating and about which he was curiously lacking in the scepticism characteristic of his outlook generally.[67] Its central article of faith, common to both the *philosophes* and their Christian enemies, is that 'the basic values of civilised human beings are essentially identical'.[68] For Gray, it was this faith in universal civilisation and emancipation that unites the Enlightenment and Christianity. Both are forms of ethical monism – the belief that 'a single way of life was best for all humankind' – whose adherents believed with a zealous and unshakeable conviction that 'the good was one, not many'.[69] That is why they also shared a 'deep intolerance towards anything that stood in the way of their universal ambitions'.[70] The *philosophes* could not accept cultural or ethical pluralism any more than the Christians they reviled, and both crusaded to 'supplant the diverse traditions and religious beliefs by which humanity has hitherto been ruled with a new morality whose authority is rational and universal'.[71]

Not surprisingly, Gray registers his enthusiastic agreement with Alasdair MacIntyre's account of both the Enlightenment project – 'the project of an independent rational justification of morality' – and its purported failure. He concurs with MacIntyre (and Crocker) that it not only failed but was doomed to fail, although, contrary to MacIntyre, he claims that this is because it is part of the same self-defeating Western universalist project to which MacIntyre remains committed in some Counter-Enlightenment form. Gray and MacIntyre also share the view that it is in liberalism that 'the Enlightenment project is now most powerfully, and certainly most pervasively, embodied'.[72] For both, contemporary liberal civilisation is but 'a relic of Enlightenment rationalism' and shares all of its pathologies, plus a few of its own.[73] Gray argues that the Whiggish self-conception of liberal civilisation as uniquely universal, rather than as just another historically contingent form of life among others – no better and no worse – depends upon a progressive view of history which it inherited from the Enlightenment and which is 'a central element in the self-conception of enlightened liberal cultures'.[74] That is why the failure of the Enlightenment project necessarily undermines the superior self-understanding of the liberal societies that are its natural heirs and successors. This directly contradicts the position of Richard Rorty, whom Gray faults for seriously underestimating the importance of the Enlightenment in conferring a coherent identity and legitimacy on liberal civilisation. As we have seen, Rorty is unperturbed by what he sees as the collapse of the philosophical foundations of the Enlightenment project which, for Gray, are indispensable pillars holding up the values and practices of liberal societies. Gray is convinced that such a loss of faith in the grounds of belief is necessarily fatal to the values once thought to depend on them for support, and he points to a serious 'crisis of legitimacy' that afflicts contemporary liberalism in the wake of the Enlightenment to support his argument against Rorty. Rorty's historicisation of the Enlightenment – his denial that its beliefs are really 'true' in a metaphysical sense – although sound in itself, in Gray's view, must necessarily weaken our commitment to it. 'What Christianity and the dwindling cultural legacy of the Enlightenment did,' he argues, 'was to confer on the most central practices of Western societies the imprimatur of universal authority. ... Can we reasonably expect Western liberal institutions to survive unchanged a cultural mutation in which their universal claims are abandoned?'[75] The 'no' to which he answers this question is as emphatic as Rorty's 'yes'. Although Gray interprets the failure of the 'Enlightenment Project' as a disaster for liberalism, he does not see this as a disaster for humanity, since he is opposed to both the Enlightenment and its offspring liberalism.

Gray also endorses MacIntyre's conviction that the best account of the consequences of the failure of the Enlightenment project is to be found in the work of Nietzsche, which is 'unavoidably and rightly the starting-point of serious reflection for us'.[76] Not only did Nietzsche provide 'the definitive critique of the Enlightenment project',[77] but its self-destruction was consummated in his thought.[78] For Gray Nietzsche is the 'owl of Minerva' who took flight at the dusk of the Western philosophical tradition in the wake of the Enlightenment and revealed its true, self-destructive nature.

Despite these similarities, Gray is as dismissive as Crocker would have been of MacIntyre's call for a revival of Aristotle's naturalistic ethics. MacIntyre's flight from Nietzsche's profoundly disturbing nihilistic vision of modernity back to pre-modern Aristotelianism is simply 'hopeless' and 'delusive', in Gray's view. For Gray there is no road back, so we must resign ourselves to our fate as Nietzsche has described it, 'with all its consequences in terms of disenchantment and ultimate groundlessness'.[79] This is what Nietzsche called '*amor fati*' – love of fate – the heroic and unflinching acceptance of what could not have been otherwise. Besides, even if MacIntyre's neo-Aristotelianism was intellectually tenable, it is part of the same 'Western humanist project' as the Enlightenment. Reinstituting Aristotle's naturalistic ethics would simply amount to putting the needle back several grooves on the same old record; it would not solve the fundamental problems that have plagued the West for over two millennia. At most it would just buy time.

Under the influence of Martin Heidegger's postwar critique of modern technological civilisation, Gray blames the West's aggressive, Promethean outlook for destroying traditional cultures and its 'Baconian instrumentalist understandings' of nature as mere dead matter in 'standing reserve' (*Berstand*[80]) for human use for devastating the natural environment. For Gray, the 'Westernising project of Enlightenment humanism' is a juggernaut crushing whatever lies in its path, imperiously sweeping aside as illegitimate everything but the one supremely authoritative source of human knowledge: modern Western experimental science. In its wake the Enlightenment has left a world 'ruled by calculation and wilfulness which is humanly unintelligible and destructively purposeless'.[81]

> Though the Enlightenment project of constructing a universal civilisation has manifestly failed, the Westernising impulse that it embodied has transmitted to nearly all cultures the radical modernist project of subjugating nature by deploying technology to exploit the earth for human purposes. This is, in fact, the real legacy of the Enlightenment project to humankind – the Baconian and Nietzschean, but also Christian and Marxian humanist project of turning nature into an object of human will. ... Westernisation impacts on the world's non-Occidental cultures in the late modern period as a form of revolutionary nihilism.[82]

Although Gray believes that the 'universalist project' of the Enlightenment has ended in total failure and is now intellectually discredited, it still has a posthumous practical authority and 'continues to inform many areas of thought and discourse aside from the increasingly culturally marginal activity of academic philosophy'.[83] It is like the ghost of Christianity, which Nietzsche believed would haunt the West for centuries after the 'death of God'. As such, the Enlightenment remains a serious threat to the few traditional cultures that remain relatively untouched by it and to the world's dwindling and beleaguered natural environment. Having already hollowed out 'the public culture of modern Western societies of their animating conceptions of science and morality', the rapacious revolutionary nihilism of enlightened modernity has moved on to other domains which are now in imminent threat of destruction too.[84] While it is too late to rescue the West, Gray believes that it may yet be possible to protect surviving traditional communities and natural habitats from the ravages of Western nihilism. Indeed, he believes that the only realistic prospect of a 'cultural recovery from the nihilism that the Enlightenment has spawned' now lies outside of the West, above all in Asia.[85]

Gray's assertion that the nihilistic destructiveness of the Enlightenment is still a grave threat to precarious and diminishing human and natural environments echoes Heidegger's earlier assault on the modern West's technological will-to-power and has recently been echoed by many environmentalists, who see it as symptomatic of a predatory and deeply pathological

Western attitude towards the non-human world.[86] For example, in his *Requiem for Modern Politics* (1997) William Ophuls argues that the most serious problems of our age are a consequence of 'the way in which the Enlightenment in general and Hobbesian politics in particular have encouraged the worst tendencies of human nature to flourish in the modern era'.[87] Among the specific maladies that he lays at the feet of the Enlightenment are explosive and uncontrolled population growth, widespread environmental destruction, pollution, increasing crime and violence, runaway addictions of all kinds, the neglect and abuse of children, social breakdown, antimonianism, nihilism, millenarianism, and all varieties of ideological excess, hyperpluralism, factionalism, administrative despotism and every other manifestation of democratic decay, weapons of mass destruction, terrorism, and structural poverty and underdevelopment – to name just a few.[88] At the root of all of these problems, which have plunged Western civilisation into 'the crisis of crises',[89] is the Enlightenment drive to master nature in order to exploit it for human purposes.[90]

Despite Gray's bleak assessment of the Enlightenment's legacy, he sees a faint silver lining in the dark cloud that it has cast over the modern world. While he bitterly regrets the enormous destruction that 'the Enlightenment project' to construct a single universal civilisation has wrought since the eighteenth century, he draws some consolation from the fact that it has finally collapsed, leaving in its wake a plurality of incommensurable perspectives and cultures that, he hopes, will be viewed as 'an historical gift to be enjoyed rather than merely as a fate to be accepted and endured'.[91] Gray is a pluralist like Berlin, whom he greatly admires.[92] Both affirm the existence of a plurality of incompatible and incommensurable universal goods between which we are often forced to make tragic choices. Like postmodern critics of the Enlightenment, Gray welcomes cultural diversity and difference, which the hegemony of 'Enlightenment liberalism' has long suppressed and devalued. However, he is not a postmodernist, since he believes in the universality of some values, like Berlin. He rejects value monism but not value objectivity.

9 Conclusion

Hits and misses

In much wisdom is much grief, and he that increaseth knowledge increaseth sorrow.

(Ecclesiastes 1: 18)

Introduction

The Great War between the Enlightenment and its enemies, which still shows little sign of abating 250 years after it began, sometimes resembles the struggle between Eurasia and Oceania in George Orwell's *1984*, which only intensified the longer it ran and involved the society of Big Brother in perpetual 'combat' with an imaginary enemy of its own creation. Orwell wished to underscore the fact that it is often very convenient to have it believed that one is constantly threatened by a powerful opponent. Advances in Enlightenment scholarship in the past quarter century have exposed the largely mythical character of this enemy, which rarely bears much resemblance to what was actually advocated in the eighteenth century. Yet not every charge that has been laid at the feet of the Enlightenment is a travesty. Its opponents have scored some palpable hits against it, making it very hard for us to swallow the Enlightenment whole now. Even its most sophisticated contemporary defenders, such as Jürgen Habermas, grant this. So the analogy with *1984* is not perfect; the Enlightenment of its enemies is not *wholly* imaginary. It is more of a distortion of the truth (often a very grotesque distortion of it) than a complete fabrication.

The necessity of faith

Many of the Enlightenment's early opponents were devout Christians who made little, if any, distinction between opposition to their faith and opposition to religion in general. Although the large majority of *philosophes* and *Aufklärer* were deists who believed in God but not in Christianity, they have routinely been attacked by such opponents for being atheists and held accountable for the purported consequences of their disbelief. They were constantly charged with seeking 'the utter extirpation of religion', as Burke put it.[1] As a rhetorical strategy this unfair attribution of atheism (and consequent blame for its alleged effects) was very effective in an age when most people were still religious. Of course there *were* atheists among the *philosophes*, such as Helvétius, the Baron d'Holbach, La Mettrie, Naigeon and, eventually, Diderot, and they *did* become more assertive in the latter half of the eighteenth century, but they were always in a small minority of the eighteenth-century 'society of men of letters', as the *philosophes* called themselves. In fact, the line of demarcation between atheists and their opponents on the question of God's existence, if on nothing else, split the *philosophes*, with most on the side of orthodox religion and a small but determined côterie against them.

A classic case of Enlightenment anti-atheism is Voltaire, a man taken by so many of the orthodox enemies of the Enlightenment as its most important and representative figure. His hostility to Christianity is famous; he spent much of his life campaigning to crush it, and in so doing earned the enmity of orthodox Christians right down to the present. But his harsh attacks on atheism are commonly overlooked by his religious enemies. In his *Histoire de Jenni* (1775), for example, he referred to atheism as one of the 'two poles of a universe of confusion and horror', the other being fanaticism. Deism is the 'narrow zone of virtue in between those two poles'.[2] Voltaire objected to atheism on grounds of both belief and utility. '[T]here is nothing good in atheism', he wrote to Jean-François Dufour, Seigneur de Villevieille, in 1768 regarding the former:

> It is a very bad system both physically and morally. An upright man may very well rebel against superstition and fanaticism; he may detest superstition; he does mankind a service if he spreads the humane principles of tolerance. But what service can he render if he spreads atheism? Will men be any more virtuous for not recognising a God who prescribes virtue? Doubtless not.[3]

Voltaire feared that atheism would probably lead to immorality among the uneducated masses. So great was this concern that he quipped that 'If God did not exist, it would be necessary to invent him'.[4] In *The A B C* (1768), he wrote: 'I want my attorney, my tailor, my servants, even my wife, to believe in God, and I fancy that as a result I shall suffer less theft and less cuckoldry.'[5] This utilitarian belief in the belief in God – that 'religion, even a false one, is the best warrant men can have of the integrity of men', as Montesquieu put it – was common among the pragmatic mainstream of the Enlightenment. Even the sceptical d'Alembert thought that 'nothing is more necessary than a revealed religion, which may instruct us concerning so many diverse objects'.[6]

Although Voltaire was far from alone among the *philosophes* in his belief that popular scepticism about the existence of God would be morally disastrous, this view did not command universal support, even among fellow deists. Many agreed with Pierre Bayle's argument in *Various Thoughts on the Occasion of a Comet* (1682) that religious beliefs are irrelevant to human behaviour because our actions are entirely determined by our passions and temperaments, not our beliefs. Montesquieu and Voltaire vigorously denied this, as did atheists like Diderot, who argued from the opposite end of the spectrum of belief that religion in general, and not just Christianity, is very destructive – 'a buttress which always ends up bringing the house down'.[7] Yet the conservative views of Voltaire, Montesquieu and d'Alembert on the moral necessity of religion found wide acceptance among the *philosophes*, as it did among the *dévots* who usually opposed them, and may fairly be described as the dominant view on both sides. If the Enlightenment is vulnerable here, it is not for disregarding the importance of religion for moral, social and political order, as many of its religious opponents unfairly charged, but for overstating its importance. Most of the *philosophes* and *Aufklärer* erred on the side of excessive conservatism in their views on religion because they feared that, if God is dead, everything is permitted, a fear rooted in their dim view of the unenlightened masses.

However, even if most of the *philosophes* and *Aufklärer* had been atheists, or if their sceptical approach towards religious beliefs tended to promote atheism, it does not follow that social disorder, widespread immorality and political revolution would have been the likely – let alone necessary – consequences. It is certainly not self-evident that the goods of social harmony, political stability and moral order require a belief in God, which is not to deny that a widespread and precipitate loss of faith may sometimes have destabilising and demoralising effects. Even if God is dead, it is not necessarily the case that everything is permitted. There is no good reason to believe that a society of atheists is per se impossible, as the existence of many stable and (more or less) peaceful secular societies with non-believing or sceptical majorities today proves.[8] It may be the case that belief in God tends to enhance or strengthen these goods, but that does not make it indispensable to them.

A very cautious optimism

Like atheism, it is hard to make the common charge of facile optimism stick to very many of the *philosophes*, whose views on progress covered a broad range, from the resigned scepticism of Voltaire's *Candide* (1759) to the defiant optimism of Condorcet's *Sketch for a Historical Picture of the Progress of the Human Mind* (1795). Neither work is really typical of the period, which could best be described as one of very cautious optimism about the future. Their optimism was rooted in a belief that by the eighteenth century great progress had been made in the arts and sciences in the West, which even Voltaire conceded in his upbeat moods, and that further progress was likely in the future, although it was by no means assured. Their caution sprang from a realistic appreciation of how long, slow and costly that ascent had been and of the many obstacles remain in our path. None believed that progress was inevitable, although most thought that it was likely, even though it would not be easy and could not be taken for granted. Even Condorcet reluctantly accepted that progress is slow and uneven, and admitted that 'thick darkness still covers an immense stretch of the horizon'.[9] But this is the only cloud darkening the otherwise clear sky that illuminates his deliriously optimistic *Sketch*.[10] Aware though he was of the many obstacles that have always stood – and still stand – on the road to progress, Condorcet remained remarkably sanguine about the ability of humans to overcome them eventually. 'Each century will add now enlightenment to that of the century preceding it', he concluded. '[A]nd this progress, which nothing from now on can stop or suspend, will have no other limits than those of the duration of the universe.'[11] Such hyperbole makes an easy target for sceptics who, by the mid-twentieth century, could point to a long succession of tragedies and atrocities since the eighteenth century, from the Reign of Terror to the Holocaust and beyond, that flatly contradict such naïve optimism. But Condorcet's *Sketch* is hardly typical of the Enlightenment view of history. It is likely that most of the *philosophes* would have expressed more dismay than surprise at the dark history of Europe since the deaths of Voltaire and Rousseau in 1778. Most were too well aware of the power of the forces that have always retarded human progress – ignorance, greed, selfishness, superstition – to be too sanguine about the future. It is likely that Condorcet's *Sketch* would have met with much sceptical derision among the *philosophes* had they had a chance to read it.

Enlightenment without revolution

Historians have not stopped debating the causes of the French Revolution since it began. Even though it is still a matter of intense dispute, it is certainly not unreasonable (outside of orthodox Marxist circles) to attribute *some* causal role to Enlightenment ideas in the downfall of the *ancien régime*. It is not self-evidently absurd to claim that the scepticism of the *philosophes* and their incessant and irreverent attacks on traditional institutions and beliefs contributed to a serious 'crisis of legitimacy' in pre-revolutionary France that helped to undermine support for the regime, at least among the educated elites and professional classes. What seems unreasonable, given what we now know about the complex social, economic and political circumstances of France in the second half of the eighteenth century, is the belief that the ideas of the *philosophes* were the *primary* cause, let alone the *only* cause, of the French Revolution, that it was simply 'la faute à Voltaire, la faute à Rousseau'. It is highly unlikely that they had the straightforword causal impact so often attributed to them by many of the Revolution's opponents, who have tended to exaggerate the importance of moral and intellectual factors, and to neglect more concrete material causes such as the *ancien régime*'s increasingly precarious finances, in the second half of the eighteenth century.

It is far from clear that all (or even most) of the *philosophes* would have rallied to the cause of the Revolution had they lived to see it. Although we can only speculate on this, it seems quite likely that it would have split their ranks. We know that some, like Condorcet, supported it, but it is unlikely that many others would have jumped on the revolutionary bandwagon if they had had the chance. With few exceptions the *philosophes* were reformers rather than revolutionaries, possessing a deep, visceral fear of (and in some cases robust contempt for) the masses and a strong commitment to *ordered* liberty. The fact that the French revolutionaries 'pantheonised' Voltaire (in 1791) and Rousseau (in 1794) has served to entrench the belief that they were 'fathers of the French Revolution'. This is a patrimony which both would have probably disowned, since Rousseau admitted to having 'the greatest aversion to revolution' and Voltaire was a proponent of enlightened monarchy. The fact that the French revolutionaries wrapped themselves in the mantle of the Enlightenment to give legitimacy to their cause does not mean that the two were consistent or causally connected.

Reason perverted

Of the many forms of what I have been calling 'the Enlightenment perversion of reason', three stand out as favourite targets of the Enlightenment's enemies. Some, like Rousseau and Maistre, have accused the *philosophes* of greatly exaggerating the power and influence of reason and underestimating the importance of non-rational influences on human behaviour such as conscience, in Rousseau's case, or sin, in Maistre's. Others such as Horkheimer and Adorno have alleged that the Enlightenment had a narrowly instrumental conception of reason incapable of providing insight into objective truths about morality, justice, beauty, or the proper ends of life, and that this conception has become dominant since the Enlightenment, turning the West into an 'iron cage'. Finally, writers such as Hamann and Flax have accused the *philosophes* of propounding a view of reason as 'pure', when in fact it is inextricably mixed with power and interests, as Nietzsche and Foucault correctly understood. In each of these cases the proper role, character and importance of reason have been grossly distorted, usually with disastrous consequences.

The problem here, as virtually everywhere when talking about the Enlightenment in general, is that the views of the *philosophes* covered such a broad range. While Condorcet and Turgot conform quite well to the usual stereotype of the Enlightenment as coldly rationalistic, they were not representative of the mainstream. Nor was David Hume at the other extreme, believing that reason is the slave of the passions and that it is completely powerless to motivate human action. Most of the *philosophes* lay somewhere between these two poles, valuing reason while acknowledging the power of the passions. Although the eighteenth century is often regarded as 'the Age of Reason', it was also an 'Age of the Passions', as Peter Gay and

Lester Crocker have reminded us.[12] Many *philosophes* were acutely aware of both the power of the passions and the limitations of reason. Very few agreed with Descartes that reason is, or ever could be, absolutely sovereign. It was often valued precisely because the passions were seen as so powerful and therefore in need of restraint and guidance by reason, which might 'check, delib'rate and advise' them.[13] Many *philosophes* went further and defended the passions from the proponents of Christian virtue and Cartesian rationalism. Diderot's *Pensées philosophiques* (1746) is full of passionate praise of the passions, just as Helvétius' *De l'esprit* (1758) defends them dispassionately. While Jean d'Alembert's *Preliminary Discourse* to the *Encyclopédie* describes reason as the highest of the three faculties of the human mind, above memory and imagination, he adds that 'men feel before they think' and notes that 'the imagination moves much faster than reason once it has made its first steps'.[14] Kant's *Critique of Pure Reason* (1781) defends reason, but only as a purely procedural faculty that is powerless to lead us to the truths of traditional metaphysics, such as God and the soul.

For many of the Enlightenment's opponents a narrow and minimalistic conception of reason lay at the heart of the problems that have plagued Western modernity since the eighteenth century. According to this view, it is the Enlightenment's *deflation* of reason, not its exaggeration, that is to blame for many of the pathologies of our civilisation, and it has left us bereft of access to objective truths about religion, nature, beauty and justice. We have seen versions of this charge across the entire spectrum of the Enlightenment's enemies. Coleridge's deep dissatisfaction with eighteenth-century epistemology was partly rooted in his belief that its conception of reason cut humans off from apprehension of 'invisible realities' and 'spiritual objects'. However, it was only in the twentieth century that this type of criticism became central to Counter-Enlightenment thought. Many theorists of totalitarianism writing in the shadow of Weber made what they saw as the *philosophes'* anaemic and impoverished understanding of reason the focus of their attacks on the Enlightenment's legacy in the twentieth century. This is most evident in the case of Max Horkheimer, who viewed the eclipse of 'objective reason' by an impotent 'subjective reason' as crucial to the advent of twentieth-century totalitarianism.

Hume's *Treatise of Human Nature* and Kant's *Critique of Pure Reason* offer deflated conceptions of reason of the kind condemned by many such critics of the Enlightenment, but neither is typical of the mainstream of the Enlightenment, which produced relatively little original thought on the question of reason's nature. Most were not philosophers but 'men of letters' whose importance lay more in their popularisation and dissemination of ideas inherited from earlier thinkers than in the depth or profundity of their own theories and conceptions. There were few intellectual giants of the stature of Descartes, Newton and Locke among the *philosophes* in eighteenth-century France, who put their faith in the senses at least as much as in the faculty of reason, without delving very deeply into its nature.

There was a very broad consensus among the *philosophes* in favour of empiricism. John Locke's *Essay Concerning Human Understanding* (1690) was universally admired for its depiction of the mind as a passive *tabula rasa* and its account of sensory experience as the principal source of knowledge. This view emerged in reaction to an overly essentialised conception of human nature found among seventeenth-century rationalists like Descartes, who believed in innate ideas, and orthodox Christians, who believed in the existence of original sin. The *philosophes* wiped the slate of the human mind clean of all such beliefs.

Unfortunately, the *philosophes* wiped out a large part of our humanity at the same time, as many Romantic writers of the late eighteenth and early nineteenth centuries complained. Even before them, Kant had taken a decisive step away from empiricism in his *Critique of Pure Reason* by arguing that it overlooked the indispensable contribution of the mind to knowledge. By the end of the twentieth century, this trend had turned into a full-blown epistemological revolution against empiricism. Evolutionary psychology, cognitive neuroscience and behavioural genetics have all been busily filling up our minds again, so that the twentieth-century mind looks very different from that of the eighteenth century.

For example, recent discoveries in human genetics have revealed the extent to which each of us is the bearer of a natural inheritance that heavily conditions much of our behaviour, personality and even our beliefs. Our brains are hard-wired in ways that strongly influence what we think and how we act.[15] This is confirmed by recent studies of identical twins, which have caused a revolution in our understanding of personality.[16] It has been discovered that genetically identical twins raised apart are much more similar in both physical and personality traits than fraternal twins raised apart, strongly suggesting the existence of innate characteristics.[17] Noam Chomsky's influential arguments for the existence of innate ideas about the grammar of language point in the same anti-empiricist direction, as does Steven Pinker's concept of a natural 'language instinct'.[18] Chomsky's sympathetic references to the seventeenth-century Rationalists (about whom most of the *philosophes* were very critical) reveals just how far modern thought has taken us away from the empiricist assumptions of the eighteenth-century Enlightenment, which have few serious defenders today. This does not mean that environmental factors are irrelevant. Natural instincts are triggered by them, like switches, without which they cannot develop. Thus it is a matter of 'nature *via* nurture' rather than 'nature *or* nurture'.[19] But the best scientific evidence now points overwhelmingly to the existence of natural instincts, an active mind and some innate knowledge.

Truth and tolerance

A great many of the Enlightenment's opponents over the centuries have accused it of intolerance. Most of its early religious critics believed (rightly) that the *philosophes* wanted to crush Christianity – *écrasez l'infâme!* – because they were convinced that such false beliefs damage human well-being and impede the advance of knowledge. Hamann complained bitterly about the intolerant despotism of Frederick II's secular state. In the twentieth century the *philosophes* have often been seen as arrogant, dogmatic and intolerant of diversity and difference. This view lies at the heart of Isaiah Berlin's contrast between liberal pluralism on the one hand, and what he sees as the fanatical monism of the *philosophes* on the other. John Gray's portrait of the Enlightenment, which is derivative of Berlin's, repeats this view, which he shares with many postmodernists. Foucault's portrait of the 'classical age' in the eighteenth century emphasises the ways and extent to which the 'Other' of reason was sequestered and 'disciplined' in the eighteenth century in order to purify and 'normalise' society. Horkheimer and Adorno's account of the alleged totalitarianism of Western enlightenment since antiquity leaves virtually no space within which diversity, difference and individuality can flourish.

It is fair to say that most of the *philosophes* regarded most error as harmful, and had great confidence in the human capacity to acquire knowledge and power when our minds are unfettered by false beliefs. (Their views on the *prospects* for such unfettering were less optimistic.) As Isaiah Berlin has argued, very few of them dissented from the belief that the truth is one and that there is one certain method for discovering it, a method pioneered by Newton and Bacon in the seventeenth century. It was their self-appointed mission to expose and discredit those false beliefs, particularly in matters of faith, that they regarded as inimical to human improvement and happiness. Why should error be tolerated when we know the truth, ignorance of which is a major obstacle to our well-being? This reasoning applied not only to natural science, but to morality, religion and art as well.

Such confidence in the objectivity and universality of truth and humanity's capacity to discern it is much less common in the West today, after so many bloody attempts to 'unbend the crooked timber of humanity' to make it conform to the truth as understood by those with great power and the will to employ it. On the ambitious metaphysical questions about religion, morality, beauty and politics we are more the heirs of Hume and Kant than Condorcet and the Baron d'Holbach. In addition, Western societies are now much more culturally, ethnically and ethically diverse than they were in Voltaire's time. Much modern theorising about politics starts from the 'fact of diversity' and a scepticism about grand metaphysical assumptions that were commonly taken for granted in the eighteenth century. This outlook has been taken furthest by postmodernists, whose extreme scepticism towards universal notions of truth and morality has led them into cognitive and ethical relativism. Liberals and social democrats such as John Rawls and Jürgen Habermas, writing in the tradition of Kant, are 'post-metaphysical', side-stepping many contentious and essentially contestable metaphysical beliefs while stopping (just) short of relativism.[20] While most postmodernists have been happy to bid farewell to the Enlightenment, more moderate writers like Habermas have been anxious to hold on to some of its values and beliefs while jettisoning others. Yet even the latter would agree, I think, that the *philosophes* were dogmatic in some of their assumptions and had a confidence in their knowledge of the truth and how to acquire it that is no longer warranted by philosophy or science. There is, at the very least, a tension between a total commitment to the truth and the eradication of error on the one hand, and an open-minded tolerance of difference on the other, even when you believe that the other is wrong. But this is a tension *within* the Enlightenment itself, which had both tendencies, although the former was dominant. It is a tension between Gotthold Ephraim Lessing and the Baron d'Holbach, for example, between Enlightenment monism and Enlightenment pluralism. While it is not at all far-fetched to say that the Enlightenment was intolerant, even authoritarian at times, it was also tolerant and pluralistic. This is because there was a liberal, sceptical Enlightenment *and* an illiberal, dogmatic Enlightenment.[21] Many of the enemies of 'the Enlightenment' are really only enemies of the latter.

Knowledge and happiness

While virtually all of the *philosophes* expected great things from modern science, and pinned many of their hopes for the future health and happiness of the species on it, none predicted (or could have predicted) the sheer scale and consequences of the advances that science and technology would make in the centuries ahead. Even Condorcet did not foresee the strides in store for science and technology. Had they anticipated the staggering scale and range of these developments, perhaps they would have been more ambivalent about their consequences.

Today we live in an age of 'Big Science' – of particle accelerators, satellites, jet aircraft and nuclear reactors – a far cry from the quaint image of Benjamin Franklin flying a kite with a key attached to it during a storm. The power and scale of science in our times is unlike anything known, or even imagined, in the eighteenth century. It is arguable that there is no greater force in our lives today than science, which is supported by a colossal infrastructure and funded with billions of dollars every year from governments, businesses and universities. It is integrated into the lives of ordinary people to an unprecedented degree, and (in the West at least) faces few of the traditional religious, moral and intellectual obstacles and stigmas that inhibited it in early modernity. The pace of scientific discovery and application is now dizzying, as it daily breaks new ground in fields such as interplanetary exploration, genetic science and nano-technology, to name just three.

In the eighteenth century, the status and power of science, although growing, were very far from secure. As Dorinda Outram writes of the period:

The intellectual status of science was contested, its institutional organisations often weak and certainly thin on the ground, and the nature of its relations with the economy and with government often tenuous. No institution of science was a major employer of labour, and educational structures in most countries paid little attention to disseminating scientific knowledge.[22]

The situation could not be more different today when the position of science is not only secure but dominant, if not hegemonic.

It was much easier to sustain a benign conception of science in the eighteenth century than it is in our age of Big Science. In the eighteenth century, science was seen by an enlightened minority of influential writers, scientists and thinkers as the exemplar of clear, rational thought, grounded in concrete experience and governed by laws, just as they regarded Christianity as the worst kind of superstitious dogmatism with no basis in reason or experience. The *philosophes* believed that the world is governed by natural laws, knowledge of which (gathered by means of the scientific method of disinterested experiment and observation) would enhance human power, which includes the power to ameliorate suffering and hardship. If anti-clericalism and religious scepticism represent the destructive, critical side of the Enlightenment, then science was its positive, constructive side. And if religious superstition and dogma set an unacceptably low standard of belief that left most people prey to manipulation and exploitation, then the modern scientific method set a new, higher standard that promised to empower humans through knowledge.

But power includes the power to destroy as well as to create. The enhancement of our knowledge means the enhancement of our capacity to destroy as well as to build, harm as well as cure. This has been demonstrated time and again in the twentieth century, when we have finally attained the ability efficiently to destroy human life and civilisation many times over. It is simply not the case that knowledge and power *necessarily* lead to a decrease in violence and destruction. If this power is put in the service of a darker conception of human nature than was prevalent in the eighteenth century, then the *philosophes*' faith in science looks increasingly Panglossian to our weary eyes, which have seen too much since 1750 to warrant their faith in the prospect of science to promote human well-being.

Apart from the destructive *application* of knowledge is the question of whether merely *possessing* it is a necessary, let alone a sufficient, condition for happiness. Often it undermines it; knowledge of the truth can be depressing, demoralising and disorienting. In such cases, ignorance really is bliss. 'In much wisdom is much grief,' the Old Testament warns, 'and he that increaseth knowledge increaseth sorrow' (Ecclesiastes 1: 18). This view found an eloquent modern proponent in Michel de Montaigne (1533–1592), who influenced Rousseau's *Discourse on the Sciences and the Arts*, a Jeremiad against the dangers of modern science and a hymn of praise to ignorance.[23]

Many Romantics sympathised with this position, lamenting the loss of enchantment that often follows when we allow our minds 'to indulge in unbounded curiosity', as Chateaubriand put it.[24] The same sentiment lies behind Hardenberg's *Hymns to the Night*.

Between these Enlightenment and Counter-Enlightenment extremes lies a balanced appreciation of the benefits and dangers of knowledge, and its variegated effects on human psychology and morale. Yet even if knowledge makes us unhappy, it does not follow that it should be suppressed and shunned. The question of whether the possession of some knowledge is demoralising and disempowering is distinct from the question of what should be done about it if it is. On this first question, many of the *philosophes* are as vulnerable to the charge of understating the potentially negative effects of knowledge as their enemies are of exaggerating them. However, it would be wrong to assume that it automatically follows that ignorance is preferable to knowledge, even when that knowledge undermines happiness. As Socrates was at pains to demonstrate, it is not necessarily the case that being happily ignorant of the truth is better than being unhappily enlightened about it. However, it is naïve to assume, as most of the *philosophes* did, that no choice needs to be made between knowledge and happiness.

Notes

Preface

1 Isaiah Berlin, 'Joseph de Maistre and the Origins of Fascism', in *The Crooked Timber of Humanity*, ed. H. Hardy (London: John Murray, 1990). A version of this essay was reprinted in the *New York Review of Books* on 27 September 1990, 11 October 1990 and 25 October 1990. It is based on a BBC radio series on 'Freedom and Its Betrayal' first broadcast four decades earlier. The edited radio broadcasts have been published as *Freedom and Its Betrayal: Six Enemies of Human Liberty*, ed. H. Hardy (London: Chatto & Windus, 2002). Another version was published as the introduction to a translation of Maistre's *Considerations on France*, trans. R. A. Lebrun (Cambridge: Cambridge University Press, 1994). See Graeme Garrard, 'Isaiah Berlin's Joseph de Maistre', in *Isaiah Berlin's Counter-Enlightenment*, eds J. Mali and R. Wokler (Philadelphia, PA: American Philosophical Association, 2003).

2 Raymond Tallis, *Enemies of Hope: A Critique of Contemporary Pessimism* (Basingstoke: Macmillan, 1997), p. 411n2.

3 See Darrin McMahon, *Enemies of the Enlightenment: The French Counter-Enlightenment and the Birth of the European Right, 1778–1830* (New York: Oxford University Press, 2001).

4 As Hans Sluga points out, 'neither in *Being and Time* nor in the writings of the decades that follows does [Heidegger] reveal a substantive interest in the Enlightenment or any of its French or British protagonists' ('Heidegger and the Critique of Reason', in *What's Left of Enlightenment: A Postmodern Question*, eds K. M. Baker and P. H. Reill (Stanford, CA: Stanford University Press, 2001), p. 51).

5 John Burrow, *The Crisis of Reason: European Thought 1848–1914* (New Haven, CT: Yale University Press, 2000), p. xiv.

1 Introduction

1 Michel Foucault, 'What is Enlightenment?' in *The Foucault Reader*, ed. P. Rabinow (Harmondsworth: Penguin, 1984), p. 32.

2 The inclusion of separate entries on 'Counter-Enlightenment' in the Blackwell *Companion to the Enlightenment*, the Oxford *Encyclopaedia of the Enlightenment*, the *Histoire de la philosophie* and the *Dictionnaire de philosophie politique* attests to the degree of its scholarly acceptance. See Jean Deprun, 'Les Anti-Lumières', in *Histoire de la philosophie*, vol. 2: *De la Renaissance à la Révolution Kantienne*, ed. Y. Belaval (Paris: Bibliothèque de la Pléiade, 1973), pp. 717–27; Karina Williamson, 'The Counter-Enlightenment', in *The Companion to the Enlightenment*, ed. J. Yolton *et al.* (Oxford: Blackwell, 1991), pp. 108–9; Mark Lilla, 'Anti-Lumières', in *Dictionnaire de philosophie politique* (3rd edn), ed.

P. Raymond and S. Rials (Paris: Quedrige/Presses Universitaires de France, 1996), pp. 16–19; and Sylviane Albertan-Coppola, 'Counter-Enlightenment', trans. C. Porter, in *The Encyclopaedia of the Enlightenment*, vol. 1, ed. A. Kors (Oxford: Oxford University Press, 2003), pp. 307–11.

3 Berlin, 'The Counter-Enlightenment', in *Against the Current*, ed. H. Hardy (New York: Viking, 1980). This essay was first published in the *Dictionary of the History of Ideas*, vol. 2 (New York: Scribner's, 1973), pp. 100–12.

4 William Barrett, 'Art, Aristocracy and Reason', *Partisan Review*, 16/6 (1949), pp. 663–4.

5 Barrett, *Irrational Man* (New York: Doubleday, 1958), p. 244.

6 Friedrich Nietzsche, *Nachgelassene Fragmente* (1877), in *Werke: Kritische Gesamtausgabe*, vol. 2, eds G. Colli and M. Montinari (Berlin: Walter de Gruyter, 1967–), p. 478. Robert Wokler discovered this reference to 'gegin-aufklärung' in Nietzsche ('Isaiah Berlin's Enlightenment and Counter-Enlightenment', in *Isaiah Berlin's Counter-Enlightenment*, eds J. Mali and R. Wokler (Philadelphia, PA: American Philosophical Association, 2003), p. 26n4).

7 Berlin mentions Beck's *Early German Philosophy* in a footnote to the revised edition of his essay on Vico, published in 1976 (*Vico and Herder: Two Studies in the History of Ideas*, ed. H. Hardy (London: Hogarth, 1976)). A version of the essay on Vico was first published in 1960 as 'The Philosophical Ideas of Giambattista Vico', in *Art and Ideas in Eighteenth Century Italy* (Rome: Edizioni di Storia, 1960). The essay on Herder first appeared in a version published as 'Herder and the Enlightenment', in *Aspects of the Eighteenth Century*, ed. E. Wasserman (Baltimore, MD: Johns Hopkins University Press, 1965). The most recent version of these two essays was published in *Three Critics of the Enlightenment: Vico, Hamann, Herder*, ed. H. Hardy (Princeton, NJ: Princeton University Press, 2000).

8 Lewis White Beck, *Early German Philosophy: Kant and His Predecessors* (Cambridge, MA: Belknap Press of Harvard University Press, 1969), p. 362.

9 Berlin, *Against the Current: Essays in the History of Ideas*, ed. H. Hardy (Oxford: Oxford University Press, 1981).

10 Berlin, 'European Unity and its Vicissitudes', in *The Crooked Timber of Humanity*, ed. H. Hardy (London: John Murray, 1990), pp. 196–7.

11 Berlin, *The Magus of the North: J. G. Hamann and the Origins of Modern Irrationalism*, ed. H. Hardy (London: Fontana Press, 1994), p. 1.

12 See Chapter 6 below.

13 Steven Seidman, *Liberalism and the Origins of European Social Theory* (Berkeley: University of California Press, 1983), pp. 52–3.

14 Seidman, *Liberalism and the Origins of European Social Theory*, pp. 43–4.

15 Seidman, *Liberalism and the Origins of European Social Theory*, p. 44.

16 Seidman, *Liberalism and the Origins of European Social Theory*, p. 51.

17 John Gray, *Enlightenment's Wake: Politics and Culture at the Close of the Modern Age* (London and New York: Routledge, 1995), p. 165.

18 Robert Darnton, *The Literary Underground of the Old Regime* (Cambridge, MA: Harvard University Press, 1982), p. 1.

19 See McMahon, *Enemies of the Enlightenment*.

20 Arthur Lovejoy, 'On the Discrimination of Romanticisms', *Proceedings of the Modern Language Association*, 39 (1924), pp. 229–53, reprinted in *Essays in the History of Ideas* (New York: Putnam, 1960).

21 Daniel Conway, *Nietzsche and the Political* (London and New York: Routledge, 1997), pp. 126–7.

22 G. W. F. Hegel, *The Phenomenology of Spirit*, trans. A. V. Miller (Oxford: Clarendon Press, 1977), p. 348.

23 Charles Frankel, *The Faith of Reason* (New York: Octagon Books, 1969), p. 11.

24 George Friedman, *The Political Philosophy of the Frankfurt School* (Ithaca, NY, and London: Cornell University Press, 1981), pp. 134–5.

25 The concept/conception distinction comes from John Rawls, *A Theory of Justice* (Cambridge, MA: Harvard University Press, 1971), p. 5.

26 Hans-Georg Gadamer, *Truth and Method* (2nd edn), trans. Joel Weinsheimer and Donald Marshall (New York: Continuum, 1999), p. 272, and *Gesammelte Werke. Vol. 1: Hermeneutik I: Wahrheit und Methode* (Tubingen: J. C. B. Mohr (Paul Siebeck), 1986), p. 276.

27 Gadamer, 'Science as an Instrument of Enlightenment', in *In Praise of Theory: Speeches and Essays*, trans. C. Dawson (New Haven, CT: Yale University Press, 1998), pp. 71–83. In this essay (first presented at a conference in 1972), Gadamer distinguishes between the 'Greek Enlightenment', the 'eighteenth-century Enlightenment' and the 'twentieth-century Enlightenment'. Max Horkheimer and Theodor Adorno's *Dialectic of Enlightenment* assumes the existence of a Greek enlightenment, which they associate with Homer's Odysseus. Hegel also refers to an enlightenment in ancient Greece (*Hegel's Lectures on the History of Philosophy*, vol. 1, trans. E. S. Haldane and F. H. Simson (London: Routledge & Kegan Paul, 1892; New York: Humanities Press, 1974), p. 366).

28 William Mahony, *The Encyclopedia of Religion*, vol. 5, ed. M. Eliade (New York: Macmillan, 1987), p. 107.

29 John Lough, 'Reflections on Enlightenment and Lumières', *British Journal for Eighteenth Century Studies*, 8/1 (1985), pp. 1–15.

30 John Sibree, the translator of an English translation of Hegel's *Philosophy of History* (first edition published in 1837, and based on notes of lectures Hegel presented in the winter of 1830–1831), wrote at the time: 'There is no current term in English denoting that great intellectual movement which dates from the first quarter of the eighteenth century, and which, if not the chief cause, was certainly the guiding genius of the French Revolution. The word "Illuminati" (signifying the members of an imaginary confederacy for propagating the open secret of the day), might suggest "Illumination", as an equivalent for the German "Aufklärung"; but the French "Eclaircissement" conveys a more specific idea' (*The Philosophy of History*, trans. J. Sibree (New York: Dover Publications, 1956), p. 438).

31 Alfred Cobban, *Edmund Burke and the Revolt Against the Eighteenth Century* (London: George Allen & Unwin, 1960 [1929]).

32 Carl Becker, *The Heavenly City of the Eighteenth Century Philosophers* (New Haven, CT, and London: Yale University Press, 1932); Ernst Cassirer, *The Philosophy of the Enlightenment*, trans. F. C. A. Koelln and J. P. Pettegrove (Princeton, NJ: Princeton University Press, 1951). The first use of the term 'the Enlightenment' in English appears to have been in James Tufts' 1894 translation of Wilhelm Windelband's *Geschichte der Philosophie* (1892). See James Schmidt, 'Inventing the Enlightenment: Anti-Jacobins, British Hegelians and the Oxford English Dictionary', *Journal of the History of Ideas*, 64/3 (2003), pp. 421–43.

33 The literature on this subject is now vast, even oceanic. Particularly noteworthy is *The Enlightenment in National Context*, eds. R. Porter and M. Teich (Cambridge: Cambridge University Press, 1981). See also Carmen Blacker, *The Japanese Enlightenment: A Study of the Writings of Fukuzawa* (Cambridge: Cambridge University Press, 1964); *Latin America and the Enlightenment*, ed. A. Whitaker (Ithaca, NY: Great Seal Books, 1961); Henry Farnham May, *The Enlightenment in America* (New York: Oxford University Press, 1976); Robert Ferguson, *The American Enlightenment: 1750–1820* (Cambridge, MA: Harvard University Press, 1997); Franco Venturi, *Italy and the Enlightenment*, trans. S. Corsi (New York: New York University Press, 1972); Peter Hanns Reill, *The German Enlightenment and the Rise of Historicism* (Berkeley, Los Angeles, London:

University of California Press, 1975); *The Scottish Enlightenment, 1730–1790*, ed.
D. Daiches (Edinburgh: Saltire Society, 1996); David Elder, *Scottish Enlighten-
ment and Other Essays* (Edinburgh: Polygon, 1991); Ronald Hamowy, *The Scottish
Enlightenment and the Theory of Spontaneous Order* (Carbondale: Southern Illinois
University Press, 1987).

34 For a good overview of this literature, see Chapter 2 of Dorinda Outram's *The
Enlightenment* (Cambridge: Cambridge University Press, 1995). Particularly
worthy of note here are the following works by Robert Darnton: 'In Search of
Enlightenment: Recent Attempts to Create a Social History of Ideas', *Journal of
Modern History*, 43 (1971), pp. 113–32; 'The High Enlightenment and the Low-
Life of Literature in Pre-Revolutionary France', *Past and Present*, 51 (1971), pp.
81–115; *The Business of Enlightenment* (Cambridge, MA: Harvard University
Press, 1979); *The Literary Underground of the Old Regime* (Cambridge, MA:
Harvard University Press, 1982); and *The Great Cat Massacre and Other Episodes
in French Cultural History* (New York: Basic Books, 1984). Also noteworthy are
Roger Chartier's *Cultural History: Between Practices and Representations*, trans. L.
Cochrane (Cambridge: Polity Press, 1988) and *The Cultural Origins of the French
Revolution*, trans. L. G. Cochrane (Durham, NC: Duke University Press, 1991),
as well as Robert Muchembled, *Culture populaire et culture des élites dans la France
moderne* (Paris: Flammarion, 1978); and David Roche, *Le Siècle des lumières en
province: Academies et academiciens provinciaux 1680–1789*, 2 vols (The Hague:
Mouton, 1978).

35 See J. G. A. Pocock, 'The Tell-Tale Article: Reconstructing (. . .) Enlightenment', Plenary Address to the 29th annual meeting of the American Society for
Eighteenth-Century Studies, University of Notre Dame, 2 April 1998.

36 Sankar Muthu, 'Enlightenment Anti-Imperialism', *Social Research*, 66/4 (1999),
p. 999.

37 H. L. A. Hart, *The Concept of Law* (2nd edn) (Oxford: Clarendon Press, 1994),
p. 128.

38 In defence of the existence of an Enlightenment project, see Robert Wokler,
'The Enlightenment Project and Its Critics', *Poznan Studies in the Philosophy of the
Sciences and the Humanities*, 58 (1997), pp. 13–30; Wokler, 'The Enlightenment
Project as Betrayed by Modernity', *History of European Ideas*, 24 (1998), pp.
301–13, and John Robertson, 'The Case for the Enlightenment: A Comparative
Approach', in *Isaiah Berlin's Counter-Enlightenment*, eds J. Mali and R. Wokler
(Philadelphia, PA: American Philosophical Association, 2003).

39 Augustin Barruel, *Memoirs Illustrating the History of Jacobinism*, vol. 1, trans. R.
Clifford (London: T. Burton, 1798), ch. 19, p. 399.

40 Barruel, *Memoirs Illustrating the History of Jacobinism*, vol. 4, p. 561. Barruel once
wrote about the *philosophes* as follows: 'Writers of this species, so far from
enlightening the people, only contribute to lead them into the path of error'
(*Memoirs*, vol. 4, Conclusion, p. 569).

41 Jürgen Habermas, *The Philosophical Discourse of Modernity*, trans. F. Lawrence
(Cambridge, MA: MIT Press, 1987), p. 87.

42 Isaiah Berlin, 'Reply to Hans Aarsleff', in *London Review of Books*, 20/3 (5–18
November 1981), pp. 7–8.

43 Mark Hulliung puts Rousseau in this camp of 'friendly critics' of the Enlighten-
ment, an interpretation I obviously do not endorse. See his *The Autocritique of
Enlightenment: Rousseau and the Philosophes* (Cambridge, MA: Harvard University
Press, 1994).

44 See Lovejoy, 'On the Discrimination of Romanticisms'.

45 Although the expression 'Counter-*the* Enlightenment' would be the most logical
formulation of the outlook that I am addressing, I have chosen not to use it
owing to its stylistic clumsiness and its potential to create confusion.

46 Coleridge, *The Courier*, 21 October 1814, in *Collected Works of Samuel Taylor Coleridge*, vol. 3: *Essays on His Times*, vol. 2, ed. D. Erdman (London: Routledge & Kegan Paul, 1978, and Princeton, NJ: Princeton University Press, 1978), p. 388. Hereafter referred to as *CWSTC*.

47 George Crowder, *Isaiah Berlin: Liberty and Pluralism* (Cambridge: Polity Press, 2004), pp. 68–71. James Schmidt very cleverly calls this 'the perversity thesis' of the Enlightenment, an idea first set out by Albert Hirshman in *The Rhetoric of Reaction: Perversity, Futility, Jeopardy* (Cambridge, MA: Belknap Press, 1991), which Schmidt has applied to the enemies of the Enlightenment. See Schmidt, 'What Enlightenment Project?', *Political Theory*, 28/6 (2000), pp. 734–57.

48 Michel Foucault, 'Conversazione con Michel Foucault', *Il Contributo* (1980), pp. 23–84, in *Power*, vol. 3 of *The Essential Works of Foucault, 1954–1984*, ed. J. Faubion, trans. R. Hurley *et al.* (London: Allen Lane, 2001), pp. 273–4.

2 First shots

1 Hamann to Christian Jacob Kraus, 18 December 1784, in *What is Enlightenment?*, ed. J. Schmidt (Berkeley and London: University of California Press, 1996), p. 147.

2 Berlin, *The Magus of the North: J. G. Hamann and the Origins of Modern Irrationalism*, ed. H. Hardy (London: Fontana, 1993), p. 7.

3 Jean-Jacques Rousseau, *Confessions*, in *Collected Writings of Rousseau*, vol. 5, eds C. Kelly, R. D. Masters and P. Stillman, trans. C. Kelly (Hanover and London: University Press of New England, 1995), p. 294. Hereafter referred to as *CWR*. Diderot wrote of this encounter with Rousseau as follows: 'The Academy of Dijon proposed as the subject for its prize, Whether the arts and sciences are more harmful than useful to society. I was then in the chateau of Vincennes. Rousseau came to see me and used the opportunity to consult with me about which side of the question he would take. "Don't hesitate", I said to him. "You'll take the side no one will take". "You're right", he responded; and he went to work accordingly' (*Réfutation suivie de l'ouvrage d'Helvétius intitulé l'Homme*, in *Oeuvres complètes*, ed. R. Lewinter, vol. 2 (Paris: Le Club français du livre, 1969–1973), p. 475).

4 Rousseau, *Discourse on the Sciences and the Arts*, in *CWR*, vol. 2, trans and ed. C. Kelly and R. D. Masters (Hanover and London: University Press of New England, 1992), p. 7 (*Œuvres complètes de Jean-Jacques Rousseau*, eds B. Gagnebin and M. Raymond, vol. 3 (Paris: Plèiade, 1959–1995), p. 9). Hereafter referred to as *OC*.

5 Jean-Jacques Rousseau, *Discourse on the Origin and Foundations of Inequality*, in *CWR*, vol. 3, trans. J. Bush, C. Kelly and R. D. Masters (Hanover and London: University Press of New England, 1992), p. 48 (*OC*, III, p. 170).

6 See Frederick Beiser, *The Fate of Reason: German Philosophy From Kant to Fichte* (Cambridge, MA: Harvard University Press, 1987), p. 20.

7 J. G. Hamann, *Gedanken über meinen Lebenslauf*, in *Johann Georg Hamann: Sämtliche Werke*, vol. 2, ed. Josef Nadler (Vienna: Verlag Herder, 1949–1957), p. 40.

8 Frederick Beiser writes that 'It was from these two experiences – appropriately, two flashes of insight and inspiration – that the *Sturm und Drang* was born' (*The Fate of Reason*, p. 19).

9 Berlin, *The Magus of the North*, pp. xv, 1.

10 Berlin, *The Magus of the North*, pp. 22–3.

11 See Graeme Garrard, *Rousseau's Counter-Enlightenment: A Republican Critique of the* Philosophes (Albany, NY: State University of New York Press, 2003).

12 Beiser, *The Fate of Reason*, p. 17. On Hamann's relationship to the *Aufklärung*,

see Rudolf Unger, *Hamann und die Aufklärung: Studien zur Vorgeschichte de romantischen Geistes im 18 Jahrhundert*, 2 vols (Halle: Niemeyer, 1925 [1911]).

13 Rousseau, *Julie, or the New Héloïse*, in *CWR*, vol. 6, eds R. D. Masters and C. Kelly, trans. P. Stewart and J. Vaché (Hanover and London: University Press of New England, 1997), p. 222 (*OC*, II, p. 270).

14 Rousseau, *Letter to d'Alembert on the Theatre*, in *Politics and the Arts*, trans. A. Bloom (Glencoe, IL: The Free Press, 1960), pp. 58–9 (*OC*, V, p. 54).

15 Rousseau, *Preface to Narcissus*, in *CWR*, vol. 2, p. 188 (*OC*, II, p. 962).

16 Voltaire to d'Alembert, 19 March 1761, in *The Complete Works of Voltaire*, vol. 107, D9682, ed. T. Besterman (Banbury, Oxon: Voltaire Foundation, 1968–), p. 107. Hereafter referred to as *CWV*.

17 Voltaire to E. N. Damilaville, 16 August 1765 (*CWV*, vol. 113, D12938, p. 346).

18 Voltaire to Thieriot, 17 September 1758 (*CWV*, vol. 103, D7864, p. 160).

19 Voltaire to Mme d'Epinay, 14 July 1760 (*CWV*, vol. 105, D9064, p. 467). In a letter written a decade later, Voltaire refers to Rousseau as 'a dangerous madman' (4 August 1770 (*CWV*, vol. 120, D16562, pp. 366–7)).

20 Voltaire to Théodore Tronchin, 30 June 1764, *CWV*, vol. III, p. 458.

21 Jean d'Alembert, quoted in R. Grimsley, *Jean D'Alembert 1717–83* (Oxford: Clarendon Press, 1963), p. 146. Unfortunately, Grimsley does not provide a reference for this quotation, which I have not been able to confirm.

22 Hume to Turgot, 22 May 1767, in *Correspondence complètes de Jean-Jacques Rousseau*, vol. 33, letter 5870, ed. R. A. Leigh (Geneva, and Banbury, Oxon: Voltaire Foundation, 1965–). Hereafter referred to as *CC*.

23 Peter Gay, *The Enlightenment: An Interpretation*, vol. 1: *The Rise of Modern Paganism* (New York and London: W. W. Norton, 1966), p. 25.

24 Rousseau, *Discourse on Inequality*, pp. 33–4 (*OC*, III, p. 151).

25 Rousseau, *Emile*, trans. A. Bloom (New York: Basic Books, 1979), p. 278 (*OC*, IV, p. 583).

26 Marie-Jean-Antoine-Nicolas de Caritat, Marquis de Condorcet, *Sketch for a Historical Picture of the Progress of the Human Mind*, trans. J. Barraclough (London: Weidenfeld & Nicolson, 1955), p. 164.

27 Darnton, *The Business of Enlightenment*, p. 522.

28 A conservative estimate of the number of copies of the *Encyclopédie* in circulation between 1751 and 1789 has been put at 15,000 to 20,000 (John Lough, 'The Contemporary Influence of the *Encyclopédie*', *Studies on Voltaire and the Eighteenth Century*, 26 (1963), pp. 1071–83).

29 Omer Joly de Fleury, quoted in Arthur Wilson, *Diderot: The Testing Years 1713–1759* (New York: Oxford University Press, 1957), p. 333.

30 Rousseau, *Discourrse on the Sciences and the Arts*, p. 12 (*OC*, III, p. 17).

31 Rousseau, *Preface to Narcissus*, p. 192 (*OC*, II, p. 967).

32 Rousseau, *Final Reply*, in *Discouse on the Sciences and the Arts*, p. 111 (*OC*, III, p. 73).

33 Rousseau, *Discourse on the Sciences and the Arts*, p. 46 (*OC*, III, p. 46).

34 Rousseau, *Rousseau, Judge of Jean-Jacques*, in *CWR*, vol. 1, trans. J. Bush, C. Kelly and R. D. Masters, ed. R. D. Masters and C. Kelly (Hanover and London: University Press of New England, 1990), p. 179 (*OC*, I, p. 890).

35 Rousseau, *Emile*, p. 312 (*OC*, IV, p. 633).

36 Rousseau, *Emile*, p. 167 (*OC*, IV, p. 428).

37 Rousseau, *Observations by Jean-Jacques Rousseau of Geneva on the Reply Made to his Discourse*, in *Discourse on the Sciences and the Arts*, pp. 51–2 (*OC*, III, p. 54).

38 Rousseau, *Final Reply*, in *Discourse on the Sciences and the Arts,* p. 113 (*OC*, III, p. 76).

39 Rousseau, *Discourse on the Sciences and the Arts*, p. 5 (*OC*, III, p. 7).

40 Rousseau, *Political Fragments*, in *CWR*, vol. 4, trans. J. Bush, C. Kelly and R. D. Masters, ed. R. D. Masters and C. Kelly (Hanover and London: University Press of New England, 1994), pp. 72–3 (*OC*, III, p. 557).
41 Rousseau, *Discourse on the Sciences and the Arts*, p. 14 (*OC*, III, p. 19).
42 Rousseau, *Political Fragments*, p. 70 (*OC*, III, pp. 552–3).
43 Rousseau to Jacob Vernes, 18 February 1758, letter 616 (*CC*, V. pp. 32–3). In *Reveries of a Solitary Walker*, written at the end of his life, Rousseau claims that, with regard to ethical questions, 'I have always found it best to be guided by the voice of conscience rather than the light of reason' (*Reveries of a Solitary Walker*, trans. P. France (Harmondsworth: Penguin, 1979), p. 68 (*OC*, I, p. 1028)).
44 Rousseau, *Discourse on Inequality*, p. 37 (*OC*, III, pp. 155–6).
45 Rousseau, *Discourse on the Sciences and the Arts*, p. 9 (*OC*, III, p. 12).
46 Rousseau, *Discourse on the Sciences and the Arts*, p. 8 (*OC*, III, p. 11).
47 This is consistent with the view that Rousseau eventually abandoned what little hope he had of such a regime under modern conditions. In his *Preface to Narcissus*, he states that 'a vicious people never returns to virtue' (p. 196 (*OC*, II, pp. 971–2)). In his *Final Reply*, he writes that 'learned and Philosophical Peoples finally come to ridicule and scorn it [virtue]. It is when a nation has once reached this point that corruption can be said to be at its peak and there is no hope for remedies' (p. 76 (*OC*, III, p. 76)). Given that Rousseau thought that the enlightened civilisation of Europe was irredemably corrupt (except for Corsica, Poland and, possibly, Geneva), he must have ended in resignation. The chronology of his works supports this interpretation. His political essays were written between 1758 and 1771. His last work, the unfinished *Reveries of a Solitary Walker*, was written between 1776 and 1778, and suggests that he may have come to the final conclusion that modern civilisation is incorrigibly corrupt, in which case escape from society into rustic isolation was the only option.
48 Rousseau, *Emile*, p. 40 (*OC*, IV, p. 249).
49 Rousseau, *Emile*, p. 252 (*OC*, IV, p. 547).
50 Rousseau, *Discourse on Political Economy*, in *CWR*, vol. 3, p. 151 (*OC*, III, pp. 254–5).
51 Rousseau, *Discourse on Political Economy*, p. 151 (*OC*, III, p. 255).
52 Rousseau, *The Government of Poland*, trans. W. Kendall (Indianapolis and New York: Bobbs-Merrill, 1972), p. 8. (*OC*, III, p. 958).
53 Rousseau, *The Government of Poland*, p. 87 (*OC*, III, p. 1019).
54 Rousseau, *The Government of Poland*, p. 19 (*OC*, III, p. 966).
55 Voltaire, *Epître à l'auteur du livre des trois imposteurs*, in *Oeuvres complètes de Voltaire*, vol. 10 (Paris: Garnier, 1877), pp. 402–3. For Voltaire's own comment on this statement, see Voltaire to Frederick-William, Crown Prince of Prussia, 28 November 1770 (*CWV*, 121, D16792, p. 104).
56 Charles Louis de Secondat, baron de Montesquieu, *The Spirit of the Laws*, trans. A.C. Cohler, B. C. Miller and H. S. Stone (Cambridge: Cambridge University Press, 1989), p. 465. See also pp. 460–1 and pp. 463–4.
57 Rousseau, *The Social Contract*, in *CWR*, vol. 4, trans. J. Bush, C. Kelly and R. D. Masters (Hanover, NH, and London: University Press of New England, 1994), pp. 219–20 (*OC*, III, pp. 464–5).
58 George Havens, *Voltaire's Marginalia on the Pages of Rousseau: A Comparative Study of Ideas* (Columbus: Ohio State University Press, 1933), p. 68.
59 Diderot to Sophie Volland, 18 July 1762, *Correspondance de Denis Diderot*, vol. 4, ed. G. Roth (Paris: Les Editions de Minuit, 1958), p. 55.
60 Voltaire to Thieriot, 17 September 1758 (*CWV*, 103, D7864, p. 160).
61 Rousseau, *Confessions*, p. 329 (*OC*, I, p. 392).
62 Rousseau, *Geneva MS of The Social Contract*, p. 117 (*OC*, III, p. 336).

63 Rousseau, *Discourse on Inequality*, pp. 60–1 (*OC*, III, p. 186). Italics added.
64 Klaus Epstein, *The Genesis of German Conservatism* (Princeton, NJ: Princeton University Press, 1966), p. 38.
65 Berlin, *The Roots of Romanticism*, ed. H. Hardy (London: Chatto & Windus, 1999), p. 36.
66 Hamann, *Gedanken über meinen Lebenslauf*, in *Johann Georg Haman: Sämtliche Werke*, vol. 2, p. 41.
67 Beiser, *The Fate of Reason*, p. 19. Beiser describes Hamann as 'the father of the *Sturm und Drang*' (p. 16, and says that he 'gave a mighty stimulus to the currents of irrationalism that were present in the Sturm und Drang and Romanticism' p. 17). This is notwithstanding the fact that Hamann actually referred to the movement he is alleged to have fathered as 'the ridiculous "Storm and Stress"' (Hamann to Jacobi, 18 February 1786, *Hamann's Briefwechsel mit Friedrich Heinrich Jacobi*, vol. 5 of *Johann Georg Hamann's, des Magus in Norden, Leben und Schriften*, ed. C. H. Gildemeister (Gotha: Perthes, 1868), p. 227).
68 Hamann to Jacobi, 18 January 1786, *Hamann's Briefwechsel mit Friedrich Heinrich Jacobi*, p. 199.
69 Hamann to Jacobi, 15 January 1786, *Hamann's Briefwechsel mit Friedrich Heinrich Jacobi*, p. 195.
70 Hamann, *Glose Philippique*, in *Johann Georg Hamann: Sämtliche Werke*, vol. 2, p. 297.
71 Hamann, *Glose Philippique*, in *Johann Georg Hamann: Sämtliche Werke*, vol. 2, p. 293.
72 Hamann to C. J. Kraus, 18 December 1784, in Schmidt, *What is Enlightenment?*, p. 147.
73 Hamann, *Aesthetica in Nuce*, in *Johann Georg Hamann: Sämtliche Werke*, vol. 2, p. 208.
74 Hamann, *Golgatha und Schlebimini!*, in *Johann Georg Hamann: Sämtliche Werke*, vol. 3, pp. 299–300.
75 Hamann, *Glose Philippique*, in *Johann Georg Hamann: Sämtliche Werke*, vol. 2, p. 295.
76 Hamann, *Hierophantische Briefe*, in *Johann Georg Hamann: Sämtliche Werke*, vol. 3, p. 159.
77 Hamann, *Glose Philippique*, in *Johann Georg Hamann: Sämtliche Werke*, vol. 2, p. 294.
78 Hamann, *Biblische Betrachtungen*, in *Johann Georg Hamann: Sämtliche Werke*, vol. 1, p. 22.
79 Hamann, *Golgatha und Schlebimini!*, in *Johann Georg Hamann: Sämtliche Werke*, vol. 3, p. 296.
80 Hamann, *Gedanken über meinen Lebenslauf*, in *Johann Georg Hamann: Sämtliche Werke*, vol. 2, p. 52.
81 Hamann, *Sokratische Denkwürdigkeiten*, in *Johann Georg Hamann: Sämtliche Werke*, vol. 2, p. 62.
82 Hamann to Jacobi, 23 April 1787, *Hamann's Briefwechsel mit Friedrich Heinrich Jacobi*, p. 497.
83 Hamann to Jacobi, 14–15 November 1784, *Hamann's Briefwechsel mit Friedrich Heinrich Jacobi*, vol. 5, pp. 13–19.
84 Hamann, *Hierophantische Briefe*, in *Johann Georg Hamann: Sämtliche Werke*, vol. 3, p. 165.
85 Hamann, *Hierophantische Briefe*, in *Johann Georg Hamann: Sämtliche Werke*, vol. 3, p. 164.
86 Hamann to Jacobi, 18 February 1786, in *Hamann's Briefwechsel mit Friedrich Heinrich Jacobi*, p. 228.

87 Hamann, *Golgatha und Schlebimini!*, in *Johann Georg Hamann: Sämtliche Werke*, vol. 3, p. 317.
88 Hamann, *Königsberg Selehrte und Politische Beitungen*, 13 February 1764, in *Johann Georg Hamann: Sämtliche Werke*, vol. 4, pp. 271–2.
89 Hamann, *Socratic Memorabilia*, in *Johann Georg Hamann: Sämtliche Werke*, vol. 2, p. 77.
90 Hamann, *Socratic Memorabilia*, in *Johann Georg Hamann: Sämtliche Werke*, vol. 2, p. 78.
91 Hamann to Lindner, 3 July 1759 in *Briefwechsel*, vol. 2, eds W. Ziesemer and A. Henkel (Wiesbaden: Insel-Verlag, 1955–79), p. 355.
92 Hamann, *Wolken*, in *Johann Georg Hamann: Sämtliche Werke*, vol. 2, p. 98.
93 Hamann to Herder, October 1784, *Briefwechsel*, vol. 5, p. 108.
94 Hamann to J. F. Hartknoch, 25 September 1786, in *Briefwechsel*, vol. 7.
95 Hamann to Jacobi, 29 April 1787, *Hamann's Briefwechsel mit Friedrich Heinrich Jacobi*, p. 513.
96 Hamann, *Konxompax*, in *Johann Georg Hamann: Sämtliche Werke*, vol. 3, p. 218.
97 Hamann, *Neue Apologie des Buchstaben h*, *Johann Georg Hamann: Sämtliche Werke*, vol. 3, pp. 105–6.
98 Hamann, *Konxompax*, in *Johann Georg Hamann: Sämtliche Werke*, vol. 3, p. 225.
99 David Hume, *A Treatise of Human Nature*, ed. E. Mossner (Harmondsworth: Penguin, 1969), p. 462. Hamann claimed that he was 'full of Hume' in 1784 (Hamann to Jacobi, 5 December 1784, (*Hamann's Briefwechsel mit Friedrich Heinrich Jacobi*, p. 27) and 'steeped in Hume when I wrote the *Socratic Memoribilia*' (Hamann to Jacobi, 27 April 1787 (*Hamann's Briefwechsel mit Friedrich Heinrich Jacobi*, vol. 5, p. 506).
100 Hamann to H. J. von Auerswald, 28 July 1785, in *Briefwechsel*, vol. 6, p. 27.
101 Hamann, *Metakritik über den Purismum der Vernunft*, in *Johann Georg Hamann: Sämtliche Werke*, vol. 3, p. 284.
102 Hamann, *Zweifel und Einfalle uber eine vermischte Nachricht der allgemeinen deutschen Bibliothek*, in *Johann Georg Hamann: Sämtliche Werke*, vol. 3, p. 191.
103 Hamann, *Sokratische Denkwürdigkeiten*, in *Johann Georg Hamann: Sämtliche Werke*, vol. 2, p. 74.
104 Hamann, to Johann Gottfried Herder, 10 May 1781, in *Johann Georg Hamann. Briefwechsel*, vol. 4, p. 294.
105 Hamann, *Golgatha und Schlebimini!*, in *Johann Georg Hamann: Sämtliche Werke*, vol. 3, p. 301.
106 See Chapter 4 below.
107 Hamann, *Neue Apologie des Buchstaben h*, in *Johann Georg Hamann: Sämtliche Werke*, vol. 3, p. 105.
108 Hamann, *Neue Apologie des Buchstaben h*, in *Johann Georg Hamann: Sämtliche Werke*, vol. 3, p. 94.
109 Hamann, *Kreuzzüge des Philologen, Johann Georg Hamann: Sämtliche Werke*, vol. 2, p. 136.
110 Hamann, *Neue Apologie des Buchstaben h*, in *Johann Georg Hamann: Sämtliche Werke*, vol. 3, p. 107.
111 Hamann, *Neue Apologie des Buchstaben h*, in *Johann Georg Hamann: Sämtliche Werke*, vol. 3, p. 100.
112 Hamann, *Metakritik über den Purismum der Vernunft*, in *Johann Georg Hamann: Sämtliche Werke*, vol. 3, p. 286. See Rousseau's *Essay on the Origin of Languages*, in *CWR*, vol. 7, trans. J. T. Scott (Hanover, NH, and London: University Press of New England, 1998) (*OC*, V, pp. 371–429).
113 Hamann, *Aesthetica in Nuce*, in *Johann Georg Hamann: Sämtliche Werke*, vol. 2, p. 197.
114 Berlin, *The Magus of the North*, p. 40.

115 Hamann, *Aesthetica in Nuce*, in *Johann Georg Hamann: Sämtliche Werke*, vol. 2, p. 213.
116 Ronald Gregor Smith, *J. G. Hamann 1730–1788: A Study in Christian Experience* (New York: Harper and Brothers, 1960), p. 22.
117 Hamann, *Sprüche Galomonis*, in *Johann Georg Hamann: Sämtliche Werke*, vol. 1, p. 165.
118 Hamann, *Kreuzzüge des Philologen, Johann Georg Hamann: Sämtliche Werke*, vol. 2, p. 150.
119 Hamann to J. G. Lindner, 12 October 1759, in *Briefwechsel*, vol. 1.
120 Hegel, *Sämtliche Werke*, vol. 11 ed. J. Hoffmeister (Hamburg: Frommanns, 1956), p. 226. '[Hamann] fights against the precepts of the Enlightenment [*die Aufklärung, welche Hamann dekämft*]. This movement, which strives to assert the freedom of thought in all intellectual matters, together with the advance made by Kant to enforce the freedom of thought – despite his achievement remaining merely formal – is completely overlooked by Hamann ... he rants and raves indiscriminately *against thinking and reason in general*' (G. W. F. Hegel, 'Hamann Schriften' [1828], in *Berliner Schriften 1818–1831*, vol. 11, eds E. Moldenhauer and K. M. Michel (Frankfurt am Main: Suhrkamp, 1986), p. 331).
121 Hamann to Jacobi, 18 February 1786, *Hamann's Briefwechsel mit Friedrich Heinrich Jacobi*, vol. 6, p. 276.
122 Hamann to Scheffner, 11 February 1785, *Briefwechsel*, vol. 5, p. 359.
123 Hamann, *Beurteilung der Kreuzzüge des Philologen*, in *Johann Georg Hamann: Sämtliche Werke*, vol. 2, p. 272.
124 Hamann, *Sokratische Denkwürdigkeiten*, in *Johann Georg Hamann. Sämtliche Werke*, vol. 2, p. 61.

3 Counter-Enlightenment and Counter-Revolution

1 Barruel, *Memoirs*, vol. 3, ch. 14, p. 304.
2 The French revolutionary government decreed that a statue of Rousseau be erected in the National Assembly with the inscription 'La Nation Française Libre à J.-J. Rousseau'. At the Festival of Triumph on 14 July 1790, a bust of Rousseau, carved from Bastille stone and crowned with laurels, was borne through the streets of Paris, attended by 600 white-gowned girls and troops of Guardsmen, their firearms wreathed with flowers. The revolutionary cult of Rousseau peaked in 1794, when his remains were ceremoniously transferred to the Panthéon in Paris and laid to rest next to the other great 'heroes of the French Revolution' such as Voltaire, despite the fact that they detested each other. (See Carole Blum in *Rousseau and the Republic of Virtue* (Ithaca, NY, and London: Cornell University Press, 1986), p. 280.) On the 'pantheonisation' of Voltaire in July 1791, see James Leith, 'Les trois apothèoses de Voltaire', *Annales historiques de la Révolution française*, 236 (1979), pp. 161–209.
3 Thomas Saine, *Black Bread–White Bread: German Intellectuals and the French Revolution* (Columbia, SC: Camden House, 1988), p. 282.
4 Rousseau, *Rousseau, Judge of Jean-Jacques*, p. 213 (*OC*, I, p. 935). As one study of his influence notes, 'Jean-Jacques Rousseau as prophet and founder of the French Revolution was thus a creation of the Revolution itself' (G. H. McNeil, 'The Anti-Revolutionary Rousseau', *American Historical Review*, 58 (1953), p. 808). Some conservatives even tried to appropriate Rousseau's name when attacking the Revolution, most notably the comte d'Antraigues (1753–1812). See Paul Beik, 'The comte d'Antraigues and the Failure of French Conservatism in 1789', *American Historical Review*, 56 (1951), pp. 767–87; Joan

McDonald, *Rousseau and the French Revolution 1762–1791* (London: Athlone, 1965); Alfred Cobban, *Rousseau and the Modern State* (London: George Allen & Unwin, 1965), pp. 171–7; and Roger Barny, *Le Comte d'Antraigues: Un Disciple aristocrate de J.-J. Rousseau*, in *Studies on Voltaire and the Eighteenth Century*, 281 (1991).

5 Burke's *Reflections* went through eleven editions within a year of its publication in Britain, and soon sold over 30,000 copies. A French translation appeared within a month of the original English edition, selling 10,000 copies in Paris and 6000 in Lyon and Strasbourg by February 1791. In Germany the influence of Burke's *Reflections* was both immediate and significant. (See Jacques Godechot, *The Counter-Revolution: Doctrine and Action 1789–1804*, trans. S. Attanasio (London: Routledge & Kegan Paul, 1972), pp. 63–6, 108–19.)

6 In a letter written early in 1790, Burke accounts for the awkward fact that Montesquieu was admired by many revolutionaries by arguing that 'they do not understand him. He is often obscure; sometimes misled by system; but, on the whole, a learned, and ingenious writer, and sometimes a most profound thinker' (Burke to Unknown, January 1790, in *The Correspondence of Edmund Burke*, vol. 6, ed. A. Cobban and R. A. Smith (Cambridge, and Chicago, IL: Cambridge University Press and University of Chicago Press, 1967), pp. 80–1). Burke also praises the 'genius' of Montesquieu in his *An Appeal From the New to the Old Whigs*, in *The Writings and Speeches of Edmund Burke*, vol. 4 (London: Bickers and Son, 1887), p. 211.

7 Conor Cruise O'Brien, *The Great Melody: A Thematic Biography and Commented Anthology of Edmund Burke* (Chicago, IL: University of Chicago Press, 1992), p. 595n1. C. P. Courtney argues that Burke was in the mainstream of the moderate Enlightenment prior to the Revolution ('Edmund Burke and the Enlightenment', in *Statesmen, Scholars and Merchants*, ed. A. Whiteman *et al.* (Oxford: Oxford University Press, 1973)).

8 Epstein, *The Genesis of German Conservatism*, p. 504.

9 Burke to Lord Charlemont, 9 August 1789, in *The Correspondence of Edmund Burke*, vol. 6, eds. A. Cobban and R. A. Smith (Cambridge, and Chicago, IL: Cambridge University Press and University of Chicago Press, 1967), p. 10.

10 Burke to William Windham, 27 September 1789, in *The Correspondence of Edmund Burke*, vol. 6, p. 25.

11 Burke to Richard Burke, *c.*10 October 1789, in *The Correspondence of Edmund Burke*, vol. 6, p. 30.

12 O'Brien, *The Great Melody*, pp. 394–5.

13 Burke, *An Appeal From the New to the Old Whigs*, p. 150.

14 Burke, *An Appeal From the New to the Old Whigs*, p. 150.

15 Burke, *Reflections on the Revolution in France*, ed. C. C. O'Brien (Harmondsworth: Penguin, 1968), p. 237.

16 Burke to William Elliot, 26 May 1795, in *The Writings and Speeches of Edmund Burke*, vol. 5, p. 118.

17 Burke, *A Letter to a Member of the National Assembly*, in *The Writings and Speeches of Edmund Burke*, vol. 4, p. 22.

18 Burke, *Reflections on the Revolution in France*, pp. 211–12.

19 Burke, *Reflections on the Revolution in France*, p. 348.

20 Burke, *A Letter to a Member of the National Assembly*, p. 12.

21 Burke, *Three Letters Addressed to A Member of the Present Parliament on the Proposals for Peace with the Regicide Directory of France*, Letter 1, in *The Writings and Speeches of Edmund Burke*, vol. 5, p. 317.

22 Burke, *Reflections on the Revolution in France*, p. 345.

23 Burke, *A Letter to a Member of the National Assembly*, p. 41.

24 Burke, *Thoughts on French Affairs*, in *The Writings and Speeches of Edmund Burke*, vol. 4, p. 319.
25 Burke to William Elliot, 26 May 1795, in *The Writings and Speeches of Edmund Burke*, vol. 5, p. 122.
26 Burke, *A Letter to a Noble Lord*, in *The Writings and Speeches of Edmund Burke*, vol. 5, p. 213.
2/ Burke, *A Letter to a Noble Lord*, pp. 216–17.
28 Burke, *A Letter to a Member of the National Assembly*, p. 26.
29 Burke to Richard Burke, 18 August 1791, in *The Correspondence of Edmund Burke*, vol. 6, pp. 363–4.
30 Burke, *Reflections on the Revolution in France*, p. 284.
31 Burke, *A Letter to a Member of the National Assembly*, p. 26.
32 Burke, *A Letter to a Member of the National Assembly*, p. 26.
33 Burke, *A Letter to a Member of the National Assembly*, p. 30. On Rousseau's political theory, see Burke to Unknown, January 1790, in *The Correspondence of Edmund Burke*, vol. 6, p. 81. See also David Cameron, *The Social and Political Thought of Rousseau and Burke: A Comparative Study* (Toronto: University of Toronto Press, 1973).
34 Burke, *A Letter to a Noble Lord*, p. 227.
35 Burke to Claude-Constant Rougane, 1791, in *The Correspondence of Edmund Burke*, vol. 6, p. 478.
36 Burke, *An Appeal From the New to the Old Whigs*, p. 95.
37 Burke, *An Appeal From the New to the Old Whigs*, pp. 80–1.
38 Burke, *An Appeal From the New to the Old Whigs*, p. 202.
39 Burke, *Reflections on the Revolution in France*, p. 345.
40 Burke to William Smith, 29 January 1795, in *The Correspondence of Edmund Burke*, vol. 8, ed. R. B. McDowell (Cambridge, and Chicago, IL: Cambridge University Press and University of Chicago Press, 1969), pp. 129–30.
41 Burke, *An Appeal From the New to the Old Whigs*, p. 206.
42 Burke, *Reflections on the Revolution in France*, pp. 211–12.
43 Burke, *Three Letters Addressed to A Member of the Present Parliament*, pp. 361–3.
44 Burke to William Smith, 29 January 1795, in *The Correspondence of Edmund Burke*, vol. 8, p. 131.
45 Burke to William Elliot, 26 May 1795, in *The Writings and Speeches of Edmund Burke*, vol. 5, p. 122.
46 Burke to Barruel, 1 May 1997, in *The Correspondence of Edmund Burke*, vol. 10, ed. B. Lowe *et al.* (Chicago, IL, and Cambridge: University of Chicago Press and Cambridge University Press, 1958–1978), pp. 38–9. Burke visited France in 1773, where he met Mirabeau, Morellet and Thomas Paine, all of whom he implicated in the plot. He may also have met Diderot, Necker, Turgot and the duc d'Orléans.
47 Amos Hofman, 'The Origins of the Theory of the *Philosophe* Conspiracy', *French History*, 2 (1988), p. 170.
48 Barruel, *Memoirs*, vol. 3, p. xiv.
49 Robison's *Proofs of a Conspiracy* was republished in 1967 by Western Islands Press, the publishing arm of the American right-wing John Birch Society.
50 Barruel, *Memoirs*, vol. 1, ch. 18, p. 363.
51 Barruel, *Memoirs*, vol. 1, prelim disc, p. xiii.
52 Barruel, *Memoirs*, vol. 1, ch. 3, p. 48.
53 Barruel, *Memoirs*, vol. 2, ch. 4, p. 138.
54 Barruel, *Memoirs*, vol. 2, prelim disc, p. 7.
55 Barruel, *Memoirs*, vol. 2, ch. 14, pp. 461–2.
56 Barruel, *Memoirs*, vol. 1, ch. 19, p. 398.
57 Barruel, *Memoirs*, vol. 1, ch. 1, p. 4.

58 Barruel, *Memoirs*, vol. 4, ch. 12, p. 399.
59 Barruel, *Memoirs*, vol. 1, ch. 1, p. 2.
60 Barruel, *Memoirs*, vol. 4, Conclusion, p. 561.
61 Barruel, *Memoirs*, vol. 1, ch. 18, p. 359.
62 Barruel, *Memoirs*, vol. 2, ch. 4, p. 132.
63 Barruel, *Memoirs*, vol. 2, ch. 1, p. 40.
64 Barruel, *Memoirs*, vol. 1, ch. 15, p. 285.
65 Barruel, *Memoirs*, vol. 1, ch. 5, p. 79.
66 Barruel, *Memoirs*, vol. 1, chap. 5, p. 77.
67 Barruel, *Memoirs*, vol. 1, chap. 5, p. 80.
68 Barruel, *Memoirs*, vol. 1, chap. 6, p. 113.
69 Barruel, *Memoirs*, vol. 1, chap. 14, p. 243.
70 Barruel, *Memoirs*, vol. 2, chap. 5, p. 159.
71 Barruel, *Memoirs*, vol. 1, chap. 4, p. 57.
72 Barruel, *Memoirs*, vol. 4, chap. 13, pp. 547–8.
73 Barruel, *Memoirs*, vol. 1, chap. 4, p. 55.
74 Barruel, *Memoirs*, vol. 4, chap. 12, p. 432.
75 Barruel, *Memoirs*, vol. 4, Conclusion, p. 562.
76 Barruel, *Memoirs*, vol. 1, ch. 15, pp. 307–8.
77 Barruel, *Memoirs*, vol. 2, chap. 4, pp. 136–7.
78 Barruel, *Memoirs*, vol. 4, Conclusion, pp. 556–7. See also vol. 1, chap. 15, p. 289 and vol. 4, chap. 12, p. 410.
79 Barruel, *Memoirs*, vol. 1, chap. 15, p. 285.
80 Barruel, *Memoirs*, vol. 1, prelim disc, p. xv.
81 Barruel, *Memoirs*, vol. 4, Conclusion, p. 584.
82 Barruel, *Memoirs*, vol. 2, chap. 14, p. 423.
83 Barruel, *Memoirs*, vol. 2, chap. 14, p. 421.
84 Barruel, *Memoirs*, vol. 3, Chap. 1, p. 16.
85 Barruel, *Memoirs*, vol. 4, Conclusion, p. 574.
86 Barruel, *Memoirs*, vol. 4, chap. 13, pp. 527–8.
87 Barruel, *Memoirs*, vol. 4, chap. 13, p. 523.
88 Barruel, *Memoirs*, vol. 1, chap. 3, p. 50.
89 Barruel, *Memoirs*, vol. 1, chap. 10, p. 157.
90 Barruel, *Memoirs*, vol. 1, chap. 3, p. 51.
91 See Emile Dermehngem, *Joseph de Maistre mystique* (Paris: La connaissance, 1923), pp. 78–94.
92 See the unpublished Maistre archive file 2J11, which contains eight pages of notes on Barruel's *Mémoires* in Maistre's own hand.
93 *Ecrits maçonniques de Joseph de Maistre et de quelques-un de ses amis franc maçons*, ed. J. Rebotton (Geneva: Slatkine, 1983). On Maistre's involvement with the Freemasons, see Richard Lebrun, *Joseph de Maistre: An Intellectual Militant* (Montreal and Kingston: McGill-Queen's University Press, 1988), pp. 53–69; and Antoine Faivre, 'Joseph de Maistre et l'illuminisme: rapports avec Willermoz', *Revue des études maistriennes*, 5–6 (1980), pp. 125–32.
94 On 21 January 1791 Maistre wrote about Burke's *Reflections* to his friend Joseph-Henry Costa as follows: 'I was delighted, and I can hardly find words to convey to you the extent to which it reinforced my anti-democratic, anti-Gallican ideas. My aversion for everything that is being done in France is turning to loathing' (quoted in Jean-Louis Darcel, 'Catalogue de la Bibliothèque de Joseph de Maistre', *Etudes maistriennes*, 1 (1975), pp. 1–91). However, Richard Lebrun doubts the influence of Burke on Maistre, noting that 'there are very few references to Burke in Maistre's published works' and '[i]n more than 5,000 pages of Maistre's *Registres de lectures*, I have found only four brief references to the *Reflections*' (*Joseph de Maistre: An Intellectual Militant*, pp. 102,

296n143). See also Bruce Mazlish, 'Burke, Bonald and de Maistre: A Study in Conservatism', Ph.D. thesis, Columbia University, 1955; Michel Fuchs, 'Edmund Burke et Joseph de Maistre', *Revue de l'Université d'Ottawa*, 54 (1984), pp. 49–58; and Lebrun, 'Joseph de Maistre and Edmund Burke: A Comparison', in *Joseph de Maistre's Life, Thought and Influence: Selected Studies*, ed. R. A. Lebrun (Montreal and Kingston: McGill-Queen's University Press, 2001), pp. 3–12.

95 Joseph de Maistre, 'Réflexions sur le Protestantisme dans ses rapports avec la Souveraineté' (dated 1798), in *Oeuvres completes de Joseph de Maistre*, vol. 8 (Lyon: Vitte et Perussel, 1884–1887), p. 99.

96 Maistre, *St. Petersburg Dialogues*, trans. R. A. Lebrun (Montreal: McGill-Queen's University Press, 1993), p. 217.

97 Berlin, 'Joseph de Maistre and the Origins of Fascism', p. 62.

98 Jean-Louis Darcel, 'Sources of Maistrian Sensibility', trans. R. A. Lebrun, in *Maistre Studies*, ed. R. A. Lebrun (Lanham, New York, London: University Press of America, 1988), p. 119. Darcel writes: 'Nourished in the thought of the Enlightenment, Joseph de Maistre saw the certitudes he had inherited from his father shaken by the arguments of the *philosophes* – the idea of the relativity of beliefs and of cultures, and the birth of a secular humanism menacing the theological-political order on which the old European monarchies rested after 1770 he little by little surmounted this conflict, which could have led him to scepticism, by betting resolutely on faith' (pp. 119–20).

99 See Darcel, 'Maistre and the French Revolution', in *Maistre Studies*, pp. 177–92.

100 R. A. Lebrun writes that 'it was the revolutionary legislation of the night of 4 August 1789 that appears to have been decisive in turning Maistre against the Revolution' (Introduction to *St. Petersburg Dialogues*, p. xiii).

101 See Graeme Garrard, 'Rousseau, Maistre and the Counter-Enlightenment', *History of Political Thought*, 15 (1994), pp. 97–120.

102 Maistre, 'On the Sovereignty of the People', in *Against Rousseau*, trans. R. A. Lebrun (Montreal: McGill-Queen's University Press, 1996), p. 106.

103 Maistre, 'On the Sovereignty of the People', pp. 111–12.

104 Maistre, *Considerations on France*, trans. R. A. Lebrun (Cambridge: Cambridge University Press, 1994), p. 31.

105 Maistre, *Essay on the Generative Principle of Political Constitutions*, reprint of 1847 edn (Delmas, NY: New York Scholars' Facsimiles and Reprints, 1977), p. 41.

106 Maistre, *Considerations on France*, pp. 7–8.

107 David Edwards, 'Count Joseph de Maistre and Russian Educational Policy 1803–1828', *Slavic Review*, 36 (1977), p. 58.

108 Edwards, 'Count Joseph de Maistre and Russian Educational Policy 1803–1828', p. 61.

109 Maistre, 'Mémoire sur la liberté de l'enseignement publique', in *Oeuvres complètes de Joseph de Maistre*, vol. 8, p. 272.

110 Maistre, *St. Petersburg Dialogues*, p. 303.

111 Maistre, *St. Petersburg Dialogues*, p. 301.

112 Maistre, 'On the Sovereignty of the People', p. 82.

113 Maistre, 'On the Sovereignty of the People', p. 76.

114 Maistre, 'On the Sovereignty of the People', p. 81.

115 Maistre, *Considerations on France*, pp. 45, 47.

116 Maistre, 'On the Sovereignty of the People', pp. 87–8.

117 Maistre, *St. Petersburg Dialogues*, p. 24.

118 Maistre, *Considerations on France*, p. 31.

119 Maistre, *St. Petersburg Dialogues*, pp. 216–17.

4 The return of faith and feeling

1 Novalis, *Hymns to the Night*, trans. D. Higgins (New York: McPherson & Co, 1988), p. 29.

2 Frederick Beiser, *Enlightenment, Revolution and Romanticism* (Cambridge, MA: Harvard University Press, 1992), p. 49.

3 Theophile Gautier, *Histoire du Romanticisme* (Paris: Charpentier, 1884), p. 4.

4 Frederick Beiser describes the demise of the *Aufklärung* as the 'major philosophical development of the 1790s' (*Enlightenment, Revolution and Romanticism*, p. 364).

5 See Friedrich Heinrich Jacobi, *David Hume Concerning Belief, or Idealism and Realism, a Dialogue* (1787), in *The Main Philosophical Writings and the Novel Allwill: Friedrich Heinrich Jacobi*, trans. G. di Giovanni (Montreal and Kingston: McGill-Queen's University Press, 1994).

6 See Frederick Beiser's very thorough account of this controversy, and its implications for German thought, in the second and third chapters of *The Fate of Reason* (Cambridge, MA: Harvard University Press, 1987), pp. 44–126.

7 Giovanni, Introduction to *The Main Philosophical Writings and the Novel Allwill: Friedrich Heinrich Jacobi*, p. 8.

8 Beiser, *The Fate of Reason*, p. 75. Jacobi's account of his debate with Mendelssohn on this matter – *Concerning the Doctrine of Spinoza in Letters to Herr Moses Mendelssohn (Uber die Lehre von Spinoza in Briefen an Herrn Moses Mendelssohn)* – was published in 1785.

9 On Herder as a critic rather than an enemy of the Enlightenment, see Isaiah Berlin, 'Reply to Hans Aarsleff', *London Review of Books*, 20/3 (5–18 November, 1981), pp. 7–8. Of Herder's relationship to the *Aufklärung*, Frederick Beiser writes that it was 'a movement that he [Herder] embraced and disowned with equal conviction and passion' (*Enlightenment, Revolution and Romanticism*, p. 191). Robert Norton places Herder closer to the mainstream of the Enlightenment in his *Herder's Aesthetics of the European Enlightenment* (Ithaca, NY, and London: Cornell University Press, 1991).

10 It is not at all surprising that Rousseau's ideas, particularly as set forth in the 'Profession of Faith' of the Savoyard Vicar in *Emile*, made such a profound impression on Kant, and have so often been associated with him. Rousseau's strong dualism, his association of the moral law with the inner principle of conscience and his emphasis on the active, pre-experiential nature of the mind inspired Kant's own moral epistemology, by his own admission. 'I learned to honour mankind', declared Kant after reading Rousseau (First Introduction to *The Critique of Judgement*, trans. J. Haden (Indianapolis: Bobbs-Merrill, 1965), p. 44). For a very good discussion of Rousseau's influence on Kant, see Susan Shell, *The Rights of Reason: A Study of Kant's Philosophy and Politics* (Toronto: University of Toronto Press, 1980), pp. 20–32. Manfred Kuehn thinks that Rousseau's influence on Kant was not very significant (*Kant: A Biography* (Cambridge: Cambridge University Press, 2001), pp. 131–2). The classic 'Kantian' reading of Rousseau is Ernst Cassirer's *The Question of Jean-Jacques Rousseau*, trans. P. Gay (New Haven, CT, and London: Yale University Press, 1954), and *Rousseau, Kant, Goethe: Two Essays*, trans. J. Gutmann *et al.* (Princeton, NJ: Princeton University Press, 1945). More recently, Andrew Levine has presented a 'neo-Kantian' reading of Rousseau in *The Politics of Autonomy* (Amherst: University of Massachusetts Press, 1976), albeit with important modifications.

11 Beiser, 'The Enlightenment and Idealism', in *The Cambridge Companion to German Idealism*, ed. K. Ameriks (Cambridge: Cambridge University Press, 2000), p. 31.

12 Friedrich Schlegel wrote an appreciative essay on Hamann's philosophy: 'Hamann als Philosoph', *Deutsches Museum*, 3 (1813), pp. 32–52.

13 Novalis, *Hymns to the Night*, pp. 15, 11.

14 Novalis, *Christendom or Europe*, in *Novalis: Philosophical Writings*, trans. M. Stoljar (Albany, NY: State University of New York Press, 1997).

15 E. D. Schleiermacher, *On Religion, Speeches to Its Cultured Despisers*, trans. R. Crouter (Cambridge: Cambridge University Press, 1988), p. 102.

16 Schleiermacher, *On Religion*, p. 103.

17 Schleiermacher, *On Religion*, p. 105.

18 Schleiermacher, *On Religion*, p. 138.

19 Schleiermacher, *On Religion*, pp. 152–3.

20 Novalis, *Christendom or Europe*, p. 151.

21 Novalis, *Christendom or Europe*, p. 148.

22 Hardenberg mentions Burke only once in his works, as follows: 'There are many anti-revolutionary books being written in favour of the revolution. Burke has written against the revolution a revolutionary book' (*Novalis: Werke, Tagebücher und Briefe – Friedrich von Hardenberg*, vol. 2, ed. H-J. Mähl (Vienna: Earl Hanser Verlag, 1978), p. 34).

23 Novalis, *Christendom or Europe*, p. 150.

24 Novalis, *Christendom or Europe*, p. 144.

25 Novalis, *Christendom or Europe*, p. 149.

26 Novalis, *Christendom or Europe*, pp. 144–5.

27 Novalis, *Christendom or Europe*, p. 145.

28 Novalis, *Christendom or Europe*, p. 145.

29 Novalis, *Christendom or Europe*, p. 146.

30 Novalis, *Christendom or Europe*, pp. 146–7.

31 Schleiermacher, *On Religion*, p. 85.

32 Novalis, *Christendom or Europe*, p. 147.

33 Apart from Coleridge and Wordsworth, no other prominent English Romantics of the period had direct contact with German writers who did call themselves 'Romantics' at this time (Marilyn Butler, 'Romanticism in England', in *Romanticism in National Context*, eds R. Porter and M. Teich (Cambridge: Cambridges University Press, 1988), p. 37).

34 Richard Holmes, *Coleridge: Early Visions* (Harmondsworth: Penguin, 1989), p. 117.

35 Coleridge to Wordsworth, *c.*10 September 1799, *Collected Letters of Samuel Taylor Coleridge*, vol. 1, ed. E. L. Griggs (Oxford: Clarendon Press, 1956–1971), p. 527.

36 Holmes, *Coleridge*, p. 117.

37 Coleridge began to take an interest in Kant's work in 1796, before he went to Germany, but did not study it systematically until his return (Holmes, *Coleridge*, p. 368).

38 Samuel Taylor Coleridge, *Aids to Reflection*, in *The Collected Works of Samuel Taylor Coleridge*, vol. 9, ed. J. Beer (London: Routledge, and Princeton, NJ: Princeton University Press, 1993), p. 216.

39 Coleridge, *The Statesman's Manual*, December 1816, in *CWSTC*, vol. 6, ed. R. J. White (London: Routledge & Kegan Paul, and Princeton, NJ: Princeton University Press, 1967–), pp. 59–60, 67–70.

40 Coleridge, *On the Constitution of the Church and State*, in *CWSTC*, vol. 10, ed. J. Colmer (London: Routledge & Kegan Paul, and Princeton, NJ: Princeton University Press, 1976), p. 14.

41 Coleridge, *Aids to Reflection*, in *CWSTC*, vol. 9, p. 224.

42 Coleridge, *Lectures on Literature*, lecture 11 (3 March 1818), *Coleridge's Miscellaneous Criticism*, ed. T. M. Raysor (London: Constable, 1936), pp. 193–6.

43 Coleridge, *Biographia Literaria*, vol. 1, in *CWSTC*, vol. 7, ed. J. Engell and W. J. Bate (London: Routledge & Kegan Paul, and Princeton, NJ: Princeton University Press, 1983), pp. 304–5.

44 Coleridge, *The Statesman's Manual*, December 1816, in *CWSTC*, vol. 6, pp. 28–31.
45 Coleridge, *Biographia Literaria*, vol. 2, in *CWSTC*, vol. 7, p. 16.
46 Coleridge, *Biographia Literaria*, vol. 2, in *CWSTC*, vol. 7, pp. 247–8.
47 Coleridge, *The Stateman's Manual*, in *CWSTC*, vol. 6, p. 33.
48 Coleridge, *The Statesman's Manual*, in *CWSTC*, vol. 6, p. 83.
49 Coleridge, *The Courier*, 1 April 1812, in *CWSTC*, vol. 3: *Essays on His Times*, vol. 2, ed. D. Erdman (London: Routledge & Kegan Paul, 1978, and Princeton, NJ: Princeton University Press, 1978), pp. 342–3.
50 Coleridge, *The Courier*, 25 July 1816, in *CWSTC*, vol. 3, p. 432.
51 Coleridge, *The Courier*, 1 April 1812, in *CWSTC*, vol. 3, pp. 342–3.
52 Coleridge, *The Courier*, 21 October 1814, in *CWSTC*, vol. 3, p. 388.
53 Coleridge, *The Courier*, 25 July 1816, in *CWSTC*, vol. 3, p. 432.
54 Coleridge to Josiah Wedgwood, February 1801, letter 384, in *Collected Letters of Samuel Taylor Coleridge*, vol. 2, ed. E. L. Griggs (Oxford: Clarendon Press, 1956–1971), p. 702.
55 Coleridge, *The Statesman's Manual*, vol. 1, in *CWSTC*, vol. 6, pp. 74–5.
56 Coleridge, *The Courier*, 1 April 1812, in *CWSTC*, vol. 3, p. 346.
57 William Wordsworth, 'The Convention of Cintra', in *The Prose Works of William Wordsworth*, vol. 1, ed. W. J. B. Owen and J. W. Smyser (Oxford: Clarendon Press, 1974), p. 332.
58 William Blake, 'Mock On', in *Manuscript Lyrics of the Felpham Years (1800–1803)*, in *William Blake*, ed. M. Mason (Oxford and New York: Oxford University Press, 1988), pp. 284–5.

> I see thee strive upon the Brooks of Arnon. There a dread
> And awful Man I see, oercoverd with the mantle of years.
> I behold Los & Urizen. I behold Orc & Tharmas;
> The Four Zoa's of Albion & they Spirit with them striving
> In Self annihilation giving thy life to thy enemies
> Are those who contemn Religion & seek to annihilate it
> Become in their Femin[in]e portions the causes & promoters
> Of these Religions, how is this thing? this Newtonian Phantasm
> This Voltaire & Rousseau: this Hume & Gibbon & Bolingbroke
> This Natural Religion! this impossible absurdity
> Is Ololon the cause of this? O where shall I hide my face
> These tears fall for the little-ones: the Children of Jerusalem
> Lest they be annihilated in they annihilation.

(Blake, 'Milton: A Poem in 2 Books', in *The Complete Poetry and Prose of William Blake*, ed. D. Erdman, p. 141).

59 Coleridge, *The Friend*, No. 8 (5 October 1809), in *CWSTC*, vol. 4:2, ed. B. Rooke (London: Routledge & Kegan Paul, 1969), pp. 111–12.
60 Coleridge, *The Friend* (1818), vol. 1, in *CWSTC*, vol. 4:1, ed. B. Rooke (London: Routledge & Kegan Paul, 1969), p. 133n.
61 Coleridge, *The Friend* (1818), vol. 1, in *CWSTC*, vol. 4:1, p. 131.
62 Coleridge to Josiah Wedgwood, February 1801, letter 384, in *Collected Letters of Samuel Taylor Coleridge*, vol. 2, ed. E. L. Griggs (Oxford: Clarendon Press, 1956–1971), p. 702.
63 Coleridge, *The Statesman's Manual*, vol. 1, in *CWSTC*, vol. 6, pp. /4–5.
64 Coleridge, *The Friend*, No. 8 (5 October 1809), in *CWSTC*, vol. 4:2, pp. 111–12.
65 Edward Duffy writes: 'It is scarcely possible to overestimate the English influence commanded by Edmund Burke for the several decades subsequent to his *Reflections on the Revolution in France* . . . he remained the interpreter of recent

history who had to be answered, the prophet who had to be shown false'
(*Rousseau in England: The Context of Shelley's Critique of the Enlightenment* (Berkeley: University of California Press, 1979), pp. 51–2).

66 Duffy, *Rousseau in England*, p. 70.

67 For a character sketch (or rather, a character assassination) of Rousseau, see Coleridge, *The Friend* (1818), vol. 1, in *CWSTC*, vol. 4:1, pp. 133–4.

68 Coleridge, *The Friend*, No. 8 (5 October 1809), in *CWSTC*, vol. 4:2, ed. B. Rooke, pp. 111–12.

69 Coleridge, *On the Constitution of the Church and State*, in *CWSTC*, vol. 10, ed. J. Colmer (London: Routledge and Kegan Paul, and Princeton, NJ: Princeton University Press, 1976), p. 14.

70 Coleridge, *Biographia Literaria*, vol. 1, in *CWSTC*, vol. 7, p. 54.

71 N. H. Clement, *Romanticism in France* (New York: Modern Languages Association of America, 1939), p. 264. Clement writes about French Romanticism that the 'Romanticism of 1820 is monarchic and Catholic, and therefore, politically and socially, reactionary, championing the Restoration and the Church. The Romanticism of 1830 marks a return to the liberal political and social ideals of the eighteenth century. ... The first type of romanticism is more one of individualism and sensibility, and its predominantly expressed itself in poetry; the second type is more one of ideas, and its predominantly expressed itself in prose' (p. 181).

72 Chateaubriand, *An Historical, Political and Moral Essay on Revolutions, Ancient and Modern* (London: Henry Colburn, 1815), pp. 357–8.

73 Chateaubriand, *An Historical, Political and Moral Essay on Revolutions, Ancient and Modern*, p. 380.

74 Chateaubriand, *An Historical, Political and Moral Essay on Revolutions, Ancient and Modern*, pp. 357–8.

75 Chateaubriand, *An Historical, Political and Moral Essay on Revolutions, Ancient and Modern*, p. 376.

76 Chateaubriand, *An Historical, Political and Moral Essay on Revolutions, Ancient and Modern*, pp. 379–80.

77 Chateaubriand, *An Historical, Political and Moral Essay on Revolutions, Ancient and Modern*, pp. 357–8. 'While religious principles were thus combated by an association of philosophers, others attacked political principles: for it is remarkable that the atheistic sect were miserable reasoners upon affairs of state. Montesquieu, J. J. Rousseau, Mably, and Raynal unfortunately began to enlighten the minds of men, who had lost that energy and purity of soul essential towards making a good use of the truth. Since the Revolution took place, each faction has destroyed one of the greatest men belonging to this body; the Jacobins, Montesquieu, the Royalists, Rousseau. This, however, will not prevent the immortality of the *Spirit of the Laws*, and *Emilius*; works that will descend to the latest posterity. As to the *Social Contract*, of which we find a part in Emilius, in the form of an extract from a large work, it rejects every thing and proves nothing. I believe that in its present imperfect state, it has done much good and much harm. I am only astonished that the republicans took it as their guide, for no work more condemns them' (p. 390).

78 Chateaubriand, *An Historical, Political and Moral Essay on Revolutions, Ancient and Modern*, pp. 379–80.

79 Chateaubriand, *An Historical, Political and Moral Essay on Revolutions, Ancient and Modern*, pp. 388–9.

80 Clement, *Romanticism in France*, p. 193n32.

81 Chateaubriand, *The Genius of Christianity*, trans. C. I. White (New York: Howard Fertig, 1976; reprint of 2nd edn, Baltimore, MD: John Murray & Co, 1856), pt. I, bk. 1, ch. 1, p. 49.

82 Novalis, *Christendom or Europe*, p. 148.
83 Chateaubriand, *The Genius of Christianity*, pt. II, bk. 2, ch. 8, p. 255.
84 Chateaubriand, *The Genius of Christianity*, pt. III, bk. 2, ch. 2, p. 402.
85 Chateaubriand, *The Genius of Christianity*, pt. III, bk. 2, ch. 1, p. 389.
86 Chateaubriand, *The Genius of Christianity*, pt. III, bk. 1, ch. 3, p. 377.
87 Chateaubriand, *The Genius of Christianity*, pt. I, bk. 1, ch. 4, p. 64.
88 Rousseau, *Emile*, pp. 290–91 (*OC*, IV, pp. 600–1).
89 Chateaubriand, *The Genius of Christianity*, pt. I, bk. 6, ch. 2, p. 188.
90 Bernard Reardon, *Religion in the Age of Romanticism* (Cambridge: Cambridge University Press, 1985), p. 29.
91 Chateaubriand, *The Genius of Christianity*, pt. I, bk. 1, ch. 2, p. 52.
92 Chateaubriand, *The Genius of Christianity*, pt. I, bk. 1, ch. 2, p. 52.
93 Chateaubriand, *The Genius of Christianity*, pt. II, bk. 3, ch. 1, p. 271.
94 Chateaubriand, *The Genius of Christianity*, pt. III, bk. 2, ch. 1, p. 398.
95 Chateaubriand, *The Genius of Christianity*, pt. I, bk. 4, ch. 3, p. 131.
96 Chateaubriand, *The Genius of Christianity*, pt. III, bk. 2, ch. 1, p. 392.
97 See Lebrun, *Joseph de Maistre*, p. 233.
98 Chateaubriand, *The Genius of Christianity*, pt. III, bk. 2, ch. 2, p. 403.
99 Chateaubriand, *The Genius of Christianity*, pt. III, bk. 2, ch. 1, p. 392.
100 Chateaubriand, *The Genius of Christianity*, pt. IV, bk. 6, ch. 13, p. 682.
101 Chateaubriand, *The Genius of Christianity*, pt. III, bk. 4, ch. 5, p. 457.
102 Coleridge, *The Courier*, 22 December, in *CWSTC*, vol. 3, p. 81.
103 Chateaubriand, *The Genius of Christianity*, pt. I, bk. 1, ch. 1, p. 47.
104 Chateaubriand, *The Genius of Christianity*, pt. II, bk. 1, ch. 5, pp. 230–1.
105 Chateaubriand, *The Genius of Christianity*, pt. II, bk. 1, ch. 5, pp. 230–1.
106 Chateaubriand, *The Genius of Christianity*, pt. III, bk. 4, ch. 5, p. 455.
107 Chateaubriand, *The Genius of Christianity*, pt. III, bk. 4, ch. 5, p. 455.
108 Chateaubriand, *The Genius of Christianity*, pt. II, bk. 1, ch. 5, p. 228.
109 Chateaubriand, *The Genius of Christianity*, pt. II, bk. 1, ch. 5, p. 228.
110 Chateaubriand, *The Genius of Christianity*, pt. III, bk. 4, ch. 5, p. 456.
111 Chateaubriand, *The Genius of Christianity*, pt. III, bk. 4, ch. 5, p. 457.

5 The strange case of Friedrich Nietzche and the Enlightenment

1 Friedrich Nietzsche, *Human, All Too Human*, sec. 463, trans. R. J. Hollingdale (Cambridge: Cambridge University Press, 1996), p. 169.
2 Nietzsche, *The Will to Power*, sec. 117, trans. R. J. Hollingdale and W. Kaufmann (New York: Vintage Books, 1968), p. 72.
3 Nietzsche, *Human, All Too Human*, sec. 55, p 41
4 The eminent Nietzsche scholar Walter Kaufmann argues that there is a basic continuity in Nietzsche's works, and rejects as 'untenable dogma' the idea that the writings of the 'middle period' represent a distinct stage in the development of his thought (*Nietzsche: Philosopher, Psychologist, Antichrist* (New York: Meridian Books, 1956), pp. 342–3).
5 Editor's introduction to Nietzsche's *Ecce Homo*, trans. W. Kaufmann and R. J. Hollingdale (New York: Vintage Books, 1969), p. 206.
6 Nietzsche, *Beyond Good and Evil*, p.1, sec. 6, trans. R. J. Hollingsdale (Harmondsworth: Penguin, 1973), p. 19.
7 Nietzsche, *Human, All Too Human*, sec. 463, p. 169.
8 Nietzsche, *Human, All Too Human*, sec. 463, p. 169. Nietzsche also uses Voltaire's famous anti-Christian expression '*Ecrasez l'infâme*' in *Ecce Homo*, p. 335.
9 Nietzsche, *The Wanderer and His Shadow*, in *Human, All Too Human*, sec. 221, p. 376.

10 Nietzsche, *Human, All Too Human*, sec. 221, p. 367.
11 Nietzsche, *Human, All Too Human*, sec. 110, pp. 61–2.
12 Nietzsche, *Daybreak: Thoughts on the Prejudices of Morality*, sec. 197, ed. M. Clark and B. Leiter, trans. R. J. Hollingdale (Cambridge: Cambridge University Press, 1997), pp. 198.
13 Nietzsche, *Daybreak*, sec. 197, p. 198.
14 Nietzsche, *The Gay Science*, trans. J. Nauchkhoff (Cambridge: Cambridge University Press, 2001), sec. 122, p. 117.
15 Nietzsche, *Human, All Too Human*, sec. 150, p. 81.
16 Nietzsche, *The Gay Science*, bk. 3, sec. 122, p. 118.
17 Nietzsche, *Human, All Too Human*, sec. 55, p. 41.
18 Nietzsche, *Human, All Too Human*, sec. 110, pp. 61–2.
19 Nietzsche, *Daybreak*, sec. 535, p. 212.
20 Nietzsche, *Daybreak*, sec. 3, pp. 2–3.
21 Nietzsche, *The Will to Power*, sec. 101 (1887), p. 64.
22 Nietzsche, *The Will to Power*, sec. 943 (1885), p. 498.
23 Nietzsche, *The Will to Power*, sec. 104 (1888), pp. 65–6.
24 Nietzsche, *The Will to Power*, sec. 117 (1887), p. 72.
25 Nietzsche, *Beyond Good and Evil*, sec. 46, pp. 57–8.
26 Nietzsche, *The Will to Power*, sec. 184 (1888), p. 111.
27 Nietzsche, *Beyond Good and Evil*, Preface, p. 14.
28 Nietzsche, *The Will to Power*, 2nd edn, sec. 117 (1887), p. 72.
29 Nietzsche, *The Will to Power*, 2nd edn, sec. 117 (1887), p. 72.
30 Nietzsche, *The Will to Power*, sec. 117 (1887), p. 72.
31 Nietzsche, *The Will to Power*, sec. 95 (1887), p. 59.
32 Nietzsche, *The Will to Power*, sec. 98 (1887), pp. 61–2.
33 Nietzsche, *The Will to Power*, sec. 83 (1887), p. 52.
34 Nietzsche, *Ecce Homo*, p. 283.
35 Nietzsche, *Beyond Good and Evil*, sec. 224, p. 134.
36 Nietzsche, *The Will to Power*, sec. 100 (1887), p. 63.
37 Nietzsche, *The Will to Power*, sec. 123 (1887), p. 75. A major influence on Nietzsche at this time in his thinking on the problem of civilisation and the way he construes it in terms of an opposition between the spirit of Voltaire and that of Rousseau was Ferdinand Brunetière's *Etudes critiques sur l'histoire de la litterature Française* (Paris: Hachette, 1887). For a discussion of this, see E. Kuhn, 'Cultur, Civilization. Die Zweideutigkeit des "Modernen"', *Nietzsche-Studien*, 18 (1989), pp. 600–27.
38 Nietzsche, *The Will to Power*, sec. 99, sec. 100 (1887), pp. 62–4.
39 Nietzsche, *The Will to Power*, sec 100 (1887), pp. 62–4.
40 Voltaire to Rousseau, 30 August 1755 (*CWV*, 100, D6451, p. 259).

6 Enlightened totalitarianism

1 Isaiah Berlin, quoted in Humphrey Carpenter, *The Envy of the World* (London: Weidenfeld & Nicolson, 1996), p. 127.
2 Jeffrey Isaac, 'Critics of Totalitarianism', in *The Cambridge History of Twentieth Century Political Thought*, eds T. Ball and R. Bellamy (Cambridge: Cambridge University Press, 2003), p. 182.
3 According to the German historian Jens Petersen, the first use of the term 'totalitarian' appears in an essay by the anti-fascist journalist and politician Giovanni Amendola in *Il Mondo*, 12 May 1923 ('Die Entstehung des Totalitarismusbegriffs in Italien', in *Totalitarismus*, ed. M. Funke (Dusseldorf: Droste Verlag, 1978)). On the 1920s origins of '*totalitarismustheorie*', see William David Jones, *The Lost Debate: German Socialist Intellectuals and Totalitarianism* (Urbana and

Chicago, IL: University of Illinois Press, 1999), p. 6. For a general history of the concept, see Abbott Gleason, *Totalitarianism: The Inner History of the Cold War* (New York: Oxford University Press, 1995).

4 Horkheimer to Pollock, 19 November 1943, quoted in Rolf Wiggershaus, *The Frankfurt School: Its History, Theories and Political Significance*, trans. M. Robertson (Cambridge: Polity Press, 1994), p. 345.

5 Max Weber, *The Social Psychology of the World Religions*, in *From Max Weber: Essays in Sociology*, trans. and eds. H. H. Gerth and C. Wright Mills (New York: Oxford University Press, 1946), p. 293.

6 Weber, *Economy and Society*, vol. 1, eds. G. Roth and C. Wittich (Berkeley: University of California Press, 1978), p. 25.

7 Weber, 'The Meaning of "Ethical Neutrality"', in *The Methodology of the Social Science*, trans. and eds. E. Shils and H. Finch (New York: Free Press, 1949), p. 35.

8 Weber, *Economy and Society*, vol. 2, eds. G. Roth and C. Wittich (Berkeley: University of California Press, 1978), pp. 1148–9.

9 Weber, *Economy and Society*, vol. 2, p. 988.

10 Weber, *Economy and Society*, vol. 2, p. 1402.

11 Max Horkheimer, *The Eclipse of Reason*, trans. J. Cumming (New York: Seabury Press, 1974), p. 174.

12 Horkheimer, *The Eclipse of Reason*, p. 55.

13 Horkheimer, *The Eclipse of Reason*, p. 18.

14 Horkheimer, *The Eclipse of Reason*, p. 18.

15 The first version of *Dialectic of Enlightenment* appeared in December 1944 as a mimeographed typescript distributed to friends and associates of the Institute for Social Research under the title *Philosophische Fragmente*. The first chapter carried the title 'Dialektik der Auklfärung'. However, the book was published in 1947 with the title *Dialektik der Auklfärung*, the first chapter now appearing as 'The Concept of Enlightenment'. As James Schmidt notes, this change suggests that the final version 'is making a claim that applies to all societies at all times. ... To call the entire book the *Dialectic of Enlightenment* is to hold out a claim to comprehensiveness that is at odds with the previous title' ('Language, Mythology and Enlightenment: Historical Notes on Horkheimer and Adorno's *Dialectic of Enlightenment*', *Social Research*, 65/4 (1998), pp. 812–14).

16 Gunzelin Schmid Noerr, 'Editor's Afterword: The Position of "Dialectic of Enlightenment" in the Development of Critical Theory', in Max Horkheimer and Theodor Adorno, *Dialectic of Enlightenment: Philosophical Fragments*, ed. G. S. Noerr, trans. E. Jephcott (Stanford, CA: Stanford University Press, 2002), p. 221. See also Jürgen Habermas, 'Remarks on the Development of Horkheimer's Work', in *On Max Horkheimer: New Perspectives*, ed. S. Benhabib *et al.* (Cambridge, MA: MIT Press, 1993), p. 57.

17 Horkheimer, 'Reason Against Itself: Some Remarks on Enlightenment', *Theory, Culture and Society*, 10 (1993), p. 81.

18 Horkheimer and Adorno, *Dialectic of Enlightenment*, p. 8.

19 Horkheimer, 'Reason Against Itself', p. 82.

20 Horkheimer and Adorno, *Dialectic of Enlightenment*, p. 5.

21 Horkheimer and Adorno, *Dialectic of Enlightenment*, p. 65.

22 Horkheimer and Adorno, *Dialectic of Enlightenment*, pp. 74, 81.

23 Horkheimer and Adorno, *Dialectic of Enlightenment*, p. 73.

24 Horkheimer, *The Eclipse of Reason*, pp. 83–4.

25 See the account of 'identity thinking' in Theodor Adorno, *Negative Dialectics*, trans. E. B. Ashton (London: Routledge & Kegan Paul, 1973).

26 Horkheimer, *The Eclipse of Reason*, p. 71.

27 Recent works linking the Enlightenment to fascism include Athur Hertzberg, *The French Enlightenment and the Jews* (New York: Columbia University Press,

1968); George Moss, *Toward the Final Solution: A History of European Racism* (New York: Howard Fertig, 1978); Zygmunt Bauman, *Modernity and the Holocaust* (Ithaca, NY: Cornell University Press, 1989); Berel Lang, *Act and Idea in the Nazi Genocide* (Chicago, IL: University of Chicago Press, 1990); Thomas Doherty, Introduction to *Postmodernism: A Reader*, ed. T. Doherty (New York: Columbia University Press, 1993); Adam Sutcliffe, *Judaism and Enlightenment* (Cambridge: Cambridge University Press, 1993); Lawrence Birken, *Hitler as Philosophe: Remnants of the Enlightenment in National Socialism* (Westport, CT: Praeger, 1995).

28 Horkheimer, *The Eclipse of Reason*, p. v.

29 Horkheimer, *The Eclipse of Reason*, p. 134.

30 Adorno, 'Memorandum on Parts of the Los Angeles Programme of Work which Cannot be Carried Out by the Philosophers' (1942), quoted in Wiggershaus, *The Frankfurt School*, p. 315.

31 Horkheimer and Adorno, *Dialectic of Enlightenment*, p. xviii. In the Preface to *Dialectic of Enlightenment*, Horkheimer and Adorno claim that they are 'wholly convinced . . . that social freedom is inseparable from enlightened thought' (p. xiii). Horkheimer had said as much a decade earlier in an essay on 'Materialism and Morality' (1933): 'The battle cries of the Enlightenment and of the French Revolution are valid now more than ever. The dialectical critique of the world, which is borne along by them, consists precisely in demonstrating that they have retained their actuality rather than lost it on the basis of reality. These ideas and values are nothing but the isolated traits of the rational society, as they are anticipated in morality as a necessary goal. Politics in accordance with this goal must therefore not abandon these demands, but realise them' ('Materialism and Morality', in *Between Philosophy and Social Science: Selected Early Writings*, trans. G. Frederick Hunter, M. S. Kramer and J. Torpey (Cambridge, MA: MIT Press, 1993), p. 37).

32 Schmidt, 'Language, Mythology and Enlightenment', p. 835. See also Wiggershaus, *The Frankfurt School*, p. 322.

33 Wiggershaus, *The Frankfurt School*, pp. 323–4.

34 Yehoshua Arieli, 'Jacob Talmon – An Intellectual Portrait', in *Totalitarian Democracy and After: International Colloquium in Memory of Jacob L. Talmon, Jerusalem, 21–24 June 1982* (Jerusalem: Magnes Press and Hebrew University), p. 14.

35 Gleason, *Totalitarianism*, pp. 113–14.

36 Gleason, *Totalitarianism*, p. 114.

37 Alexis de Tocqueville, *The Old Regime and the French Revolution*, trans. S. Gilbert (New York and London: Doubleday, 1955), pp. 5–9, 138–69.

38 Jacob Talmon, *The Origins of Totalitarian Democracy* (London: Secker and Warburg, 1952), p. 6.

39 Talmon, *The Origins of Totalitarian Democracy*, p. 252.

40 Talmon, 'Utopianism and Politics: A Conservative View', *Commentary* (1959), p. 151.

41 Talmon, *The Origins of Totalitarian Democracy*, p. 62.

42 Talmon, *The Origins of Totalitarian Democracy*, pp. 3–4.

43 Talmon, *The Origins of Totalitarian Democracy*, p. 254.

44 Talmon, *The Origins of Totalitarian Democracy*, p. 32.

45 Talmon, *The Origins of Totalitarian Democracy*, p. 249.

46 Talmon, *The Origins of Totalitarian Democracy*, pp. 249–50.

47 Talmon, *The Origins of Totalitarian Democracy*, p. 252.

48 Isaiah Berlin, 'A Tribute to My Friend', *Forum*, 38 (1980), p. 1. Talmon acknowledges his debt to Berlin in the preface to *The Origins of Totalitarian Democracy*, p. vii.

49 Berlin, Introduction to Maistre's *Considerations on France*, p. xxxiii.
50 Berlin, *Conversations with Isaiah Berlin*, ed. Ramin Jahanbegloo (London: Peter Halban, 1992), p. 76.
51 Berlin, 'George Sorel', in *Against the Current*, pp. 323–4.
52 Berlin, *Conversations with Isaiah Berlin*, p. 74.
53 Berlin, *The Age of Enlightenment* (New York: New American Library, 1956), p. 29.
54 Berlin, *Conversations with Isaiah Berlin*, p. 70.
55 Berlin, *Conversations with Isaiah Berlin*, p. 70.
56 Berlin, *Vico and Herder: Two Studies in the History of Ideas* (New York: Viking, 1976), p. 176.
57 Berlin, 'Two Concepts of Liberty', in *Four Essays on Liberty* (Oxford: Oxford University Press, 1969), p. 152.
58 Berlin, *Conversations with Isaiah Berlin*, p. 68.
59 On the early, conservative religious critics of the Enlightenment, see Darrin McMahon, *Enemies of the Enlightenment*. On more recent English conservative criticism of the Enlightenment, see Ian Holliday, 'English Conservatism and Enlightenment Rationalism', in *The Enlightenment and Modernity*, eds R. Wokler and N. Geras (Basingstoke: Macmillan, 2000).
60 Eric Voegelin, *Autobiographical Reflections*, ed. E. Sandoz (Baton Rouge and London: Louisiana State University Press, 1989), pp. 11–13.
61 Voegelin, *Autobiographical Reflections*, pp. 11–13.
62 Voegelin, *Autobiographical Reflections*, pp. 11–13.
63 Leo Strauss makes a similar argument against Weber in Chapter 2 of his *Natural Right and History* (Chicago, IL, and London: University of Chicago Press, 1953).
64 Voegelin, *Autobiographical Reflections*, pp. 11–13.
65 Eric Voegelin, *From Enlightenment to Revolution*, ed. J. H. Hallowell (Durham, NC: Duke University Press, 1975), p. 79.
66 Hallowell, *From Enlightenment to Revolution*, p. vii.
67 David Walsh, Introduction to *Crisis and the Apocalypse of Man*, in *The Collected Works of Eric Voegelin*, vol. 26, ed. D. Walsh (Columbia and London: University of Missouri Press, 1999), p. 14.
68 Lewis Simpson, 'Voegelin and the Story of the Clerks', in *Eric Voegelin's Significance for the Modern Mind*, ed. E. Sandoz (Baton Rouge and London: Louisiana State University Press, 1991), pp. 84–5.
69 Voegelin, *From Enlightenment to Revolution*, p. 16.
70 Voegelin, *From Enlightenment to Revolution*, pp. 9–10.
71 Voegelin, *From Enlightenment to Revolution*, p. 69.
72 Voegelin, *From Enlightenment to Revolution*, pp. 301–2.
73 Voegelin, *From Enlightenment to Revolution*, p. 268.
74 Voegelin, *From Enlightenment to Revolution*, p. 52.
75 Voegelin, *From Enlightenment to Revolution*, p. 20.
76 Voegelin makes the following reference to Talmon in his *Autobiographical Reflections*: 'An important element in this first part was also my first clear understanding of Rousseau's variety of collectivism. At the time I did not go very far in the analysis, only a few pages, but it is the problem that later was worked out splendidly by J. L. Talmon in his *Origins of Totalitarian Democracy* (1952)', p. 53.
77 Voegelin, *From Enlightenment to Revolution*, p. 32.
78 Voegelin, *From Enlightenment to Revolution*, pp. 73, 62.
79 Voegelin, *From Enlightenment to Revolution*, p. 132.
80 Voegelin, *From Enlightenment to Revolution*, p. 79.
81 Voegelin, *From Enlightenment to Revolution*, p. 60.
82 Voegelin, *From Enlightenment to Revolution*, p. 60.
83 Michael Oakeshott, 'The New Bentham', in *Rationalism in Politics and Other*

Essays (Indianapolis: Liberty Fund, 1991), p. 137. This essay was first published in *Scrutiny* in 1932.

84 Oakeshott, 'The New Bentham', p. 138.
85 Oakeshott, 'The New Bentham', pp. 139–40.
86 Oakeshott, 'The New Bentham', p. 139.
87 Oakeshott, 'The New Bentham', p. 139.
88 Oakeshott, 'Rational Conduct', in *Rationalism in Politics and Other Essays*, p. 106. This essay was first published in *The Cambridge Journal* in 1950.
89 Oakeshott, 'Rational Conduct', p. 105.
90 Michael Oakeshott, 'Rationalism in Politics', p. 6. This essay was first published in *The Cambridge Journal* in 1947.
91 Oakeshott, 'Rational Conduct', pp. 129–30.
92 Oakeshott, 'Rationalism in Politics', p. 5.

7 The postmodern challenge

1 Foucault, 'Conversazione con Michel Foucault', pp. 273–4.
2 Arthur Goldhammer, 'Man in the Mirror: Language, the Enlightenment, and the Postmodern', in *Postmodernism and the Enlightenment: New Perspectives in Eighteenth-century French Intellectual History*, ed. D. Gordon (New York and London: Routledge, 2001), p. 31.
3 Slavoj Žižek, *Did Somebody Say Totalitarianism?* (London and New York: Verso, 2001), p. 39.
4 Johnson Kent Wright, 'The Pre-postmodernism of Carl Becker', in *Postmodernism and the Enlightenment*, p. 161.
5 Hugo Meynell, *Postmodernism and the New Enlightenment* (Washington, DC: Catholic University Press, 1999), p. xi.
6 One notable exception to this tendency is *Postmodernism and the Enlightenment* (2001). Daniel Gordon, the editor of this collection, writes that one of its main purposes is 'to break down the polarity of postmodernism/Enlightenment by demonstrating that the Enlightenment foreshadows the concerns of post-modernism' (p. 218).
7 Jean-François Lyotard, 'The Tomb of the Intellectual' (1983), in *Political Writings*, trans. B. Readings and K. Paul (Minneapolis: University of Minnesota Press, 1993), pp. 6–7.
8 Lyotard, *The Postmodern Condition: A Report on Knowledge*, trans. G. Bennington and B. Massumi (Minneapolis: University of Minnesota Press, 1997), pp. xxiii–xxiv. This book was first published in French as *La condition postmoderne: rapport sur le savoir* in 1979.
9 Lyotard, *Postmodern Fables*, trans. G. van Den Abbeele (Minneapolis: University of Minnesota Press, 1997), pp. 70–1. This book was first published in French as *Moralités postmodernes* (Paris: Editions Galilee, 1993).
10 Lyotard, 'The Tomb of the Intellectual', pp. 6–7.
11 Lyotard, *The Postmodern Condition*, p. xiii.
12 Foucault, 'What is Enlightenment?', pp. 42–3.
13 Alison Assiter, *Enlightened Women* (London and New York: Routledge, 1996), p. 136.
14 Foucault, *Madness and Civilization: A History of Insanity in the Age of Reason*, trans. R. Howard (New York: Vintage Books, 1988), pp. 201–2.
15 Foucault, *Madness and Civilization*, pp. 201–2.
16 See Alain Viala, 'Qu'est-ce qu'un classique?', *Littératures classiques*, 19 (1993), pp. 11–31.
17 Foucault writes in *Discipline and Punish* that 'the gradual extension of the mechanisms of discipline throughout the seventeenth and eighteenth cen-

turies, their spread throughout the whole social body, the formation of what might be called in general the disciplinary society. A whole disciplinary generalisation – the Benthamite physics of power represented an acknowledgement of this – had operated throughout the classical age' (p. 209).
18 Foucault, *Madness and Civilization*, p. 220.
19 Foucault, 'Conversazione con Michel Foucault', pp. 273–4.
20 Foucault, '"Omnes et Singulatim": Towards a Critique of Political Reason', in *Power*, vol. 3 of *The Essential Works of Michel Foucault, 1954–1984*, pp. 299–300.
21 Foucault, '"Omnes et Singulatim": Towards a Critique of Political Reason', pp. 298–9.
22 Foucault, '"Omnes et Singulatim": Towards a Critique of Political Reason', pp. 298–9.
23 Foucault, *Discipline and Punish*, trans. A. Sheridan (New York: Vintage Books, 1995), p. 169.
24 Foucault, '"Omnes et Singulatim": Towards a Critique of Political Reason', pp. 299–300.
25 Foucault, *The Order of Things: An Archaeology of the Human Sciences* (London and New York: Routledge, 2003 (1966), pp. xxiii–xxiv.
26 Foucault, *Madness and Civilization*, p. 84.
27 Foucault, *Madness and Civilization*, p. 209.
28 Foucault, *Madness and Civilization*, p. 70.
29 Foucault, *Madness and Civilization*, p. 66.
30 Foucault, *Madness and Civilization*, p. 26.
31 Foucault, *Madness and Civilization*, p. 75.
32 Foucault, *Madness and Civilization*, p. 70.
33 Foucault, *Madness and Civilization*, p. 60.
34 Foucault, *Madness and Civilization*, p. 63.
35 Foucault, *Madness and Civilization*, p. 259.
36 Foucault, *Madness and Civilization*, p. 64.
37 Foucault, *Madness and Civilization*, p. 206.
38 Foucault, *Discipline and Punish*, p. 101.
39 Foucault, *Discipline and Punish*, p. 16.
40 Foucault, *Discipline and Punish*, p. 78.
41 Foucault, *Discipline and Punish*, p. 221.
42 Foucault, *Discipline and Punish*, pp. 128–9.
43 Foucault, *Discipline and Punish*, p. 173.
44 Foucault, *Discipline and Punish*, pp. 80–1.
45 Foucault, *Discipline and Punish*, p. 184.
46 Foucault, *Discipline and Punish*, p. 183.
47 Foucault, *Discipline and Punish*, p. 184.
48 Foucault, *Discipline and Punish*, p. 125.
49 Foucault, *Discipline and Punish*, p. 304.
50 Foucault, *Discipline and Punish*, p. 209.
51 Foucault, *Discipline and Punish*, p. 223.
52 Foucault, *Discipline and Punish*, p. 130.
53 Foucault, *Discipline and Punish*, p. 216.
54 Foucault, *Discipline and Punish*, p. 209.
55 Foucault writes in the Preface to *The Order of Things* that 'the present study is, in a sense, an echo of my undertaking to write a history of madness in the Classical age [*Madness and Civilisation*]: it has the same articulations in time, taking the end of the Renaissance as its starting-point, then encountering, at the beginning of the nineteenth century, just as my history of madness did, the threshold of a modernity that we have not yet left behind' (pp. xxv–xxvi).
56 Foucault, *The Order of Things*, p. 69.

57 I am grateful to Professor Flax for confirming this for me.
58 Surprisingly, Flax makes no reference to Kant's *Observations on the Feeling of the Beautiful and the Sublime* (1764), where he presents a gendered juxtaposition of beauty (feminine) and subliminity (masculine) that most feminists have found highly questionable.
59 Jane Flax, 'Is Enlightenment Emancipatory?: A Feminist Reading of "What is Enlightenment?"', in *Postmodernism and the Re-reading of Modernity*, eds F. Barker, P. Hulme and M. Iverson (Manchester and New York: Manchester University Press, 1992), p. 240.
60 Flax, 'Is Enlightenment Emancipatory?', p. 233.
61 Flax, 'Is Enlightenment Emancipatory?', p. 242.
62 Flax, 'Is Enlightenment Emancipatory?', p. 240.
63 Flax, 'Is Enlightenment Emancipatory?', p. 244.
64 Flax, 'Is Enlightenment Emancipatory?', p. 244.
65 Flax, 'Is Enlightenment Emancipatory?', p. 244.
66 Flax, 'Is Enlightenment Emancipatory?', p. 246.
67 Flax, 'Is Enlightenment Emancipatory?', p. 246.
68 Flax, 'Is Enlightenment Emancipatory?', p. 247.
69 Sandra Harding, 'Feminism, Science and the Anti-Enlightenment Critiques', in *Feminism/Postmodernism*, ed. L. Nicholson (New York and London: Routledge, 1990), pp. 87–8.
70 Harding, 'Feminism, Science and the Anti-Enlightenment Critiques', p. 93.
71 Harding, 'Feminism, Science and the Anti-Enlightenment Critiques', p. 88.
72 Harding, 'Feminism, Science and the Anti-Enlightenment Critiques', p. 97.
73 Harding, 'Feminism, Science and the Anti-Enlightenment Critiques', p. 97.
74 Harding, 'Feminism, Science and the Anti-Enlightenment Critiques', pp. 93–4.
75 Harding, 'Feminism, Science and the Anti-Enlightenment Critiques', pp. 92–3.
76 Harding, 'Feminism, Science and the Anti-Enlightenment Critiques', p. 90.
77 Harding, 'Feminism, Science and the Anti-Enlightenment Critiques', p. 99.
78 Richard Rorty, 'Is "Postmodernism" Relevant to Politics?', in *Truth, Politics and 'Postmodernism'* (Amsterdam: Van Gorcum, 1997). A version of this essay has been republished as 'The Continuity Between the Enlightenment and "Postmodernism"', in *What's Left of Enlightenment: A Postmodern Question*, ed. K. Baker and P. H. Reill (Stanford, CA: Stanford University Press, 2001), pp. 19–36.
79 Rorty, *Contingency, Irony and Solidarity* (Cambridge: Cambridge University Press, 1989), p. 194. Rorty's frequent reference to 'throwing away the ladder' is borrowed from Ludwig Wittgenstein (*Tractatus Logico-Philosophicus*, trans. S. C. K. Ogden (New York: Routledge, 1995), p. 189).
80 Joseph Schumpeter, *Capitalism, Socialism and Democracy* (London: George, Allen & Unwin, 1943), p. 243.
81 Gray, *Enlightenment's Wake*, p. 145.
82 Berlin's comment on Schumpeter's claim about our commitments also elicits Rorty's approval. Berlin writes: 'To demand more than this is perhaps a deep and incurable metaphysical need; but to allow it to determine one's practice is a symptom of an equally deep, and more dangerous, moral and political immaturity' ('Two Concepts of Liberty', in *Four Essays on Liberty* (Oxford: Oxford University Press, 1969), p. 172).
83 Rorty, *Contingency, Irony and Solidarity*, pp. 45–7.
84 Rorty, *Contingency, Irony and Solidarity*, p. 57.
85 Rorty, *Contingency, Irony and Solidarity*, p. 57.
86 Rorty, *Contingency, Irony and Solidarity*, p. 46.
87 Rorty, *Contingency, Irony and Solidarity*, p. 52.

88 Rorty, *Contingency, Irony and Solidarity*, p. 44.
89 Rorty, *Objectivity, Relativism and Truth: Philosophical Papers*, vol. 1 (Cambridge: Cambridge University Press, 1991), p. 34.
90 Rorty, *Objectivity, Relativism and Truth*, p. 23.
91 Rorty, 'The Priority of Democracy to Philosophy', in *Reading Rorty: Critical Responses to Philosophy and the Mirror of Nature*, ed. A. Malachowski (Oxford: Blackwell, 1990), p. 279.
92 Rorty, *Contingency, Irony and Solidarity*, p. 87.
93 Rorty, *Contingency, Irony and Solidarity*, p. 53.
94 Rorty, *Contingency, Irony and Solidarity*, p. 73.
95 Rorty, *Contingency, Irony and Solidarity*, pp. 73–4.
96 Rorty, *Contingency, Irony and Solidarity*, p. 87.
97 Gray, 'Why Irony Can't Be Superior', *Times Literary Supplement*, 3 November 1995, p. 4.
98 Rorty, *Contingency, Irony and Solidarity*, p. 88; italics added.
99 Rorty, *Contingency, Irony and Solidarity*, p. 61.
100 Rorty, *Contingency, Irony and Solidarity*, p. 84.
101 Rorty, *Contingency, Irony and Solidarity*, p. 189.
102 Rorty, *Contingency, Irony and Solidarity*, p. 86.
103 For Rorty, Jürgen Habermas is typical of the other point of view on this matter: 'Habermas shares with the Marxists, and with many of those whom he criticizes, the assumption that the real meaning of a philosophical view consists in its political implications, and that the ultimate frame of reference within which to judge a philosophical, as opposed to a merely "literary" writer, is a political one. For the tradition within which Habermas is working, it is as obvious that political philosophy is central to philosophy as, for the analytic tradition, that philosophy of language is central' (*Contingency, Irony and Solidarity*, p. 83). This misrepresents Habermas' position, which he summarised in an interview in terms that sound much closer to Rorty's view than the latter would admit: 'Philosophers are not teachers of the nation. They can sometimes – if only rarely – be useful people. . . . This is what I think philosophers should also do: forget about their professional role and bring what they can do better than others into a common business. But the common business of political discourses among citizens nevertheless stays what it is. It is not a philosophical enterprise. . . . But it is fair to ask: how could anyone focus on moral intuitions and reconstruct them, before having them – and how do we get them? Not from philosophy, and not by reading books. We acquire them just by growing up in a family. This is the experience of everyone, except perhaps the limit-cases of psychopaths with no moral sensibility whatsoever' (*Autonomy and Solidarity: Interviews with Jürgen Habermas*, ed. P. Dews (New York: Verso, 1986), pp. 199–202).
104 Rorty, *Contingency, Irony and Solidarity*, p. 198.
105 Rorty, *Contingency, Irony and Solidarity*, p. 208.
106 Rorty, *Objectivity, Relativism and Truth*, p. 33n16. On Hans Blumenberg's distinction between self-foundation and self-assertion, see his *The Legitimation of the Modern Age*, trans. R. Wallace (Cambridge, MA: MIT Press, 1983).

8 From Enlightenment to nothingness

1 Gray, *Enlightenment's Wake*, p. 145.
2 Jacobi, *David Hume on Faith, Or Idealism and Realism*, p. 583.
3 Ernst Bloch, *Subjekt-Objekt. Erlauterungen zu Hegel* (Frankfurt, am Main: Suhrkamp, 1962), p. 59.
4 Hegel, *The Phenomenology of Spirit*, trans. A.V. Miller (Oxford: Clarendon Press, 1977), sec. 594, p. 362.

5 In his posthumously published notes, *The Will to Power*, Nietzsche writes that '[s]cepticism regarding morality is what is decisive. The end of the moral interpretation of the world . . . leads to nihilism. "Everything lacks meaning"' (p. 7). He also writes that 'Radical nihilism is the conviction of an absolute untenability of existence when it comes to the highest values one recognises; plus the realization that we lack the least right to posit a beyond or an in-itself of things that might be "divine" or morality incarnate' (p. 9).

6 Lester Crocker, *Nature and Culture: Ethical Thought in the French Enlightenment* (Baltimore, MD: Johns Hopkins University Press, 1963), pp. 326–7.

7 Crocker, *Nature and Culture*, p. 518.

8 Crocker, *An Age of Crisis: Man and World in Eighteenth Century French Thought* (Baltimore, MD: Johns Hopkins University Press, 1959), p. 471.

9 Crocker, *Nature and Culture*, p. 512.

10 Alasdair MacIntyre, *After Virtue: A Study in Moral Theory* (Notre Dame, Indiana: University of Notre Dame Press, 1981), p. 38.

11 Gray, *Enlightenment's Wake*, pp. 165–6.

12 Nietzsche, *The Will to Power*, see. 91 (1885), pp. 55–6.

13 Gray, *Enlightenment's Wake*, p. 152.

14 Lester Crocker was born in New York in 1912. He graduated from New York University with a BA (1932) and, after a year at the University of Paris, received an MA from NYU (1934) and a Ph.D. from the University of California at Berkeley (1936). He taught at Wittenberg College, Queen's College, New York, Sweet Briar College, Groucher College, Western Reserve University, and the University of Virginia, where he was Kenan Professor of French. His principal publications include *La Correspondance de Diderot: son intérêt documentaire, psychologique et littéraire* (1939), *Two Diderot Studies: Ethics and Esthetics* (1953), *The Embattled Philosopher: A Biography of Denis Diderot* (1954), *An Age of Crisis: Man and World in Eighteenth-Century French Thought* (1959), *Nature and Culture: Ethical Thought in the French Enlightenment* (1963), *Jean-Jacques Rousseau: The Quest (1712–1758)* (1968), *Rousseau's 'Social Contract': An Interpretive Essay* (1968), *Jean-Jacques Rousseau: The Prophetic Voice (1758–1778)* (1973), and *Diderot's Chaotic Order: Approach to Synthesis* (1974).

15 Crocker, *Nature and Culture*, p. 500.

16 Crocker wrote in *Nature and Culture* that he was 'pleased to acknowledge my debt to Prof. Talmon's epoch-making book', although he adds that his own study 'was completed before I read his work' (p. 433). Although he paints a more balanced picture of the Enlightenment than does Talmon, whom he reproaches for brushing over its many 'cross-currents, contradictions, and antitheses' (p. 509), Crocker's basic thesis about the pivotal role of eighteenth-century thought in the development of twentieth-century totalitarianism is fundamentally the same as Talmon's, albeit with an important twist.

17 Crocker, *Nature and Culture*, p. 452.

18 Crocker, Introduction to *The Age of Enlightenment*, ed. L. Crocker (New York: Walker and Co, 1969), p. 28.

19 Crocker, *Nature and Culture*, p. 433.

20 Crocker, *Nature and Culture*, p. 519.

21 Crocker, *Nature and Culture*, p. 493.

22 Crocker, *An Age of Crisis*, p. 16.

23 Crocker, *Nature and Culture*, p. 334.

24 Crocker, *An Age of Crisis*, p. 402.

25 Crocker, *Nature and Culture*, p. 489.

26 Crocker, *Nature and Culture*, pp. 418–19.

27 Crocker, *Nature and Culture*, pp. 418–19.

28 Crocker, *Nature and Culture*, p. 423.

29 Crocker, *Nature and Culture*, p. 420.
30 Crocker, *Nature and Culture*, p. 396.
31 Crocker, *Nature and Culture*, p. 396.
32 Crocker, *An Age of Crisis*, p. 217.
33 Crocker, *Nature and Culture*, p. 455.
34 Crocker, *Nature and Culture*, pp. 397–8.
35 Crocker, *Nature and Culture*, p. 428.
36 Crocker, *An Age of Crisis*, p. 448.
37 Crocker, *An Age of Crisis*, p. 457.
38 Crocker, *An Age of Crisis*, p. 400.
39 Crocker, *An Age of Crisis*, p. 451.
40 Crocker, *An Age of Crisis*, p. 473.
41 Crocker, *The Age of Enlightenment*, p. 30.
42 Crocker, *Nature and Culture*, p. 521.
43 Alasdair MacIntyre is Research Professor of Philosophy at Notre Dame University. He was born in Scotland in 1929. He taught in Britain (Manchester, Leeds, Oxford, Essex) before emigrating to the USA in 1970, where he has taught at Brandeis University, Boston University, Wellesley College, Vanderbilt University and Duke University. His principal works include *Marxism and Christianity* (1954), *The Unconscious: A Conceptual Analysis* (1958), *A Short History of Ethics* (1965), *Secularisation and Moral Change* (1967), *Marcuse: An Exposition and a Polemic* (1970), *Against the Self-images of the Age* (1971), *After Virtue* (1981), *Whose Justice? Which Rationality?* (1988), *Three Rival Versions of Moral Enquiry* (1990), *First Principles, Final Ends and Contemporary Philosophical Issues* (1990), *Dependent Rational Animals: Why Human Beings Need the Virtues* (1999).
44 Hume, *A Treatise of Human Nature*, pp. 520–1.
45 G. E. Moore, *Principia Ethica*, ed. T. Baldwin (Cambridge: Cambridge University Press, 1993 [1903]), pp. 53–110.
46 MacIntyre, *After Virtue*, p. 54.
47 MacIntyre, *After Virtue*, p. 56.
48 MacIntyre, *After Virtue*, p. 53.
49 MacIntyre, *After Virtue*, pp. 52–3.
50 MacIntyre, *After Virtue*, pp. 51–2.
51 MacIntyre states that: 'From 1977 onwards I have been engaged in a single project to which *After Virtue* [1981], *Whose Justice? Which Rationality?* [1988], and *Three Rival Versions of Moral Enquiry* [1990] are central' ('An Interview with Alasdair MacIntyre', *Cogito*, 5 (1991), pp. 268–9).
52 MacIntyre, *Whose Justice? Which Rationality?* (London: Duckworth, 1988), p. 6.
53 MacIntyre, *Three Rival Versions of Moral Enquiry: Encyclopaedia, Genealogy and Tradition* (Note Dame: University of Notre Dame Press, 1990), pp. 23–4. This book is based on MacIntyre's 1988 Gifford Lectures at the University of Edinburgh.
54 MacIntyre, *Whose Justice? Which Rationality?*, p. 6.
55 There are striking similarities between MacIntyre's account of the role of tradition and Hans-Georg Gadamer's attack on 'the Enlightenment prejudice against prejudice' in *Truth and Method*, pp. 271–85.
56 MacIntyre, *Whose Justice? Which Rationality?*, p. 7.
57 MacIntyre, *Whose Justice? Which Rationality?*, p. 403.
58 For a very incisive and convincing critique of the conception of rationality that MacIntyre propounds, see Mark Colby, 'Moral Traditions, MacIntyre and Historicist Practical Reason', *Philosophy and Social Criticism*, 21 (1995), pp. 53–78.
59 MacIntyre, *After Virtue*, pp. 65–6.
60 MacIntyre, *After Virtue*, pp. 65–6.
61 John Gray is Professor of European Thought at the LSE. Before that he was

Tutor and Fellow in Political Theory at Jesus College, Oxford, from which he received both his BA and his D. Phil. He is the author of: *Mill on Liberty: A Defence* (1983), *Conceptions of Liberty in Political Philosophy* (co-edited with Z. Pelczynski) (1984), *Hayek on Liberty* (1984), *Liberalism* (1986), *Liberalisms: Essays in Political Philosophy* (1989), *J. S. Mill, On Liberty in Focus* (edited with G. W. Smith) (1991), *On Liberty and Other Essays/John Stuart Mill* (edited) (1991), *Post-Liberalism: Studies in Political Thought* (1993), *Beyond the New Right: Markets, Government and the Common Environment* (1993), *Berlin* (1995), *Enlightenment's Wake: Politics and Culture at the Close of the Modern Age* (1995), *Endgames: Questions in Late Modern Political Thought* (1997), *False Dawn: The Delusions of Global Capitalism* (1998), *Voltaire: Voltaire and Enlightenment* (1998), *Voltaire* (1999), *Two Faces of Liberalism* (2000), *Straw Dogs: Thoughts on Humans and Other Animals* (2002), and *Al Qaeda and What it Means to be Modern* (2003).

62 Gray, *Enlightenment's Wake*, p. 162.
63 Gray, *Enlightenment's Wake*, p. 152.
64 Gray, *Voltaire* (London: Phoenix, 1998), p. 52.
65 Carl Becker, *The Heavenly City of the Eighteenth Century Philosophers* (New Haven, CT, and London: Yale University Press, 1964), p. 31.
66 Becker, *The Heavenly City of the Eighteenth Century Philosophers*, pp. 41–2.
67 Gray, *Voltaire*, p. 1.
68 Gray, *Voltaire*, p. 17.
69 Gray, *Voltaire*, p. 19.
70 Gray, *Voltaire*, pp. 1–2.
71 Gray, *Voltaire*, p. 17.
72 Gray, *Enlightenment's Wake*, p. 150.
73 Gray, *Enlightenment's Wake*, p. 156.
74 Gray, *Enlightenment's Wake*, p. 169.
75 Gray, 'Why Irony Can't Be Superior', pp. 4–5.
76 Gray, *Enlightenment's Wake*, p. 152.
77 Gray, *Enlightenment's Wake*, p. 164.
78 Gray, *Enlightenment's Wake*, pp. 151–2.
79 Gray, *Enlightenment's Wake*, p. 147.
80 Martin Heidegger, 'The Question Concerning Technology', in *The Question Concerning Technology and Other Essays*, trans. W. Lovill (New York: Harper Torch Books, 1977), p. 17.
81 Gray, *Enlightenment's Wake*, p. 146.
82 Gray, *Enlightenment's Wake*, p. 178.
83 Gray, *Enlightenment's Wake*, p. 144.
84 Gray, *Enlightenment's Wake*, p. 164.
85 Gray, *Enlightenment's Wake*, p. 184.
86 See Michael Zimmerman, 'Toward a Heideggerian Ethos for Radical Environmentalism', *Environmental Ethics*, 5 (1983), pp. 99–131.
87 William Ophuls, *Requiem for Modern Politics: The Tragedy of the Enlightenment and the Challenge of the New Millennium* (Boulder, CO: Westview Press, 1997), p. 268.
88 Ophuls, *Requiem for Modern Politics*, pp. 267–8.
89 Ophuls, *Requiem for Modern Politics*, p. 1.
90 See Lewis Hinchman and Sandra Hinchman, 'Should Environmentalists Reject the Enlightenment?', *Review of Politics*, 63 (2001), pp. 663–92, and Chapter 5 of Adrian Atkinson, *Principles of Political Ecology* (London: Belhaven Press, 1991).
91 Gray, *Enlightenment's Wake*, p. 157.
92 See Gray, *Isaiah Berlin* (London: HarperCollins, 1995).

9 Conclusion: hits and misses

1 Burke, *Three Letters Addressed to A Member of the Present Parliament on the Proposal for Peace with the Regicide Directory of France*, in *The Writings of Edmund Burke* (London: Bickers and Sons, 1887), pp. 361–3.

2 Voltaire, *Historie de Jenni* (1775), in *Oeuvres complètes de Voltaire*, vol. 21, ed. L. Moland (Paris: Garnier, 1877–1886), p. 574.

3 Voltaire to Jean-François Dufour, Seigneur de Villevieille, 26 August 1768 (*Voltaire's Correspondence*, vol. 70, ed. T. Besterman (Geneva: Institut et Musée Voltaire, 1953–1957, pp. 30–2). Besterman adds the following note to this page: '[I]t is the present editor's opinion that Voltaire was himself for all practical purposes an atheist.'

4 Voltaire, *A l'auteur du livre des trois imposteurs* (1769), in *Œuvres complètes de Voltaire*, vol. 10, p. 403. Voltaire comments on this remark in his letter to Frederick-William of Prussia, 28 November 1770 (*Voltaire's Correspondence*, vol. 77, p. 120). Peter Gay writes about it that it is 'not a cynical injunction to rulers to invent a divine policeman for their ignorant subjects. Rather, it is part of a vehement diatribe against an atheist, written in the midst of Voltaire's dialogue with d'Holbach' (*Voltaire's Politics: The Poet as Realist* (New Haven, CT: Yale University Press, 1988), p. 265).

5 Voltaire, *The A B C, or Dialogues between A B C* (1768), in *Voltaire: Political Writings*, trans. D. Williams (Cambridge: Cambridge University Press, 1994), p. 190. Peter Gay interprets this remark as follows: 'This is the declaration of a believer who has previously declared his own certainty that God exists, not the disillusioned observation of a worldling who distrusts mankind' (*Voltaire's Politics*, p. 265). Voltaire also wrote that the doctrine of immortality is useful 'to keep the peasants from stealing wheat and wine' (*Philosophical Dictionary*, trans. P. Gay (New York: Basic Books, 1962), p. 605).

6 D'Alembert, *Preliminary Discourse to the Encyclopedia of Diderot*, trans. R. N. Schwab (Indianapolis: Bobbs-Merrill, 1963), p. 26.

7 Denis Diderot, *Diderot: Political Writings*, trans. J. H. Mason and R. Wokler (Cambridge: Cambridge University Press, 1992), p. 83. For Montesquieu's views on this subject, see *The Spirit of the Laws*, trans. A. Cohler, B. C. Miller and H. S. Stone (Cambridge: Cambridge University Press, 1989), p. 465. See also pp. 460–1 and 463–4.

8 A recent study (commissioned by the Welsh television channel SC4) found that only 29 per cent of people in Britain believe in God (*The Times*, 4 October 2004).

9 Condorcet, *Sketch for a Historical Picture of the Progress of the Human Mind*, p. 169.

10 Condorcet writes that 'if we survey in a single sweep the universal history of peoples, we see them sometimes making fresh progress, sometimes plunging back into ignorance, sometimes surviving somewhere between these extremes or halted at a certain point, sometimes disappearing from the earth under the conqueror's heel ... or sometimes receiving knowledge from some more enlightened people in order to transmit it in their turn to other nations' (*Sketch for a Historical Picture of the Progress of the Human Mind*, p. 8).

11 Condorcet, *Discours prononcé dans l'Académie francaise, de Jeudi 21 février 1782, à la réception de M. le marquis de Condorcet*, in *Oeuvres de Condorcet*, vol. 1, eds A. Condorcet O'Connor and M. F. Arago (Paris: Firmin Didot, 1847–1849), pp. 390–1.

12 Peter Gay, *The Enlightenment: An Interpretation*, vol. 2: *The Science of Freedom* (London: Wildwood House, 1969), pp. 187–207 and 281–90; Crocker, *An Age of Crisis*, pp. 218–55.

13 Alexander Pope, *An Essay on Man* (1733–1734), in *The Enlightenment: A Source-*

book and Reader, ed. P. Hyland *et al.* (London and New York: Routledge, 2003), p. 14.

14 D'Alembert, *Preliminary Discourse to the Encyclopedia of Diderot*, p. 70.
15 W. R. Clark and Michael Grunstein, *Are We Hard-wired? The Role of Genes in Human Behaviour* (Oxford: Oxford University Press, 2000).
16 Matt Ridley, *Nature Via Nurture: Genes, Experience and What Makes Us Human* (London: Harper Perennial, 2004), p. 82. See also T. J. Bouchard, D. T. Lykken, M. McGue, N. L. Segal and A. Tellegen, 'Sources of Human Psychological Differences: The Minnesota Study of Twins Reared Apart', *Science*, 250 (1990), pp. 223–8.
17 Ridley, *Nature Via Nurture*, pp. 82–3.
18 See Noam Chomsky, *Aspects of the Theory of Syntax* (Cambridge, MA: MIT Press, 1965); Steven Pinker, *How the Mind Works* (London: Allen Lane, 1998); Pinker, *The Language Instinct: How the Mind Creates Language* (New York: Perennial Classics, 2000); and Pinker, *The Blank Slate: The Modern Denial of Human Nature* (London: Allen Lane, 2002).
19 Matt Ridley, *Nature Via Nurture*, p. 49.
20 See Rawls, *A Theory of Justice*, and Jürgen Habermas, *The Philosophical Discourse of Modernity*, trans. F. G. Lawrence (Cambridge, MA: MIT Press, 1995).
21 Charles Griswold distinguishes between liberal and illiberal Enlightenments in *Adam Smith and the Virtues of Enlightenment* (Cambridge: Cambridge University Press, 1999), p. 2.
22 Outram, *The Enlightenment*, p. 48.
23 See Chapter 3, on 'The Futility of Learning', in Michel de Montaigne, *In Defence of Raymond Sebond*, trans. A. H. Beattie (New York: Ungar, 1959).
24 Chateaubriand, *The Genius of Christianity*, pt. II, bk. 3, ch. 1, p. 271.

Bibliography

Adorno, Theodor. *Negative Dialectics*. Translated by E. B. Ashton. London: Routledge & Kegan Paul, 1973.

Adorno, Theodor and Max Horkheimer. *Dialectic of Enlightenment: Philosophical Fragments*. Edited by G. S. Noerr. Translated by E. Jephcott. Stanford, CA: Stanford University Press, 2002.

Ages, Arnold. 'Chateaubriand and the *Philosophes*'. In *Chateaubriand Today*. Edited by R. Switzer. Madison, Milwaukee and London: University of Wisconsin Press, 1970.

Albertan-Coppola, Sylviane. 'Counter-Enlightenment'. Translated by C. Porter. In *The Encyclopaedia of the Enlightenment*, vol. 1. Edited by A. Kors. Oxford: Oxford University Press, 2003.

Alembert, Jean d'. *Preliminary Discourse to the Encyclopedia of Diderot*. Translated by R. N. Schwab. Indianapolis: Bobbs-Merrill, 1963.

Arendt, Hannah. *Totalitarianism: Part Three of The Origins of Totalitarianism*. San Diego: Harcourt, Brace, Jovanovich, 1968.

Arieli, Yehoshua. 'Jacob Talmon – An Intellectual Portrait'. In *Totalitarian Democracy and After: International Colloquium in Memory of Jacob L. Talmon, Jerusalem, 21–24 June 1982*. Jerusalem: Magnes Press and the Hebrew University, 1984.

Assiter, Alison. *Enlightened Women*. London and New York: Routledge, 1996.

Atkinson, Adrian. *Principles of Political Economy*. London: Belhaven Press, 1991.

Austern, Donald. 'The Political Theories of Edmund Burke and Joseph de Maistre As Representative of the Schools of Conservative Libertarianism and Conservative Authoritarianism'. Ph.D. diss, University of Massachusetts, 1974.

Baker, Keith. 'Enlightenment and Revolution in France: Old Problems, Renewed Approaches', *Journal of Modern History*, 53 (1981): 281–303.

Baker, Keith. *Inventing the French Revolution: Essays on French Political Culture in the Eighteenth Century*. Cambridge: Cambridge University Press, 1990.

Baker, Keith and P. H. Reill, eds. *What's Left of Enlightenment: A Postmodern Question*. Stanford, CA: Stanford University Press, 2001.

Barny, Roger. *Le Comte d'Antraigues: Un Disciple aristocrate de J.-J. Rousseau*, in *Studies on Voltaire and the Eighteenth Century*, 281 (1991).

Barrett, William. 'Art, Aristocracy and Reason', *Partisan Review*, 16/6 (1949): 663–4.

Barrett, William. *Irrational Man*. New York: Doubleday, 1958.

Barruel, Augustin. *Memoirs Illustrating the History of Jacobinism*, 4 vols. Translated by R. Clifford. London: T. Burton, 1798.

Bates, David. *Enlightenment Aberrations: Error and Revolution in France*. Ithaca, NY: Cornell University Press, 2002.

Bauman, Zygmunt. *Modernity and the Holocaust*. Ithaca, NY: Cornell University Press, 1989.

Bayle, Pierre. *Various Thoughts on the Occasion of a Comet*. Translated by R. C. Bartlett. Albany, NY: SUNY Press, 2000.

Beck, Lewis White. *Early German Philosophy: Kant and His Predecessors*. Cambridge, MA: Belknap Press of Harvard University Press, 1969.

Becker, Carl. *The Heavenly City of the Eighteenth Century Philosophers*. New Haven and London: Yale University Press, 1932.

Beik, Paul. 'The comte d'Antraigues and the Failure of French Conservatism in 1789', *American Historical Review*, 56 (1951): 767–87.

Beiser, Frederick. *The Fate of Reason: German Philosophy From Kant to Fichte*. Cambridge, MA: Harvard University Press, 1987.

Beiser, Frederick. *Enlightenment, Revolution and Romanticism: The Genesis of Modern German Political Thought, 1790–1800*. Cambridge, MA: Harvard University Press, 1992.

Beiser, Frederick. 'The Enlightenment and Idealism'. In *The Cambridge Companion to German Idealism*. Edited by K. Ameriks. Cambridge: Cambridge University Press, 2000.

Berlin, Isaiah. Introduction to *The Age of Enlightenment*. New York: New American Library, 1956.

Berlin, Isaiah. 'The Philosophical Ideas of Giambattista Vico'. In *Art and Ideas in Eighteenth Century Italy*. Rome: Edizioni di Storia, 1960.

Berlin, Isaiah. 'Herder and the Enlightenment'. In *Aspects of the Eighteenth Century*. Edited by E. Wasserman. Baltimore, MD: Johns Hopkins University Press, 1965.

Berlin, Isaiah. 'Two Concepts of Liberty'. In *Four Essays on Liberty*. Oxford: Oxford University Press, 1969.

Berlin, Isaiah. *Vico and Herder: Two Studies in the History of Ideas*. Edited by H. Hardy. London: Hogarth, 1976.

Berlin, Isaiah. 'A Tribute to My Friend', *Forum*, 38 (1980): 1.

Berlin, Isaiah. 'Reply to Hans Aarsleff'. In *London Review of Books*, 20/3 (5–18 November, 1981): 7–8.

Berlin, Isaiah. 'George Sorel'. In *Against the Current: Essays in the History of Ideas*. Edited by H. Hardy. Oxford: Oxford University Press, 1981.

Berlin, Isaiah. 'The Counter-Enlightenment'. In *Against the Current: Essays in the History of Ideas*. Edited by H. Hardy. Oxford: Oxford University Press, 1981.

Berlin, Isaiah. 'European Unity and its Vicissitudes'. In *The Crooked Timber of Humanity*. Edited by H. Hardy. London: John Murray, 1990.

Berlin, Isaiah. 'Joseph de Maistre and the Origins of Fascism'. In *The Crooked Timber of Humanity: Chapters in the History of Ideas*. Edited by H. Hardy. London: John Murray, 1990.

Berlin, Isaiah. *Conversations with Isaiah Berlin*. Edited by Ramin Jahanbegloo. London: Peter Halban, 1992.

Berlin, Isaiah. *The Magus of the North: J. G. Hamann and the Origins of Modern Irrationalism*. Edited by H. Hardy. London: Fontana, 1993.

Berlin, Isaiah. Introduction to Joseph de Maistre's *Considerations on France*. Translated by R. A. Lebrun. Cambridge: Cambridge University Press, 1994.

Berlin, Isaiah. *The Roots of Romanticism.* Edited by H. Hardy. London: Chatto & Windus, 1999.

Berlin, Isaiah. *Three Critics of the Enlightenment: Vico, Hamann, Herder.* Edited by H. Hardy. Princeton, NY: Princeton University Press, 2000.

Birken, Lawrence. *Hitler as Philosophe: Remnants of the Enlightenment in National Socialism.* Westport, CT: Praeger, 1995.

Blacker, Carmen. *The Japanese Enlightenment: A Study of the Writings of Fukuzawa.* Cambridge: Cambridge University Press, 1964.

Blake, William. 'The Song of Los'. In *The Complete Poetry and Prose of William Blake.* Edited by D. Erdman. Berkeley and Los Angeles: University of California Press, 1982.

Blake, William. 'Mock On'. In *Manuscript Lyrics of the Felpham Years (1800–1803).* In *William Blake.* Edited by M. Mason. Oxford and New York: Oxford University Press, 1988.

Blanc, Louis. *Histoire de la Révolution française.* Paris: A. Lacroix, 1878.

Blum, Carole. *Rousseau and the Republic of Virtue.* Ithaca, NY, and London: Cornell University Press, 1986.

Blumenberg, Hans. *The Legitimacy of the Modern Age.* Translated by R. Wallace. Cambridge: MIT Press, 1983.

Bouchard, T. J. D., T. Lykken, M. McGue, N. L. Segal and A. Tellegen. 'Sources of Human Psychological Differences: The Minnesota Study of Twins Reared Apart', *Science*, 250 (1990): 223–8.

Brandom, Robert, ed. *Rorty and His Critics.* Oxford: Blackwell, 2000.

Bronner, Stephen. 'The Great Divide: The Enlightenment and Its Critics', *New Politics*, 5/3 (1995): 65–86.

Bronner, Stephen. *Reclaiming the Enlightenment: Toward a Politics of Radical Engagement.* New York: Columbia University Press, 2004.

Brown, Marshall. 'Romanticism and Enlightenment'. In *The Cambridge Companion to British Romanticism.* Edited by S. Curran. Cambridge: Cambridge University Press, 1993.

Brunetière, Ferdinand. *Etudes critiques sur l'histoire de la littérature française.* Paris: Hachette, 1887.

Burke, Edmund. *An Appeal From the New to the Old Whigs.* In *The Writings and Speeches of Edmund Burke*, vol. 4. London: Bickers and Son, 1887.

Burke, Edmund. *A Letter to William Elliot.* In *The Writings and Speeches of Edmund Burke*, vol. 5. London: Bickers and Son, 1887.

Burke, Edmund. *A Letter to a Member of the National Assembly.* In *The Writings and Speeches of Edmund Burke*, vol. 4. London: Bickers and Son, 1887.

Burke, Edmund. *Three Letters Addressed to A Member of the Present Parliament on the Proposals for Peace with the Regicide Directory of France.* In *The Writings and Speeches of Edmund Burke*, vol. 5. London: Bickers and Son, 1887.

Burke, Edmund. *Thoughts on French Affairs.* In *The Writings and Speeches of Edmund Burke*, vol. 4. London: Bickers and Son, 1887.

Burke, Edmund. *A Letter to a Noble Lord.* In *The Writings and Speeches of Edmund Burke*, vol. 5. London: Bickers and Son, 1887.

Burke, Edmund. *Reflections on the Revolution in France.* Edited by C. C. O'Brien. Harmondsworth: Penguin, 1968.

Burke, Edmund. *The Correspondence of Edmund Burke*, vol. 6. Edited by A. Cobban and R. A. Smith. Cambridge: Cambridge University Press and Chicago, IL: University of Chicago Press, 1967.

Burke, Edmund. *The Correspondence of Edmund Burke*, vol. 8. Edited by R. B. McDowell. Cambridge: Cambridge University Press and Chicago, IL: University of Chicago Press, 1969.

Burke, Edmund. *The Correspondence of Edmund Burke*, vol. 10. Edited by B. Lowe *et al.* Chicago, IL: University of Chicago Press, and Cambridge: Cambridge University Press, 1958–1978.

Butler, Marilyn. 'Romanticism in England'. In *Romanticism in National Context*. Edited by Roy Porter and M. Teich. Cambridge: Cambridge University Press, 1988.

Cameron, David. *The Social and Political Thought of Rousseau and Burke: A Comparative Study*. Toronto: University of Toronto Press, 1973.

Capaldi, Nicholas. *The Enlightenment Project in the Analytic Conversation*. Boston, MA: Dordrecht, and London: Kluwer Academic, 1998.

Carpenter, Humphrey. *The Envy of the World*. London: Weidenfeld & Nicolson, 1996.

Carr, Karen. *The Banalization of Nihilism: Twentieth-century Responses to Meaninglessness*. Albany, NY: State University of New York Press, 1992.

Cassirer, Ernst. *Rousseau, Kant, Goethe: Two Essays*. Translated by J. Gutmann, P. Oskar Kristeller and J. H. Randall. Princeton, NJ: Princeton University Press, 1945.

Cassirer, Ernst. *The Philosophy of the Enlightenment*. Translated by F. C. A. Koelln and J. P. Pettegrove. Princeton, NJ: Princeton University Press, 1951.

Cassirer, Ernst. *The Question of Jean-Jacques Rousseau*. Translated by P. Gay. New Haven, CT, and London: Yale University Press, 1954.

Chapman, Mark. 'Why the Enlightenment Project Doesn't Have to Fail', *Heythrop Journal*, 39 (1998): 379–93.

Chartier, Roger. *Cultural History: Between Practices and Representations*. Translated by L. Cochrane. Cambridge: Polity Press, 1988.

Chartier, Roger. *The Cultural Origins of the French Revolution*. Translated by L. G. Cochrane. Durham, NC: Duke University Press, 1991.

Chateaubriand, François-René, vicomte de. *An Historical, Political and Moral Essay on Revolutions, Ancient and Modern*. London: Henry Colburn, 1815.

Chateaubriand, ———. *The Genius of Christianity*. Translated by C. I. White. New York: Howard Fertig, 1976. Reprint of 2nd edn, Baltimore, MD: John Murray and Co, 1856.

Church, W. F., ed. *The Influence of the Enlightenment on the French Revolution*. Boston, MA: D. C. Heath, 1964.

Clark, W. R. and Michael Grunstein. *Are We Hard-Wired? The Role of Genes in Human Behaviour*. Oxford: Oxford University Press, 2000.

Clement, N. H. *Romanticism in France*. New York: Modern Language Association of America, 1939.

Clive, Geoffrey. *The Romantic Enlightenment*. Westport, CT: Greenwood, 1973.

Cobban, Alfred. *Edmund Burke and the Revolt Against the Eighteenth Century* (2nd edn). London: George Allen & Unwin, 1960.

Cobban, Alfred. *Rousseau and the Modern State*. London: George Allen & Unwin, 1965.

Colby, Mark. 'Moral Traditions, MacIntyre and Historicist Practical Reason', *Philosophy and Social Criticism*, 21 (1995): 53–78.

Coleridge, Samuel Taylor. *Lectures on Literature*. In *Coleridge's Miscellaneous Criticism*. Edited by T. M. Raysor. London: Constable, 1936.

Coleridge, Samuel Taylor. *Collected Letters of Samuel Taylor Coleridge*, 2 vols. Edited by E. L. Griggs. Oxford: Clarendon Press, 1956–1971.

Coleridge, Samuel Taylor. *The Statesman's Manual*. In *The Collected Works of Samuel Taylor Coleridge*, vol. 6. Edited by K. Coburn. London: Routledge & Kegan Paul, and Princeton, NJ: Princeton University Press, 1967–.

Coleridge, Samuel Taylor. *The Friend*, No. 8 (5 October 1809). In *The Collected Works of Samuel Taylor Coleridge*, vol. 4:2. Edited by B. Rooke. London: Routledge & Kegan Paul, 1969.

Coleridge, Samuel Taylor. *On the Constitution of the Church and State*. In *The Collected Works of Samuel Taylor Coleridge*, vol. 10. Edited by J. Colmer. London: Routledge & Kegan Paul, and Princeton, NJ: Princeton University Press, 1976.

Coleridge, Samuel Taylor. *The Courier*, 1 April 1812. In *The Collected Works of Samuel Taylor Coleridge*, vol. 3: *Essays on His Times*, vol. 2. Edited by D. Erdman. London: Routledge & Kegan Paul, and Princeton, NJ: Princeton University Press, 1978.

Coleridge, Samuel Taylor. *Biographia Literaria*, vol. 1. In *The Collected Works of Samuel Taylor Coleridge*, vol. 7. Edited by J. Engell and W. J. Bate. London: Routledge & Kegan Paul, and Princeton, NJ: Princeton University Press, 1983.

Coleridge, Samuel Taylor. *Aids to Reflection*. In *The Collected Works of Samuel Taylor Coleridge*, vol. 9. Edited by J. Beer. London: Routledge, and Princeton, NJ: Princeton University Press, 1993.

Condorcet, M.-J.-A.-N. de Caritat, Marquis de. *Discours prononcé dans l'Académie francaise, de Jeudi 21 février 1782, à la réception de M. le marquis de Condorcet*. In *Œuvres de Condorcet*, vol. 1. Edited by A. Condorcet O'Connor and M. F. Arago. Paris: Firmin Didot, 1847–1849.

Condorcet, M.-J.-A.-N. de Caritat, Marquis de. *Sketch for a Historical Picture of the Progress of the Human Mind*. Translated by J. Barraclough. London: Weidenfeld & Nicolson, 1955.

Conway, Daniel. *Nietzsche and the Political*. London and New York: Routledge, 1997.

Courtney, C. P. 'Edmund Burke and the Enlightenment'. In *Statesmen, Scholars and Merchants*. Edited by A. Whiteman *et al*. Oxford: Oxford University Press, 1973.

Crocker, Lester. *An Age of Crisis: Man and World in Eighteenth Century French Thought*. Baltimore, MD: Johns Hopkins University Press, 1959.

Crocker, Lester. *Nature and Culture: Ethical Thought in the French Enlightenment*. Baltimore, MD: Johns Hopkins University Press, 1963.

Crocker, Lester. Introduction to *The Age of Enlightenment*. Edited by L. Crocker. New York: Walker & Co, 1969.

Crocker, Lester. 'The Enlightenment: What and Who?', *Studies in Eighteenth Century Culture*, 17 (1987): 335–47.

Crowder, George. *Isaiah Berlin: Liberty and Pluralism*. Cambridge: Polity Press, 2004.

Daiches, David, ed. *The Scottish Enlightenment, 1730–1790*. Edinburgh: Saltire Society, 1996.

Darcel, Jean-Louis. 'Catalogue de la Bibliothèque de Joseph de Maistre', *Etudes maistriennes*, 1 (1975): 1–91.

Darcel, Jean-Louis. 'Sources of Maistrian Sensibility'. Translated by R. A. Lebrun. In *Maistre Studies*. Edited by R. A. Lebrun. Lanham, New York and London: University Press of America, 1988.

Darcel, Jean-Louis. 'Maistre and the French Revolution'. Translated by R. A.

Lebrun. In *Maistre Studies*, translated and edited by R. A. Lebrun. Lanham, New York, London: University Press of America, 1988.

Darnton, Robert. 'In Search of Enlightenment: Recent Attempts to Create a Social History of Ideas', *Journal of Modern History*, 43 (1971): 113–32.

Darnton, Robert. 'The High Enlightenment and the Low-life of Literature in Pre-Revolutionary France', *Past and Present*, 51 (1971): 81–115.

Darnton, Robert. *The Business of Enlightenment: A Publishing History of the Encyclopédie, 1775–1800*. Cambridge, MA: Harvard University Press, 1979.

Darnton, Robert. *The Literary Underground of the Old Regime*. Cambridge, MA: Harvard University Press, 1982.

Darnton, Robert. *The Great Cat Massacre and Other Episodes in French Cultural History*. New York: Basic Books, 1984.

Day, Aidan. *Romanticism*. London: Routledge, 1996.

Deprun, Jean. 'Les Anti-Lumières'. In *Histoire de la philosophie*, vol. 2: *De la Renaissance à la Révolution Kantienne*. Edited by Y. Belaval. Paris: Pléiade, 1973.

Dermehngem, Emile. *Joseph de Maistre mystique*. Paris: La connaissance, 1923.

Diderot, Denis. *Correspondence de Denis Diderot*, vol. 4. Edited by G. Roth. Paris: Les Editions de Minuit, 1958.

Diderot, Denis. *Political Writings*. Translated by J. H. Mason and R. Wokler. Cambridge: Cambridge University Press, 1992.

Doherty, Thomas. Introduction to *Postmodernism: A Reader*. Edited by T. Doherty. New York: Columbia University Press, 1993.

Domenech, Jacques. 'Anti-Lumières'. In *Dictionnaire européen des Lumières*. Edited by M. Delon. Paris: Presses Universitaire de France, 1997.

Drury, Shadia. 'Foucault's Critique of the Enlightenment'. In *The Philosophical Canon in the Seventeenth and Eighteenth Centuries*. Edited by G. A. J. Rogers and S. Tomaselli. Rochester, NY: University of Rochester Press, 1996.

Duffy, Edward. *Rousseau in England: The Context of Shelley's Critique of the Enlightenment*. Berkeley: University of California Press, 1979.

Dupront, Alphonse. *Qu'est-ce que les Lumières?* Paris: Gallimard, 1996.

Edwards, David. 'Count Joseph de Maistre and Russian Educational Policy 1803–1828', *Slavic Review*, 36 (1977): 54–75.

Elder, David. *Scottish Enlightenment and Other Essays*. Edinburgh: Polygon, 1991.

Engelhardt, Dietrich von. 'Romanticism in Germany'. In *Romanticism in National Context*. Edited by R. Porter and M. Teich. Cambridge: Cambridge University Press, 1988.

Epstein, Klaus. *The Genesis of German Conservatism*. Princeton, NJ: Princeton University Press, 1966.

Ferguson, Frances. 'Burke and the Response to the Enlightenment'. In *The Enlightenment World*. Edited by M. Fitzpatrick, P. Jones, C. Knellwolf and I. McCalman. London and New York: Routledge, 2004.

Ferguson, Robert. *The American Enlightenment: 1750–1820*. Cambridge, MA: Harvard University Press, 1997.

Flax, Jane. 'Is Enlightenment Emancipatory?: A Feminist Reading of "What is Enlightenment?"'. In *Postmodernism and the Re-Reading of Modernity*. Edited by F. Barker, P. Hulme and M. Iverson. Manchester and New York: Manchester University Press, 1992.

Foucault, Michel. *Folie et déraison: histoire de la folie à l'âge classique*. Paris: Librairie Plon, 1961.

Foucault, Michel. 'What is Enlightenment?' Translated by C. Porter. In *The Foucault Reader*. Edited by P. Rabinow. Harmondsworth: Penguin, 1984.

Foucault, Michel. *Madness and Civilization: A History of Insanity in the Age of Reason*. Translated by R. Howard. New York: Vintage Books, 1988.

Foucault, Michel. *The Birth of the Clinic: An Archaeology of Medical Perception*. Translated by A. M. Sheridan Smith. New York: Vintage Books, 1994.

Foucault, Michel. *Discipline and Punish*. Translated by A. Sheridan. New York: Vintage Books, 1995.

Foucault, Michel. '"Omnes et Singulatim": Towards a Critique of Political Reason'. In *The Essential Works of Michel Foucault, 1954–1984*, vol. 3: *Power*. Edited by J. Faubion. Translated by R. Hurley *et al*. New York: New Press, 2000.

Foucault, Michel. 'Conversazione con Michel Foucault', *Il Contributo* (1980), pp. 23–84, in *Power*. Vol. 3 of *The Essential Works of Foucault, 1954–1984*. Edited by J. Faubion. Translated by R. Hurley *et al*. London: Allen Lane/Penguin, 2001.

Foucault, Michel. *The Order of Things: An Archaeology of the Human Sciences*. London and New York: Routledge, 2003.

Frankel, Charles. *The Faith of Reason*. New York: Octagon Books, 1969.

Fuchs, Michel. 'Edmund Burke et Joseph de Maistre', *Revue de l'Université d'Ottawa*, 54 (1984): 49–58.

Funke, Manfred, ed. *Totalitarismus*. Dusseldorf: Droste Verlag, 1978.

Furst, Lilian. *Romanticism*. London: Methuen, 1969.

Gadamer, Hans-Georg. *Gesammelte Werke. Vol. 1: Hermeneutik I: Wahrheit und Methode*. Tubingen: J. C. B. Mohr (Paul Siebeck), 1986.

Gadamer, Hans-Georg. 'Science as an Instrument of Enlightenment'. In *In Praise of Theory: Speeches and Essays*. Translated by C. Dawson. New Haven, CT: Yale University Press, 1998.

Gadamer, Hans-Georg. *Truth and Method* (2nd edn). Translated by Joel Weinsheimer and Donald Marshall. New York: Continuum, 1999.

Garrard, Graeme. 'Maistre, Judge of Jean-Jacques: An Examination of the Relationship Between Jean-Jacques Rousseau, Joseph de Maistre and the French Enlightenment'. Oxford University D.Phil. diss, 1997.

Garrard, Graeme. 'The Counter-Enlightenment Liberalism of Isaiah Berlin', *Journal of Political Ideologies*, 2/3 (1997): 281–96.

Garrard, Graeme. *Rousseau's Counter-Enlightenment: A Republican Critique of the Philosophes*. Albany, NY: State University of New York Press, 2003.

Garrard, Graeme. 'Isaiah Berlin's Joseph de Maistre'. In *Isaiah Berlin's Counter-Enlightenment*. Edited by J. Mali and R. Wokler. Philadelphia, PA: American Philosophical Association, 2003.

Gautier, Theophile. *Histoire du Romanticisme*. Paris: Charpentier, 1884.

Gay, Peter. *The Enlightenment: An Interpretation*, vol. 1: *The Rise of Modern Paganism*. New York and London: W. W. Norton, 1966.

Gay, Peter. *The Enlightenment: An Interpretation*, vol. 2: *The Science of Freedom*. London: Wildwood House, 1969.

Gay, Peter. *Voltaire's Politics: The Poet as Realist*. New Haven, CT: Yale University Press, 1988.

German, Terence. *Hamann on Language and Religion*. Oxford: Oxford University Press, 1981.

Gillespie, Michael. *Nihilism Before Nietzsche*. Chicago, IL: University of Chicago Press, 1996.

Gleason, Abbott. *Totalitarianism: The Inner History of the Cold War*. New York: Oxford University Press, 1995.

Godechot, Jacques. *The Counter-Revolution: Doctrine and Action 1789–1804*. Translated by S. Attanasio. London: Routledge & Kegan Paul, 1972.

Goldhammer, Arthur. 'Man in the Mirror: Language, the Enlightenment, and the Postmodern'. In *Postmodernism and the Enlightenment: New Perspectives in Eighteenth-century French Intellectual History*. Edited by D. Gordon. New York and London: Routledge, 2001.

Gordon, Daniel, ed. *Postmodernism and the Enlightenment: New Perspectives in Eighteenth-century French Intellectual History*. New York and London: Routledge, 2001.

Gray, John. *Enlightenment's Wake: Politics and Culture at the Close of the Modern Age*. London and New York: Routledge, 1995.

Gray, John. *Isaiah Berlin*. London: HarperCollins, 1995.

Gray, John. 'Why Irony Can't Be Superior'. *Times Literary Supplement*, 3 November 1995.

Gray, John. *Endgames: Questions in Late Modern Political Thought*. Cambridge: Polity Press, 1997.

Gray, John. *Voltaire*. London: Phoenix, 1998.

Grimsley, Ronald. *Jean D'Alembert 1717–83*. Oxford: Clarendon, 1963.

Griswold, Charles. *Adam Smith and the Virtues of Enlightenment*. Cambridge: Cambridge University Press, 1999.

Habermas, Jürgen. *Autonomy and Solidarity: Interviews with Jürgen Habermas*. Edited by P. Dews. New York: Verso, 1986.

Habermas, Jürgen. *The Philosophical Discourse of Modernity*. Translated by F. Lawrence. Cambridge, MA: MIT Press, 1987.

Habermas, Jürgen. 'Remarks on the Development of Horkheimer's Work'. In *On Max Horkheimer: New Perspectives*. Edited by S. Benhabib *et al.* Cambridge, MA: MIT Press, 1993.

Hallowell, John. Editor's preface to Eric Voegelin's *From Enlightenment to Revolution*. Edited by J. H. Hallowell. Durham, NC: Duke University Press, 1975.

Hamann, Johann Georg. *Hamann's Schriften*, 8 vols. Edited by F. Roth and G. A. Weiner. Berlin: G. Reimer, 1821–1843.

Hamann, Johann Georg. *Hamann's Briefwechsel mit Friedrich Heinrich Jacobi*, vol. 5 of *Johann Georg Hamann's, des Magus in Norden, Leben und Schriften*. Edited by C. H. Gildemeister. Gotha: Perthes, 1868.

Hamann, Johann Georg. *Sämtliche Werke*, 6 vols. Edited by Josef Nadler. Vienna: Herder, 1949–1957.

Hamann, Johann Georg. *Briefwechsel*, 6 vols. Edited by Walther Ziesemer and Arthur Henkel. Wiesbaden: Insel-Verlag, 1955–1979.

Hamann, Johann Georg. *Socratic Memorabilia: Compiled for the Boredom of the Public by a Lover of Boredom*. Translated by J. O'Flaherty. In James O'Flaherty. *Hamann's Socratic Memorabilia: A Translation and Commentary*. Baltimore, MD: Johns Hopkins University Press, 1967.

Hamann, Johann Georg. *Golgotha and Scheblimini!* Translated by S. N. Dunning. In Stephen Dunning. *The Tongues of Men: Hegel and Hamann on Religious Language and History*. Missoula, Montana: Scholars Press, 1979.

Hamann, Johann Georg. *Aesthetica in Nuce: A Rhapsody in Cabbalistic Prose*. Translated by J. P. Crick. In *German Aesthetic and Literary Criticism: Winckelmann,*

Lessing, Hamann, Herder, Schiller and Goethe. Edited by H. B. Nisbet. Cambridge: Cambridge University Press, 1985.

Hamann, Johann Georg. *Metacritique of the Purism of Reason.* Translated by K. Haynes. In *What is Enlightenment?* Edited by J. Schmidt. Berkeley; University of California Press, 1996.

Hamowy, Ronald. *The Scottish Enlightenment and the Theory of Spontaneous Order.* Carbondale: Southern Illinois University Press, 1987.

Harding, Sandra. 'Feminism, Science and the Anti-Enlightenment Critiques'. In *Feminism/Postmodernism.* Edited by L. Nicholson. New York and London: Routledge, 1990.

Harrison, Paul. *The Disenchantment of Reason.* Albany, NY: State University of New York Press, 1994.

Hart, Herbert. *The Concept of Law* (2nd edn). Oxford: Clarendon Press, 1994.

Hatier, Cécile. 'Isaiah Berlin and the Totalitarian Mind', *The European Legacy*, 9/6 (2004), pp. 767–82.

Havens, George. *Voltaire's Marginalia on the Pages of Rousseau: A Comparative Study of Ideas.* Columbus: Ohio State University Press, 1933.

Hegel, G. W. F. *Sämtliche Werke.* vol. 11. Edited by J. Hoffmeister. Hamburg: Frommanns, 1956.

Hegel, G. W. F. *The Philosophy of History.* Translated by J. Sibree. New York: Dover Publications, 1956.

Hegel, G. W. F. *Lectures on the History of Philosophy*, vol. 1. Translated by E. S. Haldane and F. H. Simson. London: Routledge & Kegan Paul, 1892; New York: Humanities Press, 1974.

Hegel, G. W. F. *The Phenomenology of Spirit.* Translated by A. V. Miller. Oxford: Clarendon Press, 1977.

Hegel, G. W. F. 'Hamann Schriften'. In *Berliner Schriften 1818–1831*, vol. 11. Edited by E. Moldenhauer and K. M. Michel. Frankfurt am Main: Suhrkamp, 1986.

Heidegger, Martin. 'The Question Concerning Technology'. In *The Question Concerning Technology and Other Essays.* Translated by W. Lovill. New York: Harper Torch Books, 1977.

Heilke, Thomas. *Eric Voegelin: In Quest of Reality.* Lanham, Boulder, New York and Oxford: Rowman and Littlefield, 1999.

Hertzberg, Arthur. *The French Enlightenment and the Jews.* New York: Columbia University Press, 1968.

Hibben, John Grier. *The Philosophy of the Enlightenment.* New York: Charles Scribner's Sons, 1910.

Hinchman, Lewis and Sandra Hinchman. 'Should Environmentalists Reject the Enlightenment?', *Review of Politics*, 63 (2001): 663–92.

Hirschman, Albert. *The Rhetoric of Reaction: Perversity, Futility, Jeopardy.* Cambridge, MA: Belknap Press, 1991.

Hoffman, Amos. 'The Origins of the Theory of the *Philosophe* Conspiracy', *French History*, 2 (1988): 152–72.

Holliday, Ian. 'English Conservatism and Enlightenment Rationalism'. In *The Enlightenment and Modernity.* Edited by R. Wokler and N. Geras. Basingstoke: Macmillan, 2000.

Holmes, Richard. *Coleridge: Early Visions.* Harmondsworth: Penguin, 1989.

Holub, Robert and W. Daniel Wilson, eds. *Impure Reason: Dialectic of Enlightenment in Germany.* Detroit: Wayne State University Press, 1993.

Horkheimer, Max. *The Eclipse of Reason*. Translated by J. Cumming. New York: Seabury, 1974.

Horkheimer, Max. 'Materialism and Morality'. In *Between Philosophy and Social Science: Selected Early Essays*. Translated by G. F. Hunter, M. S. Kramer and J. Torpey. Cambridge, MA: MIT Press, 1993.

Horkheimer, Max. 'Reason Against Itself: Some Remarks on Enlightenment', *Theory, Culture and Society*, 10 (1993): 79–88.

Horkheimer, Max and Theodor Adorno. *Dialectic of Enlightenment: Philosophical Fragments*. Edited by. G. S. Noerr. Translated by E. Jephcott. Stanford: Stanford University Press, 2002.

Horowitz, Asher and Terence Maley, eds. *The Barbarism of Reason: Max Weber and the Twilight of Enlightenment*. Toronto: University of Toronto Press, 1994.

Hulme, Peter and Ludmilla Jordanova, eds. *The Enlightenment and Its Shadows*. London and New York: Routledge, 1990.

Hume, David. *A Treatise of Human Nature*. Edited by E. Mossner. Harmondsworth: Penguin, 1969.

Isaac, Jeffrey. 'Critics of Totalitarianism'. In *The Cambridge History of Twentieth Century Political Thoughts*. Edited by T. Ball and R. Bellamy. Cambridge: Cambridge University Press, 2003.

Israel, Jonathan. *Radical Enlightenment: Philosophy and the Making of Modernity, 1650–1750*. Oxford: Oxford University Press, 2002.

Jacobi, Friedrich Heinrich. *The Main Philosophical Writings and the Novel* Allwill. Translated by G. di Giovanni. Montreal and Kingston: McGill-Queen's University Press, 1994.

Johnson, Pauline. 'Feminism and the Enlightenment', *Radical Philosophy*, 63 (1993): 3–12.

Jones, William David. *The Lost Debate: German Socialist Intellectuals and Totalitarianism*. Urbana and Chicago: University of Illinois Press, 1999.

Kant, Immanuel. First Introduction to *The Critique of Judgement*. Translated by J. Haden. Indianapolis: Bobbs-Merrill, 1965.

Kant, Immanuel. *Observations on the Feeling of the Beautiful and the Sublime*. Translated by J. T. Goldthwait. Berkeley: University of California Press, 1991.

Kant, Immanuel. *Critique of Pure Reason*. Translated by P. Guyer and A. Wood. Cambridge: Cambridge University Press, 1998.

Kuehn, Manfred. *Kant: A Biography*. Cambridge: Cambridge University Press, 2001.

Kuhn, Elisabeth. 'Cultur, Civilization. Die Zweideutigkeit des "Modernen"', *Nietzsche-Studien*, 18 (1989): 600–27.

Lamartine, Alphonse de. *Atheism Among the People*. Boston: Phillips, Sampson and Co, 1850.

Lamartine, Alphonse de. *Mémoires inédits de Lamartine, 1790–1815*. Edited by L. de Ronchaud. Paris: Hachette, 1909.

Lang, Berel. *Act and Idea in the Nazi Genocide*. Chicago, IL: University of Chicago Press, 1990.

Larmore, Charles. *The Romantic Legacy*. New York: Columbia University Press, 1996.

Lebrun, Richard. *Joseph de Maistre: An Intellectual Militant*. Montreal and Kingston: McGill-Queen's University Press, 1988.

Lebrun, Richard. 'Joseph de Maistre and Edmund Burke: A Comparison'. In *Joseph *de Maistre's Life, Thought and Influence: Selected Studies*. Edited by R. A. Lebrun. Montreal and Kingston: McGill-Queen's University Press, 2001.

Leith, James. 'Les trois apothèoses de Voltaire', *Annales historiques de la Révolution française*, 236 (1979): 161–209.

Levine, Andrew. *The Politics of Autonomy: A Kantian Reading of Rousseau's* Social Contract. Amherst: University of Massachusetts Press, 1976.

Liedman, Sven-Eric, ed. *Postmodernist Critique of the Project of Enlightenment*. Amsterdam and Atlanta: Rodopi, 1997.

Lilla, Mark. 'Anti-Lumières'. In *Dictionnaire de philosophie politique* (3rd edn). Edited by P. Raymond and S. Rials. Paris: Quedrige/Presses Universitaires de France, 1996.

Linker, Damon. 'The Counter-Enlightenment in Germany: Origins and Echoes'. In *Aspects of German Politics, Society and History: American Perceptions*. Bonn: Alexander von Humboldt-Stiftung, 1998.

Linker, Damon. 'From Kant to Schelling: Counter-Enlightenment in the Name of Reason', *Review of Politics*, 54 (2000): 337–77.

Lively, Jack, ed. *The Enlightenment*. London: Longmans, 1966.

Lough, John. 'The Contemporary Influence of the *Encyclopédie*', *Studies on Voltaire and the Eighteenth Century*, 26 (1963): 1071–83.

Lough, John. 'Reflections on Enlightenment and Lumières', *British Journal for Eighteenth Century Studies*, 8/1 (1985): 1–15.

Lovejoy, Arthur. 'On the Discriminations of Romanticisms'. In *Essays in the History of Ideas*. New York: Putnam, 1960.

Lyotard, Jean-François. 'The Tomb of the Intellectual'. In *Political Writings*. Translated by B. Readings and K. Paul. Minneapolis: University of Minnesota Press, 1993.

Lyotard, Jean-François. *The Postmodern Condition: A Report on Knowledge*. Translated by G. Bennington and B. Massumi. Minneapolis: University of Minnesota Press, 1997.

Lyotard, Jean-François. *Postmodern Fables*. Translated by G. van Den Abbeele. Minneapolis: University of Minnesota Press, 1997.

McDonald, Joan. *Rousseau and the French Revolution 1762–1791*. London: Athlone, 1965.

McGrath, Alister. *The Genesis of Doctrine: A Study in the Foundation of Doctrinal Criticism*. Oxford: Blackwell, 1990.

MacIntyre, Alasdair. *After Virtue: A Study in Moral Theory*. Notre Dame, IN: University of Notre Dame Press, 1981.

MacIntyre, Alasdair. *Whose Justice? Which Rationality?* London: Duckworth, 1988.

MacIntyre, Alasdair. *Three Rival Versions of Moral Enquiry: Encyclopaedia, Genealogy and Tradition*. Notre Dame: University of Notre Dame Press, 1990.

MacIntyre, Alasdair. 'An Interview with Alasdair MacIntyre', *Cogito* 5 (1991): 67–73.

Mack, Eric. 'The Limits of Diversity: The New Counter-Enlightenment and Isaiah Berlin's Liberal Pluralism'. In *The Imperiled Academy*. Edited by H. Dickman. New Brunswick, NJ, and London: Transaction, 1993.

McMahon, Darrin. *Enemies of the Enlightenment: The French Counter-Enlightenment and the Making of Modernity*. New York and Oxford: Oxford University Press, 2001.

McNeil, G. H. 'The Anti-revolutionary Rousseau', *American Historical Review*, 58 (1953): 808–23.

Mahony, William. *The Encyclopedia of Religion*, vol. 5. Edited by M. Eliade. New York: Macmillan, 1987.

Maistre, Joseph de. 'Réflexions sur le Protestantisme dans ses rapports avec la Souveraineté'. In *Oeuvres complètes de Joseph de Maistre*, vol 8. Lyon: Vitte et Perussel, 1884–1886.

Maistre, Joseph de. 'Mémoire sur la liberté de l'enseignement publique'. In *Oeuvres complètes de Joseph de Maistre*, vol. 8. Lyon: Vitte et Perussel, 1884–1886.

Maistre, Joseph de. *Essay on the Generative Principle of Political Constitutions*. Delmas, NY: New York Scholars' Facsimiles and Reprints, 1977. Reprint of 1847 edition.

Maistre, Joseph de. *St. Petersburg Dialogues: Or Conversations on the Temporal Government of Providence*. Translated by R. A. Lebrun. Montreal: McGill-Queen's University Press, 1993.

Maistre, Joseph de. *Considerations on France*. Translated by R. A. Lebrun. Cambridge: Cambridge University Press, 1994.

Maistre, Joseph de. 'On the Sovereignty of the People'. In *Against Rousseau*. Translated by R. A. Lebrun. Montreal: McGill-Queen's University Press, 1996.

Mali, Joseph and Robert Wokler, eds. *Isaiah Berlin's Counter-Enlightenment*. Philadelphia, PA: American Philosophical Society, 2003.

May, Henry Farnham. *The Enlightenment in America*. New York: Oxford University Press, 1976.

Mazlish, Bruce. 'Burke, Bonald and de Maistre: A Study in Conservatism'. Ph.D. diss, Columbia University, 1955.

Mendelssohn, Moses. *Jerusalem. Or, On Religious Power and Judaism*. Translated by A. Arkush. Hanover, NH: University Press of New England, 1983.

Merlan, Philip. 'Kant, Hamann-Jacobi, and Schelling on Hume', *Rivista Critica di Storia della Filosofia*, 22 (1967): 481–94.

Meynell, Hugo. *Postmodernism and the New Enlightenment*. Washington, DC: Catholic University Press, 1999.

Miller, John. *Ideology and Enlightenment: The Political and Social Thought of Samuel Taylor Coleridge*. New York and London: Garland, 1987.

Montaigne, Michel de. *In Defence of Raymond Sebond*. Translated by A. H. Beattie. New York: Unger, 1959.

Montesquieu, Charles Louis de Secondat, baron de. *The Spirit of the Laws*. Translated by A. C. Cohler, B. C. Miller and H. S. Stone. Cambridge: Cambridge University Press, 1989.

Moore, G. E. *Principia Ethica*. Edited by T. Baldwin. Cambridge: Cambridge University Press, 1993.

Moss, George. *Toward the Final Solution: A History of European Racism*. New York: Howard Fertig, 1978.

Muchembled, Robert. *Culture populaire et culture des élites dans la France moderne*. Paris: Flammarion, 1978.

Muthu, Sankar. 'Enlightenment Anti-Imperialism', *Social Research*, 66/4 (1999), 959–1007.

Muthu, Sankar. *Enlightenment Against Empire*. Princeton, NJ, and Oxford: Princeton University Press, 2003.

Nadler, Josef. *Johann Georg Hamann: Der Zeuge des Corpus Mysticum*. Salzburg: Muller, 1949.

Nietzsche, Friedrich. *The Will to Power* (2nd edn). Translated by R. J. Hollingdale and W. Kaufmann. New York: Vintage Books, 1968.

Nietzsche, Friedrich. *Beyond Good and Evil*. Translated by R. J. Hollingsdale. Harmondsworth: Penguin, 1973.

Nietzsche, Friedrich. *The Gay Science*. Translated by W. Kaufmann. New York: Random House, 1974.

Nietzsche, Friedrich. *Human, All Too Human*. Translated by R. J. Hollingdale. Cambridge: Cambridge University Press, 1996.

Nietzsche, Friedrich. *The Wanderer and His Shadow*. In *Human, All Too Human*. Translated by R. J. Hollingdale. Cambridge: Cambridge University Press, 1996.

Nietzsche, Friedrich. *Daybreak*. Edited by M. Clark and B. Leiter. Translated by R. J. Hollingdale. Cambridge: Cambridge University Press, 1997.

Norton, Robert. *Herder's Aesthetics and the European Enlightenment*. Ithaca, NY, and London: Cornell University Press, 1991.

Novalis. *Werke, Tagebücher und Briefe—Friedrich von Hardenberg*, vol. 2. Edited by H-J. Mähl. Vienna: Earl Hanser Verlag, 1978.

Novalis. *Hymns to the Night*. Translated by D. Higgins. New York: McPherson & Co, 1988.

Novalis. *Christendom or Europe*. In *Novalis: Philosophical Writings*. Translated by M. Stoljar. Albany, NY: State University of New York Press, 1997.

Novalis. *Philosophical Writings*. Translated by M. Stoljar. Albany, NY: State University of New York Press, 1997.

Oakeshott, Michael. 'Rationalism in Politics'. In *Rationalism in Politics and Other Essays*. Indianapolis: Liberty Fund, 1991.

Oakeshott, Michael. 'The New Bentham'. In *Rationalism in Politics and Other Essays*.

Oakeshott, Michael. 'Rational Conduct'. In *Rationalism in Politics and Other Essays*.

O'Brien, Conor Cruise. *The Great Melody: A Thematic Biography and Commented Anthology of Edmund Burke*. Chicago, IL: University of Chicago Press, 1992.

Offen, Karen. 'Reclaiming the European Enlightenment for Feminism: Or Prolegomena to any Future History of Eighteenth-century Europe'. In *Perspectives on Feminist Political Thought in European History: From the Middle Ages to the Present*. Edited by T. Akkerman and S. Stuurman. London and New York: Routledge, 1998.

O'Flaherty, James. *Johann Georg Hamann*. Boston, MA: Twayne Publishers, 1979.

Ophuls, William. *Requiem for Modern Politics: The Tragedy of the Enlightenment and the Challenge of the New Millennium*. Boulder, CO: Westview Press, 1997.

Outram, Dorinda. *The Enlightenment*. Cambridge: Cambridge University Press, 1995.

Pettit, Philip. 'Liberal/Communitarian: MacIntyre's Mesmeric Dichotomy'. In *After MacIntyre*. Edited by J. Horton and S. Mendus. Cambridge: Polity Press, 1994.

Pinkard, Terry. *German Philosophy 1760–1860: The Legacy of Idealism*. Cambridge: Cambridge University Press, 2002.

Pinker, Steven. *How the Mind Works*. London: Allen Lane, 1998.

Pinker, Steven. *The Language Instinct: How the Mind Creates Language*. New York: Perennial Classics, 2000.

Pinker, Steven. *The Blank Slate: The Modern Denial of Human Nature*. London: Allen Lane, 2002.

Pocock, J. G. A. 'The Tell-tale Article: Reconstructing (. . .) Enlightenment'. Plenary Address to the 29th annual meeting of the American Society for Eighteenth-century Studies, University of Notre Dame, 2 April 1998.

Pocock, J. G. A. 'Enlightenment and Counter-Enlightenment, Revolution and

Counter-Revolution: A Eurosceptical View', *History of Political Thought*, 20/1 (1999): 125–39.

Pope, Alexander. *An Essay on Man* (1733–1734). In *The Enlightenment: A Sourcebook and Reader*. Edited by P. Hyland *et al.* London and New York: Routledge, 2003.

Porter, Roy and Mikulás Teich, eds. *The Enlightenment in National Context*. Cambridge: Cambridge University Press, 1981.

Porter, Roy and Mikulás Teich, eds. *Romanticism in National Context*. Cambridge: Cambridge University Press, 1988.

Racevskis, Karlis. *Postmodernism and the Search for Enlightenment*. Charlottesville, VA and London: University Press of Virginia, 1993.

Rawls, John. *A Theory of Justice*. Cambridge, MA: Harvard University Press, 1971.

Reardon, Bernard. *Religion in the Age of Romanticism*. Cambridge: Cambridge University Press, 1985.

Redmond, Michael. 'The Hamann–Hume Connection', *Religious Studies*, 23 (1987): 95–107.

Reill, Peter Hanns. *The German Enlightenment and the Rise of Historicism*. Berkeley, Los Angeles, London: University of California Press, 1975.

Ridley, Matt. *Nature Via Nurture: Genes, Experience and What Makes Us Human*. London: Harper Perennial, 2004.

Ritter, Joachim. *Hegel and the French Revolution: Essays on the* Philosophy of Right. Translated by R. D. Winfield. Cambridge, MA, and London: MIT Press, 1982.

Roche, David. *Le Siècle des lumières en province: Académies et académiciens provinciaux 1680–1789*, 2 vols. The Hague: Mouton, 1978.

Rorty, Richard. *Contingency, Irony and Solidarity*. Cambridge: Cambridge University Press, 1989.

Rorty, Richard. 'The Priority of Democracy to Philosophy'. In *Reading Rorty: Critical Responses to Philosophy and the Mirror of Nature*. Edited by A. Malachowski. Oxford: Blackwell, 1990.

Rorty, Richard. *Objectivity, Relativism and Truth: Philosophical Papers*, vol. 1. Cambridge: Cambridge University Press, 1991.

Rorty, Richard. 'Is "Postmodernism" Relevant to Politics?'. In *Truth, Politics and 'Postmodernism'*. Amsterdam: Van Gorcum, 1997.

Rorty, Richard. 'The Continuity Between Enlightenment and "Postmodernism"'. In *What's Left of Enlightenment?: A Postmodern Question*. Edited by Keith Baker and P. H. Reill. Stanford, CA: Stanford University Press, 2001.

Rousseau, Jean-Jacques. *Letter to d'Alembert on the Theatre*. In *Politics and the Arts*. Translated by A. Bloom. Glencoe, IL: The Free Press, 1960.

Rousseau, Jean-Jacques. *Correspondence complètes de Jean-Jacques Rousseau*. Edited by R. A. Leigh. Geneva, Banbury, Oxford: Voltaire Foundation, 1965–1998.

Rousseau, Jean-Jacques. *Réfutation suivie de l'ouvrage d'Helvétius intitulé* l'Homme. In *Oeuvres complètes*. Edited by R. Lewinter, vol. 2. Paris: Le Club français du livre, 1969–1973.

Rousseau, Jean-Jacques. *The Government of Poland*. Translated by W. Kendall. Indianapolis and New York: Bobbs-Merrill, 1972.

Rousseau, Jean-Jacques. *Emile*. Translated by A. Bloom. New York: Basic Books, 1979.

Rousseau, Jean-Jacques. *Rousseau, Judge of Jean-Jacques*. In *The Collected Writings of Rousseau*, vol. 1. Edited by R. D. Masters and C. Kelly. Translated by J. R. Bush,

C. Kelly and R. D. Masters. Hanover and London: University Press of New England, 1990.

Rousseau, Jean-Jacques. *Discourse on the Sciences and the Arts*. In *The Collected Writings of Rousseau*, vol. 2. Translated and edited by C. Kelly and R. D. Masters. Hanover and London: University Press of New England, 1992.

Rousseau, Jean-Jacques. *Preface to Narcissus*. In *The Collected Writings of Rousseau*, vol. 2. Translated and edited by C. Kelly and R. D. Masters. Hanover and London: University Press of New England, 1992.

Rousseau, Jean-Jacques. *Final Reply*. In *The Collected Writings of Rousseau*, vol. 2. Translated and edited by C. Kelly and R. D. Masters. Hanover and London: University Press of New England, 1992.

Rousseau, Jean-Jacques. *Discourse on Political Economy*. In *The Collected Writings of Rousseau*, vol. 3. Translated by J. Bush, R. D. Masters and C. Kelly. Edited by C. Kelly and R. D. Masters. Hanover and London: University Press of New England, 1992.

Rousseau, Jean-Jacques. *Discourse on the Origin and Foundations of Inequality*. In *The Collected Writings of Rousseau*, vol. 3. Translated and edited by J. Bush, C. Kelly and R. D. Masters. Hanover and London: University Press of New England, 1992.

Rousseau, Jean-Jacques. *Political Fragments*. In *The Collected Writings of Rousseau*, vol. 4. Translated by J. Bush, C. Kelly and R. D. Masters. Edited by R. D. Masters and C. Kelly. Hanover and London: University Press of New England, 1994.

Rousseau, Jean-Jacques. *The Social Contract*. In *The Collected Writings of Rousseau*, vol. 4. Translated by J. Bush, C. Kelly and R. D. Masters. Edited by R. D. Masters and C. Kelly. Hanover and London: University Press of New England, 1994.

Rousseau, Jean-Jacques. *Confessions*. In *The Collected Writings of Rousseau*, vol. 5. Edited by C. Kelly, R. D. Masters and P. Stillman. Translated by C. Kelly. Hanover and London: University Press of New England, 1995.

Rousseau, Jean-Jacques. *Julie, or the New Héloïse*. In *The Collected Writings of Rousseau*, vol. 6. Edited by R. D. Masters and C. Kelly. Translated by P. Stewart and J. Vaché. Hanover and London: University Press of New England, 1997.

Rousseau, Jean-Jacques. *Essay on the Origin of Languages*. In *The Collected Writings of Rousseau*, vol. 7. Edited by J. T. Scott. Translated by J. T. Scott. Hanover and London: University Press of New England, 1998.

Rousseau, Jean-Jacques. *Reveries of a Solitary Walker*. In *The Collected Writings of Rousseau*, vol. 8. Edited by C. Kelly. Translated by C. E. Butterworth, A. Book and T. Marshall. Hanover and London: University Press of New England, 2000.

Saine, Thomas. *The Problem of Being Modern, or The German Pursuit of Enlightenment from Leibniz to the French Revolution*. Detroit: Wayne State University Press, 1997.

Schlegel, Friedrich. 'Hamann als Philosoph', *Deutsches Museum*, 3 (1813): 32–52.

Schleiermacher, E. D. *On Religion, Speeches to Its Cultured Despisers*. Translated by R. Crouter. Cambridge: Cambridge University Press, 1988.

Schmidt, James. 'The Question of Enlightenment: Kant, Mendelssohn and the *Mittwochsgesellschaft*', *Journal of the History of Ideas*, 50/2 (1989): 269–92.

Schmidt, James, ed. *What is Enlightenment?* Berkeley and London: University of California Press, 1996.

Schmidt, James. 'Language, Mythology and Enlightenment: Historical Notes on Horkheimer and Adorno's *Dialectic of Enlightenment*', *Social Research*, 65/4 (1998): 812–14.

Schmidt, James. 'Civility, Enlightenment and Society: Conceptual Confusions and Kantian Remedies', *American Political Science Review*, 92/2 (1998): 419–27.

Schmidt, James. 'Liberalism and Enlightenment in Eighteenth-century Germany', *Critical Review*, 13 (1999): 31–53.

Schmidt, James. 'What Enlightenment Project?' *Political Theory*, 28/6 (2000): 734–57.

Schmidt, James. 'Inventing the Enlightenment: Anti-Jacobins, British Hegelians and the Oxford English Dictionary', *Journal of the History of Ideas*, 64/3 (2003): 421–43.

Schumpeter, Joseph. *Capitalism, Socialism and Democracy*. London: George, Allen & Unwin, 1943.

Seidman, Steven. *Liberalism and the Origins of European Social Theory*. Berkeley: University of California Press, 1983.

Shackleton, Robert. 'Chateaubriand and the Eighteenth Century'. In *Chateaubriand Today*. Edited by R. Switzer. Madison, Milwaukee and London: University of Wisconsin Press, 1970.

Shell, Susan. *The Rights of Reason: A Study of Kant's Philosophy and Politics*. Toronto: University of Toronto Press, 1980.

Shklar, Judith. *After Utopia: The Decline of Political Faith*. Princeton, NJ: Princeton University Press, 1957.

Simpson, Lewis. 'Voegelin and the Story of the Clerks'. In *Eric Voegelin's Significance for the Modern Mind*. Edited by E. Sandoz. Baton Rouge and London: Louisiana State University Press, 1991.

Sluga, Hans. 'Heidegger and the Critique of Reason'. In *What's Left of Enlightenment: A Postmodern Question*. Edited by K. M. Baker and P. H. Reill. Stanford, CA: Stanford University Press, 2001.

Smith, Ronald Gregor. *J. G. Hamann 1730–1788: A Study in Christian Experience*. New York: Harper and Brothers, 1960.

Spragens, Thomas. *The Irony of Liberal Reason*. Chicago, IL, and London: University of Chicago Press, 1981.

Strauss, Leo. *Natural Right and History*. Chicago, IL, and London: University of Chicago Press, 1953.

Sutcliffe, Adam. *Judaism and Enlightenment*. Cambridge: Cambridge University Press, 1993.

Tagliacozza, Giorgio. 'Vico, the Counter-Enlightenment and Advanced Contemporary Thought'. In *Man, God and Nature in the Enlightenment*. Edited by D. Mell, T. Brown and L. Palmer. East Lansing, MI: Colleagues, 1988.

Taine, Hippolyte. *The Ancien Régime*. Translated by J. Durand. London: Daldy, Isbister and Co, 1876.

Tallis, Raymond. *Enemies of Hope: A Critique of Contemporary Pessimism, Irrationalism, Anti-Humanism and Counter-Enlightenment*. Basingstoke and London: Macmillan, 1997.

Talmon, Jacob. *The Origins of Totalitarian Democracy*. London: Secker and Warburg, 1952.

Talmon, Jacob. 'Utopianism and Politics: A Conservative View', *Commentary* (1959): 149–54.

Tate, John. 'The Hermeneutic Circle vs. The Enlightenment', *Telos*, 110 (1998): 9–38.

Taylor, Charles. *Hegel*. Cambridge: Cambridge University Press, 1975.

Thiele, Leslie Paul. 'The Agony of Politics: The Nietzschean Roots of Foucault's Thought', *American Political Science Review*, 84/3 (1990): 907–25.

Tiryakian, Edward. 'The Sociological Impact of a Metaphor: Tracking the Source of Max Weber's "Iron Cage"', *Sociological Inquiry*, 51 (1981): 27–33.

Tocqueville Alexis de. *The Old Regime and the French Revolution*. Translated by S. Gilbert. New York and London: Doubleday, 1955.

Trey, George. *Solidarity and Difference: The Politics of Enlightenment in the Aftermath of Modernity*. Albany, NY: State University of New York Press, 1998.

Tseng, Roy. *The Sceptical Idealist: Michael Oakeshott as a Critic of the Enlightenment*. Thorverton: Imprint Academic, 2003.

Unger, Rudolf. *Hamann und die Aufklärung: Studien zur Vorgeschichte de romantischen Geistes im 18 Jahrhundert*, 2 vols. Halle: Niemeyer, 1925 [1911].

Venturi, Franco. *Italy and the Enlightenment*. Translated by S. Corsi. New York: New York University Press, 1972.

Viala, Alain. 'Qu'est-ce qu'un classique?', *Littératures classiques*, 19 (1993): 11–31.

Voegelin, Eric. 'The Origins of Totalitarianism', *The Review of Politics*, 15/1 (1953): 68–85.

Voegelin, Eric. *From Enlightenment to Revolution*. Edited by J. H. Hallowell. Durham, NC: Duke University Press, 1975.

Voegelin, Eric. *Autobiographical Reflections*. Edited by E. Sandoz. Baton Rouge and London: Louisiana State University Press, 1989.

Voegelin, Eric. *The Collected Works of Eric Voegelin*, vol. 26. Edited by David Walsh. Columbia and London: University of Missouri Press, 1999.

Voltaire, François-Marie Arouet de. *Epître à l'auteur du livre des trois imposteurs*. In *Oeuvres complètes de Voltaire*, vol. 10. Paris: Garnier, 1877.

Voltaire, François-Marie Arouet de. *Voltaire's Correspondence*, vol. 70. Edited by T. Besterman. Geneva: Institut et Musée Voltaire, 1953–1957.

Voltaire, François-Marie Arouet de. *Complete Works of Voltaire*. Edited by T. Besterman. Banbury, Oxon: Voltaire Foundation, 1968–.

Voltaire, François-Marie Arouet de. *Political Writings*. Translated by D. Williams. Cambridge: Cambridge University Press, 1994.

Walsh, David. Introduction to *Crisis and the Apocalypse of Man*. In *The Collected Works of Eric Voegelin*, vol. 26. Edited by David Walsh. Columbia and London: University of Missouri Press, 1999.

Weber, Max. *Die Protestantische Ethik und der Beist des kapitalismus*. Tubingen: Verlag von J. C. B. Mohr/Paul Siebeck, 1934.

Weber, Max. *The Social Psychology of the World Religions*. In *From Max Weber: Essays in Sociology*. Translated and edited by H. H. Gerth and C. Wright Mills. New York: Oxford University Press, 1946.

Weber, Max. 'The Meaning of "Ethical Neutrality"'. In *The Methodology of the Social Science*. Translated and edited by E. Shils and H. Finch. New York: Free Press, 1949.

Weber, Max. *Economy and Society*, 2 vols. Edited by G. Roth and C. Wittich. Berkeley: University of California Press, 1978.

Wellmer, Albrecht. *The Critical Theory of Society*. Translated by J. Cumming. New York: Herder and Herder, 1969.

Whitaker, A., ed. *Latin America and the Enlightenment*. Ithaca, NY: Great Seal Books, 1961.

Wiggershaus, Rolf. *The Frankfurt School: Its History, Theories and Political Significance*. Translated by M. Robertson. Cambridge: Polity Press, 1994.

Williamson, Karina. 'The Counter-Enlightenment'. In *The Companion to the Enlightenment*. Edited by J. Yolton *et al*. Oxford: Blackwell, 1991.

Wilson, Arthur. *Diderot: The Testing Years 1713–1759*. New York: Oxford University Press, 1957.

Wilson, Susan. 'Postmodernism and the Enlightenment'. In *The Enlightenment World*. Edited by M. Fitzpatrick, P. Jones, C. Knellwolf and I. McCalman. London and New York: Routledge, 2004.

Wittgenstein, Ludwig. *Tractatus Logico-Philosophicus*. Translated by S. C. K. Ogden. New York and London: Routledge, 1995.

Wokler, Robert. 'Projecting the Enlightenment'. In *After MacIntyre*. Edited by J. Horton and S. Mendus. Cambridge: Polity Press, 1994.

Wokler, Robert. 'The Enlightenment Project and Its Critics'. In *The Postmodernist Critique of the Project of Enlightenment*. Edited by S-E. Liedman. Amsterdam and Atlanta: Rodopi, 1997.

Wokler, Robert. 'The Enlightenment Project As Betrayed by Modernity', *History of European Ideas*, 24/4–5 (1999): 301–13.

Wordsworth, William. 'The Convention of Cintra'. In *The Prose Works of William Wordsworth*, vol. 1. Edited by W. J. B. Owen and Jane Worthington Smyser. Oxford: Clarendon Press, 1974.

Wright, Johnson Kent. 'The Pre-postmodernism of Carl Becker'. In *Postmodernism and the Enlightenment: New Perspectives in Eighteenth-century French Intellectual History*. Edited by D. Gordon. New York and London: Routledge, 2001.

Zengotita, Thomas de. 'Common Ground: Finding Our Way Back to the Enlightenment', *Harper's Magazine* (January 2003): 35–44.

Zimmerman, Michael. 'Toward a Heideggerian Ethos for Radical Environmentalism', *Environmental Ethics*, 5 (1983): 99–131.

Žižek, Slavoj. *Did Somebody Say Totalitarianism?* London and New York: Verso, 2001.

Zoll, Donald Atwell. *The Twentieth Century Mind: Essays on Contemporary Thought*. Baton Rouge: Louisiana State University Press, 1967.

Index

Lightning Source UK Ltd.
Milton Keynes UK
UKOW03f0952121113

220882UK00009B/710/P